Following Luke

"Readers of William Loader's colloquial and engaging translation will find themselves experiencing Luke's story of Jesus in new and immediate ways, accompanied by his helpful explanations and suggestions for reflection as they follow Jesus in Luke's company."

—**Judith Lieu**, Professor Emerita of New Testament, Cambridge University

"In this excellent book, William Loader gives us a highly readable translation of the Gospel of Luke and an accessible guide to how to interpret the text. Packed full of understanding and insight, *Following Luke* has clear and immensely helpful discussions of both the overall message of the Gospel of Luke and of individual passages. Preachers, teachers, and students alike will find this a veritable treasure trove of wisdom and inspiration."

—**Paul Trebilco**, Professor of New Testament Studies, University of Otago, New Zealand

"'Just tell me the main things I need to know, please, without lots of padding, and in readable form.' That's the request that Bill Loader has responded to in the latest book in his *Following* series on the four Gospels. As always, he meets the brief, working his way through all twenty-four chapters of Luke's Gospel in just two hundred very readable pages. For each passage he offers his own lively original translation of a passage ('Listening to Luke'), a careful and concise reflection on that passage ('Thinking About Luke'), and a focus question to ponder or discuss. The book is in an accessible format, written in Loader's inimitable conversational style, yet touching on so many important technical issues of interpretation. Preachers will find much in this book to equip them in their important task."

—**John Squires**, Retired Minister, Uniting Church

"Bill Loader distills insights from decades of study and reflection on Luke. Juxtaposing a new translation, detailed textual analysis, and his own insights, he offers an accessible commentary for study and contemplation."

—**IAN TOZER**, Former Moderator, Uniting Church Western Australia

"Bill Loader has the rare gift of making scholarship invisible. *Following Luke* is deeply grounded in biblical scholarship yet communicates as easily and directly to the reader as the author of Luke did to Theophilus. *Following Luke* is also about much more than Luke. Loader helps us to read Luke within the context of the other Synoptic Gospels and thus serves as an introduction to all the Gospels. Just as much, Loader helps us to read Luke within the contexts of our own lives as we read Luke 'on the road.'"

—**ROB MCFARLANE**, Presbytery Relations Minister, Uniting Church Synod of NSW & ACT

Following Luke

A Commentary for People on the Road

BY
William Loader

CASCADE *Books* • Eugene, Oregon

FOLLOWING LUKE
A Commentary for People on the Road

Copyright © 2025 William Loader. All rights reserved. Except for brief quotations in critical publications or reviews, no part of this book may be reproduced in any manner without prior written permission from the publisher. Write: Permissions, Wipf and Stock Publishers, 199 W. 8th Ave., Suite 3, Eugene, OR 97401.

Cascade Books
An Imprint of Wipf and Stock Publishers
199 W. 8th Ave., Suite 3
Eugene, OR 97401

www.wipfandstock.com

PAPERBACK ISBN: 979-8-3852-4857-5
HARDCOVER ISBN: 979-8-3852-4858-2
EBOOK ISBN: 979-8-3852-4859-9

Cataloguing-in-Publication data:

Names: Loader, William R. G., 1944– [author].

Title: Following Luke : a commentary for people on the road / by William Loader.

Description: Eugene, OR: Cascade Books, 2025.

Identifiers: ISBN 979-8-3852-4857-5 (paperback) | ISBN 979-8-3852-4858-2 (hardcover) | ISBN 979-8-3852-4859-9 (ebook)

Subjects: LCSH: Bible.—Luke—Commentaries. | Commentaries.

Classification: BS2595.53 L63 2025 (paperback) | BS2595.53 (ebook)

VERSION NUMBER 12/04/25

Contents

Preface | vii

Introducing Luke | 1

1 Announcing Hope | 5
    "Come into my studio!" (Luke 1:1–24) 5
    Just a Girl (Luke 1:26–56) 10
    Hopes for Liberation (Luke 1:57–80) 16
    The Christmas Story (Luke 2:1–52) 20
    Getting Ready (Luke 3:1–38) 25
    Facing the Options (Luke 4:1–13) 32
    Jesus' Mission Statement (Luke 4:14–44) 36

2 Hope in Action | 42
    What Are God's Priorities? (Luke 5:1—6:11) 42
    Jesus' Teaching (Luke 6:12–49) 51
    Jesus and John (Luke 7:1–34) 57
    Jesus and Women (Luke 7:36—8:3) 64
    Hope and Reality (Luke 8:4–21) 69
    Worlds Apart (Luke 8:22–56) 73

3 Following the Way of the Son of Man | 79

    The Way of the Son of Man (Luke 9:1–27) 79

    Priorities and Projections (Luke 9:28–62) 86

    Liberating Mission (Luke 10:1–24) 93

    Beyond Prejudices (Luke 10:25–42) 97

    "May your kingdom come!" (Luke 11:1–26) 101

    Confrontations (Luke 11:27–54) 106

    A Call to Trust (Luke 12:1–34) 111

    Readiness (12:35–59) 116

    Warnings and Allusions to What Was to Come (Luke 13:1–35) 121

4 Conflicting Priorities | 126

    Challenging the Norms (Luke 14:1–35) 126

    Defending Love (Luke 15:1–32) 132

    Money Matters (Luke 16:1–31) 138

    Advice and Warnings (Luke 17:1–37) 143

    Colliding Values (Luke 18:1–43) 148

    Making Money Work (Luke 19:1–27) 155

5 Jesus and Jerusalem | 160

    Challenging the Jerusalem Authorities (Luke 19:28–48) 160

    Defending Jesus' Profile (Luke 20:1–44) 165

    Reflecting on Demise and Imagining Hope (Luke 20:45—21:38) 172

    Jesus' Last Meal (Luke 22:1–21) 178

    Falsely Charged with Subversion (Luke 22:22–71) 184

    A Travesty of Justice and a Model of Faithfulness in Adversity (Luke 23:1–47) 192

    Affirming Hope (Luke 23:48—24:53) 200

Where to From Here with Luke? | 209

Preface

THIS COMMENTARY IS ONE of a series on the Gospels, designed to be a resource for preachers and for people concerned to have an informed faith. It sits alongside many fine extensive commentaries by leading scholars in the field. For many today, the demands of time make it difficult for them to consult extensive commentaries. This brief commentary aims to provide them with readable up-to-date scholarship. It responds to what I often sense the need to be, "Bill, can you just tell me, please, what are the main things I need to know, and, please, without lots of padding and in readable form."

For the past two decades I have sought to do this through online commentaries on the Gospel and Epistle readings of the widely used Revised Common Lectionary as an aid for preachers and a resource for study groups who meet each week to reflect on the texts (billloader.com). I am now doing the same for each of the Gospels as a whole. This is a way of also seeing what can be treated as isolated passages in the context of the story in the particular Gospel as a whole.

For this purpose, I offer my own translation in contemporary English, seeking to keep close to the Greek text, but expressed in less formal language typical of contemporary Australian society. I also cite my own translations from the commentaries on Mark and John, already published. For texts beyond these, I cite the New Revised Standard Version, unless otherwise indicated.

I have divided the commentary into five sections, and each section has translations and commentaries on individual passages. "Listening to

Luke" brings the translation. "Thinking About Luke" brings the commentary. There follows a "Reflection," usually a question that might evoke group discussion. The best question to start with in relation to all of them is: What is new or significant for you in what you have just read?

As far as possible I have sought to help readers hear Luke's Gospel in its world, both when that may strike us as strange and remote and when it may speak to us with continuing relevance. Theirs was a world of seeing illness and disability, including mental illness, within the framework of demonology, and so seeing healing as exorcism. Their science was different from ours, including what they would have assumed, namely that the earth was flat or at most a sphere around which the sun circled. But they also saw good news in broader terms that remain challenging: as not just healing but also as societal transformation, good news for the poor, and radical inclusion of the marginalized and self-marginalizing, and ultimately as reaching out and embracing all peoples.

My own contributions to research on Luke (and Acts) have been related primarily to the way Luke depicts the Law, especially in my study *Jesus' Attitude Towards the Law: A Study of the Gospels* (Tübingen: Mohr Siebeck,1997; Grand Rapids: Eerdmans, 2002), and in *Jesus and the Fundamentalism of His Day* (Grand Rapids: Eerdmans, 2001), but I have also engaged Luke in dealing with a wide range of issues, including, for instance, attitudes to sexuality.

I am deeply grateful to colleagues in the community of research who have also written on Luke and those who have read and responded to earlier versions of this commentary, Professors Judith Lieu and Paul Trebilco, and Revd. Drs. John Squires and Ian Tozer. I also thank my proofreaders: Sharyn Robinson and my wife, Gisela.

William Loader

Introducing Luke

As with the other Gospels, Luke's Gospel is anonymous. The author is not named. One might imagine that the authors would say that the real author was Jesus. By the end of the second century, we find the name Luke associated with the Gospel. This may well have been deduced from the comment found in 2 Timothy, a letter composed in Paul's name but some decades after his death, where that "Paul" in prison in Rome states: "Only Luke is with me" (2 Tim 4:11). References in Acts where the author speaks in the first person plural about journeys Paul and he made have suggested that it must have been Luke referring to himself, and the brief reference to a Luke who was a physician in Col 4:14 led to the conclusion that this Luke is the author of Acts and so also of the Gospel. This is all very speculative, and there is nothing very medical about either writing; nor does his way of presenting the gospel give the impression that he was close to Paul.

We are best to leave the actual identity and name of the author of what we call the Gospel According to Luke an open question. For simplicity's sake, in the rest of this book I shall refer to the author as Luke. There is nevertheless much more about the author that we can say and say with confidence. To begin with, the author was sufficiently well educated to be able to write and he does so in reasonably sophisticated Greek. The way he introduces his two volumes, addressing a person called Theophilos, reflects the fact that he was familiar with how authors often introduced their works in public, either dedicating them to a patron or in some way acknowledging someone who had made the publication possible.

Luke, in fact, tell us about his intentions in writing the Gospel. He wants to reassure people about what they have been taught and to do so in an orderly manner. He is doing what others also did, namely telling the story of a famous person in a way that will help those listening appreciate that person's importance. In that sense he is writing history but also biography. To do so, he would have to have resources and find a way of putting it all together into a coherent whole.

It is widely recognized that he used Mark's Gospel for the basic outline of Jesus' life, at least his yearlong ministry. In addition, however, it is also clear that he had other sources, and one of those appears to have been used also by Matthew. It is fairly clear that Matthew organized that material to fit into five main addresses he has Jesus give during his ministry, beginning with the best known, the Sermon on the Mount (Matt 5–7). We find the same basic outline as for Matthew's Sermon on the Mount in Luke's report of Jesus' teaching in Luke 6:20–49. It also begins with statements of blessing and ends with warnings about building one's life on the right foundation. Much of the material that Matthew has brought together into that first address is not in the shorter address that Luke brings, but is found scattered in various places in Luke. As in many instances, it looks like Matthew has been using a version of their common source which has undergone further development and refinement and has reorganized it to fit his pattern of five main speeches.

Luke tended to follow Mark, but then broke off for a number of chapters where he used other sources before returning to Mark again, whereas Matthew tends to weave his sources together. When Luke is using Mark, he tends to follow Mark closely, sometimes word for word. Only occasionally does he relocate episodes, such as when he obviously decided that the discussion about which was the greatest commandment, found in Mark's account of Jesus' teaching in his last days in Jerusalem, made an excellent introduction to the parable of the good Samaritan. He brings it, therefore, in Luke 10 instead of in Luke 20, where it would have been, had he followed Mark's sequence.

Changing the order of events was not a problem, because, apart from knowing that the baptism was at the beginning and the death at the end, Mark had no detailed CV of Jesus, but had to create a narrative from the primarily oral traditions passed on to him. They already included groupings of stories and sayings with similar themes, such as the parables about seeds in Mark 4. Accordingly, Matthew and Luke felt free to change Mark's order, especially if they felt it could enhance the impact of their accounts and so the impact of Jesus. They, too, needed to make decisions about how to bring their sources together into a coherent narrative, including source material that was unique to them.

For instance, Luke takes the account of Jesus' visit to his hometown synagogue in Nazareth, which Mark presents in Mark 6:1–6, and relocates it to make it the opening scene of Jesus' ministry, and adds elaborations that point to what is to come in his two volumes (Luke 4:16–30). Similarly, Luke brings together the famous parables of the prodigal son and the lost coin, found only in his gospel, and combines them with the parable of the lost sheep in Luke 15 to form Jesus' response to one of the major criticisms that Jesus faced, namely his associating with people deemed unworthy. Much was left, therefore, to the imagination in how the authors put stories and sayings together.

Both Matthew and Luke were familiar with a common pattern of their time in portraying the lives of famous people. That was to say something about their origins, usually in a way that foreshadowed the famous people they would become, often with colorful embellishments such as signs in the heavens, divine interventions, angelic visitations, inspired predictions, or miraculous conceptions. These narrative overtures then set the scene for what would follow. We have become adept at combining Matthew's and Luke's different wonder stories into one, when we celebrate Christmas.

Luke gives particular attention to placing the story of Jesus within Israel's story and depicting him as the one who was to fulfill the hopes and dreams of the faithful of Israel. This theme colors the opening chapters celebrating Jesus' birth and meets us in the closing chapters celebrating his resurrection. While sometimes portrayed as a gentile because of the emphasis in his second volume on outreach to the world, Luke rather gives the impression that he is deeply committed to Jewish hopes and may well have been a Jew. He alone of the Gospel writers even sees hope for all humanity as taking the form of Jesus' return to rule the kingdom of God from Jerusalem.

His story claims continuity between Jesus and Israel and between the church, Jesus, and Israel, despite so many of his (probably) fellow Jews rejecting Jesus' message and, as he depicts it, their leaders being primarily responsible for his death. At many points in his story we are left imagining how his first hearers would have heard the story. That includes how it related to what were probably growing tensions with a resurgent Judaism after the debacle of Jerusalem's fall in 70 CE. It also includes how they would have struggled to assure Roman authorities that their new faith was not a danger, let alone subversive. Any actions undertaken by its officers based on such misunderstanding had to be seen as a failure of their duty to uphold justice and good order.

At the core of Luke's account is good news for the poor, which included, above all, Israel in its need, but extended also to non-Jews. It was a challenge to the status quo, a confrontation of the wealthy and powerful, a promise of a different order. Forgiveness of sins was central from the beginning, both for John and Jesus, and this entailed turning to God and becoming ready to embrace the vision of change, the kingdom of God. Luke does not confine the gospel, however, to forgiveness of sins or to only individual salvation and so does not make forgiveness of sins the primary focus in interpreting Jesus' death, as, for instance, would Paul. Luke's focus is change on a broader scale, which also shapes actions in community in the present, often with a strong ethical focus, not least in the handling of wealth. In this he has Jesus remain close to John the Baptist, but sees such change now working itself out in communities of believers. His gospel would enhance and inspire such faith in his time and in centuries to follow.

1

Announcing Hope

"Come into my studio!" (Luke 1:1–24)

Listening to Luke

^{1:1} Since many have attempted to produce an orderly report of the events that have come to fulfillment among us, ² as those who were eyewitnesses from the start and those who became servants of the message passed them on to us, ³ it seemed right also for me, in following everything closely from the beginning, to write an orderly account for you, most excellent Theophilos, ⁴ so that you could be sure that the information you have been given has a sound basis.

⁵ It happened in the days of King Herod of Judea that there was a certain priest, named Zechariah, of the Abijah order, whose wife was of Aaron's lineage, and her name was Elizabeth. ⁶ They were both upright people before God, blameless in behaving according to the Lord's commandments and laws. ⁷ And they were childless, since Elizabeth was unable to conceive and both were getting on in years.

⁸ And one time when his order was rostered, he was exercising his priestly duties before God. ⁹ And as was the custom for determining who was to enter the Lord's sanctuary to offer incense, the lot fell to him. ¹⁰ And the whole crowd of people was praying outside at the hour for offering incense ¹¹ and an angel of the Lord appeared to him

standing on the right side of the altar of incense. ¹² And Zechariah was taken aback when he saw him and became afraid. ¹³ But the angel said to him, "Don't be afraid, Zechariah. Because your prayer has been heard and your wife Elizabeth will bear you a son and you will name him John. ¹⁴ And you'll be filled with joy and gladness and many will be delighted at his birth. ¹⁵ For he will be great before the Lord. 'And he's not to drink wine and beer' [Num 6:3], and he will be filled with the Holy Spirit even from the time he leaves his mother's womb, ¹⁶ and he will turn many of Israel's folk to the Lord their God. ¹⁷ And he will go before him in the spirit of Elijah and direct the minds of fathers to their children and the disobedient to the wisdom of the upright, to make people ready for the Lord."

¹⁸ Then Zechariah said to the angel, "How will I know this? For I'm old and my wife is getting on in years." ¹⁹ And the angel responded, "I am Gabriel, the one who stands before God, and I was sent to speak with you and bring you this good news. ²⁰ And, see now, you will be struck dumb and unable to speak until the day this takes place because you didn't believe my prediction, which will come about in its own good time."

²¹ Now the people were waiting for Zechariah and were wondering why he was spending so much time in the sanctuary. ²² When he came out, he couldn't tell them anything, and they realized that he had had a vision in the sanctuary; and he was gesticulating to them and stayed silent. ²³ And when his service days were completed, he went off home.

²⁴ Some days later Elizabeth became pregnant and went into isolation for five months, saying, ²⁵ "The Lord has done this for me and has looked to remove the shame I've been feeling these days before people."

Thinking About Luke

By stopping at this point in chapter 1 we have interrupted Luke after he has scarcely begun. Had we been sitting listening to one of his readings of his gospel in the first century, we might expect to be listening for at least another hour or more. Some of those present with us would not have been surprised at how he began, namely with one big long sentence in Greek of sophisticated style (Luke 1:1–4), which I have tried to reproduce in the translation. They would be used to hearing such a preface as authors introduced their work. That was a convention, including among historians of the time.

The preface was a way of Luke's introducing us to his world and telling us what he intends. He is, in that sense, inviting us into his studio. He is going to be a good historian. That means taking into account what others have written and what has been passed down to him by word of mouth. His intent is to produce his own "orderly account." That is much more than listing events. It is, on the one hand, providing information and, on the other, doing so in a way that brings out the significance of Jesus, and that would require skill and imagination. Historians of the ancient world often wrote biographies of great people and in doing so exercised both care and creativity to ensure the legacy and significance of their subjects addressed the people who would be listening to their accounts. Luke is a historian of his time and a very good one.

We know at least some of the sources that Luke mentions. It is widely recognized that he used Mark's Gospel for his basic outline of Jesus' ministry. He has also used a collection of sayings, known also to Matthew. He would have also had sources not known to us from elsewhere. His preface tells us that he does not belong to the first generation of those who were eyewitnesses but belongs to at least a generation later. Had he invited us into his studio or his workplace, we might have seen some of these scrolls lying not too far away from where he was writing his own.

It was conventional not only to begin with a long sentence and preface, but also to make mention of a person who had also played a role in making the production possible. Luke refers very respectfully to Theophilos. His name means "Friend of God," but that may just be fortuitous, for it is highly likely that Luke mentions Theophilos as someone who has been significant for him in some way. Was Luke's studio in his house? Did Theophilos help Luke purchase the papyrus scrolls he needed? We have no idea, except that he is also identified as someone who has been instructed, that is, who has embraced the faith. It sounds like Luke has written his gospel just for him, but mentioning him is a standard convention. Luke wrote for all like Theophilos of his own day and unwittingly for all of us ever since who have come to value his work.

Luke was not a reporter of wooden style, but rather a creative writer. We see that already in his transition from the lofty style of his preface in

1:1–4 to his simple storytelling style in the verses that follow, which for many would have reminded them of the style of the Old Testament. It may well have been Luke's intention to invite his hearers to sense that they were back in the world of sacred stories.

Another convention among biographers was to tell stories about the birth of their heroes, often with creative imagination, which might include signs in the stars, appearance of gods and angels, and miraculous conceptions and births. Often the stories reflect the significance of what these heroes grew up to become. We see this already in the story of Moses' rescue from the river, foreshadowing and symbolizing his leading his people from captivity and oppression in the land of the River, as Egypt was called. People listening to Luke would recognize the convention and know that such stories were not really about the baby but about who the baby would become.

Thus, Luke follows the convention by offering stories about Jesus' birth, replete with appearance of angels and miracles of conception. He will have had Mark's Gospel before him and so prefaces Mark's story by adding two chapters that tell these wondrous stories about Jesus and John the Baptist. Mark's account begins with John the Baptist, and so it is not surprising that Luke tells stories of the wonders not only of Jesus' origins but also of John the Baptist's. It is even possible that those who in Luke's time saw themselves primarily as followers of John rather than Jesus were a source for the stories about John, but we cannot know for sure. As we go further into these chapters, we shall reflect on the way Luke compares and contrasts Jesus and John.

We have paused the story at the account of John's father, Zechariah, and his mother, Elizabeth. The story of a godly couple unable to conceive would recall for many of Luke's listeners the story of Sarah, who miraculously became pregnant in her nineties and gave birth to Isaac, or of Rebekah, enabled to conceive and give birth to Jacob, or of Hannah, who was similarly enabled to conceive and gave birth to Samuel. Some might also have known the legend of Melchizedek, preserved in the Jewish book 2 Enoch, whose mother miraculously conceived him without sleeping with her husband. The angel Gabriel announces the miracle to Zechariah.

For some of Luke's listeners, then and now, the account may touch on their own concerns about wanting to start a family. Elizabeth's concern about shame in not being able to conceive might also find echoes among those who might struggle with an unwarranted sense of inadequacy. In a healthy society we would want to encourage Elizabeth to resist such assumptions, quite apart from the fact that we know that the issue may not be with the woman at all but with the man.

Angels and miraculous conceptions belonged to such stories, but we miss their significance if we try to imagine they are historical reports about babies. They are not. They are all ways of saying something about who these babies became, so, here, about John and Jesus, and their ministry in particular, namely that we are to see the work of God in their ministries. In the case of Jesus, it was one special way of bringing to expression what Paul once declared: "God was in Christ." In the rest of Luke 1 and in the following chapter Luke will tell us much more.

Already in these initial verses we have an indication of John's role. They portray him as destined to fulfill a function that had been predicted of Elijah when he returns, as in Malachi:

> Lo, I will send you the prophet Elijah before the great and terrible day of the LORD comes. He will turn the hearts of parents to their children and the hearts of children to their parents. (Mal 4:5–6)

Mark similarly identifies John with Elijah (Mark 9:9–13) and portrays this as a living hope at the time of Jesus (Mark 6:15; 8:28; 9:4–5; 15:34–35; similarly, Luke 9:19, 30). When, in contrast, the Fourth Gospel has John emphatically deny he is Elijah, this was probably part of the author's attempt to redefine John's significance (John 1:21). When Luke has Gabriel see John's role as "to make people ready for the Lord" (Luke 1:17), this fits the way Mark and also Luke portray John's role, namely as preparing people for God's intervention, seen as expressed in Jesus' ministry. As we shall see in what follows, Luke is also concerned not to have John given greater prominence than Jesus.

Such stories of wondrous conceptions and births can sometimes contain incidental detail of historical value. Such is Luke's dating of John's birth, and so by implication also Jesus' birth, to the last years of Herod the Great, who died in 4 BCE, which corresponds to the dating of the birth of Jesus also in Matthew, and so is more correct than what Luke subsequently writes in 2:1–2, which would put it as happening in 6 CE.

Reflection: Why did ancient biographers really tell stories about babies? How can we celebrate Christmas in a way that keeps the focus not on the baby but on who the baby became?

Just a Girl (Luke 1:26–56)

Listening to Luke

1:26 When Elizabeth was six months pregnant, the angel Gabriel was sent on a mission by God to a town in Galilee called Nazareth **27** to a girl promised in marriage to a man named Joseph, of the house of David. The girl's name was Mary. **28** Approaching her, Gabriel said, "Hi, very special girl! The Lord is with you!" **29** She was taken aback at this and was wondering what this greeting was all about.

30 So the angel said to her, "Don't be afraid, Mary. God likes you. **31** And look, you're going to get pregnant and have a baby boy and you'll call him Jesus. **32** He'll be great and be called the Son of the Most High, and the Lord God will give him the throne of David his ancestor, **33** and he'll rule over the house of Jacob forever and there'll be no end to his rule."

34 Then Mary told the angel, "How can this be, because I haven't slept with anyone?"

35 The angel replied, "The Holy Spirit will come over you and the power of the Highest will overshadow you. Therefore, the holy baby you're going to have will be called the Son of God. **36** And look, in her old age Elizabeth your cousin's also become pregnant and is going to have a baby boy, too. So from once being known as not able to have a baby she's now in her sixth month, **37** because nothing will be impossible when God's with you." **38** Then Mary said, "Look, I'm the Lord's servant girl. Let it happen just as you've said it would." So the angel left her.

39 In those days Mary got up and hurried off to the hill country to a city in Judah, **40** and came into Zechariah's house and said hi to Elizabeth. **41** Now when Elizabeth heard Mary say hi, the baby did a jump in her womb, and Elizabeth was filled with the Holy Spirit **42** and declared in a loud voice, "You're really blessed among women and so will the baby be you're going to have. ⁴³ How come I'm so fortunate that the mother of my Lord has come to me? ⁴⁴ Because look, when I heard you say hi, the baby in my womb jumped for joy. ⁴⁵ And she can be really happy for believing that the Lord's promise she was told about is really going to come true."

⁴⁶ Then Mary said, "God is great! That's what fills my mind ⁴⁷ and with my whole being I'm so happy with God as my savior, ⁴⁸ because he's paid attention to me even though I'm nothing special, just like his servant girl. Gosh, from now on people are going to recognize how lucky I am, ⁴⁹ because the mighty one has done wonderful things for me; he's truly holy. ⁵⁰ And his compassion stays with those who hold him in awe forever and ever across the ages. ⁵¹ His mighty power has been doing great things; it's sent those who were full of themselves packing ⁵² and knocked the powerful off their thrones and lifted up people at the bottom of the heap. ⁵³ He's made sure hungry people get enough good food to eat and he's sent off the wealthy with nothing. ⁵⁴ He's helped his servant Jacob, and kept showing love to our fathers, ⁵⁵ to Abraham and his descendants, as he promised he would."

⁵⁶ Mary stayed with her for three months and then set off home.

Thinking About Luke

The usual age for men to marry was around thirty, so at the age when Jesus would have been expected to marry, he instead embarked on his calling (Luke 3:23). For women, marriage usually took place as soon after they began menstruating as possible, so as young as twelve. By the time Jesus is exercising his ministry, Joseph would have reached around sixty years of age, so that it should not be surprising that we hear little of him, given that many men would not survive into their sixties. He was probably dead by then.

Most people hearing Luke's story in the ancient world would have assumed that Mary was just a girl. Members of the extended family, the senior men, would usually come to an arrangement whereby a girl would be promised in marriage to an older man, sometimes called a betrothal, not really the equivalent of what we call an engagement, which assumes a mutual arrangement by the couple. The girl usually had no choice, as is still often the case in cultures where this is still the norm. Marriages those days were thus arranged, and that would have been the case also with Mary and Joseph.

The fact that Joseph is a descendant of David, which Luke signals early, is significant because it qualifies Jesus to be seen as of David's line, even though not directly Joseph's child. One may assume that most of the extended family were also of David's line, including Mary, but neither Matthew nor Luke, who both trace his ancestry through Joseph, see any problem in doing so, despite their stories suggesting he was not involved in the reproductive process.

Just as Gabriel spoke to Zechariah, so now he speaks to Mary. There are many parallels between John's story and Jesus' story. Luke even portrays them as cousins, something not attested elsewhere. The parallels between the stories of John's and Jesus' beginnings are striking. They include: Gabriel tells both Zechariah and Mary not to be afraid, announces to both a miraculous conception (though in Jesus' case it is an even greater miracle because no male is involved), tells both what to name their child, and says of both that their child will be great. Both hear Gabriel's promise, but Zechariah doubts, given Elizabeth's age, and so is struck dumb, whereas Mary believes, despite not having had sexual intercourse. The parallels extend also to their births. Both are circumcised on the eighth day, as the biblical Law required, and both are said to grow and become strong. Of John, Luke says: "The child grew and became strong in spirit" (Luke 1:80) and of Jesus: "The child grew and became strong, filled with wisdom" (Luke 2:40).

They are clearly parallel, yet consistently Luke portrays Jesus as greater than John. We may speculate about Luke's reasons for doing so. Perhaps it was to counter groups who thought the opposite. Unquestionably, Luke holds John in high regard and later in his gospel will even cite a saying of Jesus found also in Matthew in which Jesus declares: "I tell you, there's no one greater than John among all born of women," but then, however, continues: "but the one who is least in the kingdom of God is greater than he is" (Luke 7:28; Matt 11:11).

Mary's encounter with Elizabeth underlines the superiority and does so in a way that brings us into the world of family: the unborn John jumps for joy at the encounter as baby Jesus' mom and Elizabeth meet. It helps give the story a very human feel. The very human touch has already been present in Elizabeth's struggles with social shame at not being able to bear children and then her relief, and then in Mary's perplexity at being told that she would conceive without having slept with anyone. The assumption here is that betrothed couples would not have sex before marriage, a stance also reflected in Paul's advice that betrothed couples should marry if they find holding on too hard, and not feel guilty about marrying (1 Cor 7:9).

The story about Mary's miraculous conception is all about wonder and miracle and celebrates the specialness of Jesus. Nothing indicates that Luke had an anti-sexual agenda, as though sex and married life are something less than holy and that virginity is somehow superior. All of our accounts report that Mary and Joseph did marry and produce children, sons and daughters, and this was not seen as Mary then becoming unholy. Rather, Luke's story makes Mary a model of faith and willingness to follow God's will. In a world dominated by male models of greatness, Mary stands out, and her story affirms women and depicts greatness as oneness with God and God's will.

Luke indicated John the Baptist's future role is to act in the spirit of Elijah. In his depiction of Gabriel's message to Mary he indicates Jesus' role as to be the hoped for Messiah. The Messiah (Greek: Christ) means the Anointed One, and more particularly the one anointed to be king in David's line. As kings of David's line were hailed as sons of David, so the Messiah was hailed as the Son of David. Similarly, as kings were hailed as sons of God (Ps 2:7), so the Messiah would be Son of God and so Mary's son is to be the Messiah of David's line, the Son of God. Luke has Elizabeth awed at the encounter with the one who would be also her Lord, Jesus the Messiah.

The words "The Holy Spirit will come over you and the power of the Highest will overshadow you. Therefore, the holy baby you're going to have will be called the Son of God" (Luke 1:35) might sound to some of Luke's hearers like Jesus was a hybrid. This might have been especially so for those who were familiar with stories of Greek mythology about gods sleeping with women and producing hybrids, half god and half man. Nothing, however, in Luke's Gospel suggests such an understanding, and nor is that the case in Matthew, the only other place where we find the story of Mary conceiving without male sperm.

The most likely understanding, if we were to interview Luke, would be that he would have seen this as an act of creation, namely that God created the male sperm to make the birth possible, not that it was God's sperm. The most common understanding of human reproduction at the time—very different from ours—was that the man sowed the seed (semen) in the woman, who incubated and nourished it.

Suggesting that God must have intervened in the process to provide newly created human male sperm was just one of a range of secondary explanations of how it might have come about that Jesus was so special. John's Gospel attributes that specialness to the fact that in Jesus God's Wisdom/Word became flesh, and others could explain it by attributing Jesus' specialness to the Spirit. In the Jewish writing 2 Enoch, written in the early first century CE, the famous Melchizedek, priest in Salem (Jerusalem), is said to have been also conceived by a woman without her husband's sperm.

The story of Mary later took on a life of its own. Mary's virginity was celebrated and came to be seen as permanent. Those who saw it this way then chose to depict her children as cousins or to depict them as children of a previous marriage that they supposed that Joseph must have had. From being a model, she became an exception. Counter legends then also developed asserting that a Roman soldier must have raped her. Better to let Matthew and Luke's story be what it is, as belonging to the storytelling of the time about wondrous conceptions, designed to celebrate who Jesus became, rather than attempts to provide scientific prenatal data.

The role that the Messiah would perform was more important than the status indicated by titles given the Messiah: he will rule God's kingdom, and that rule will be forever. Mary's song, sometimes named by the first word of its Latin translation, the *Magnificat*, begins with Mary expressing her faith and gratitude, echoing Hannah's song, "My heart exults in the LORD; my strength is exalted in my God" (1 Sam 2:1), but then moves to acclaim what God has done and, by implication, what God would do. It is radical. It overturns the powerful and brings relief to the lowly, feeding the hungry and lifting up the lowly.

Luke portrays this hope as focused on Israel, Abraham's descendants. Mary's song speaks of this hope as having already been realized. It uses the past tense. "He's made sure hungry people get enough good food to eat and he's sent off the wealthy with nothing" (Luke 1:53). By Luke's time this had not happened, or had happened only in minor ways. Some would therefore see Luke using poetry, as employing such statements only symbolically, perhaps just as ways of saying that Jesus would bring forgiveness of sins. It is much more likely that Luke sees these statements as stating what really will happen in the future, especially when the kingdom of God comes and Jesus leads it as the Messiah. There will be real social change. It is not just about forgiveness of sins.

For Luke, this will take place when Jesus will return to Jerusalem at the climax of history. That is still to come, from Luke's perspective. It will bring blessing for Israel, but also for the nations. Luke will also go on to show that such good news and hope is, however, already starting to be realized through Jesus' earthly ministry. "Good news for the poor," meaning good news for the poor and hungry, for Israel, and for all who are downtrodden, will come. It is at the heart of the gospel as Luke portrays it.

Mary's song expresses radical hope. It can also be hijacked to serve hate, hate of the rich and powerful, and hope only for the poor and needy. Some people prefer to construct their life around love and hate. Luke clearly does not embrace such an ideology. The message and challenge of love is for all. He will show it reaching out to the poor and destitute but also calling rich Zacchaeus out of his tree. It is radical and inclusive, at every level, seeking to bring change, to put hope, healing, and goodness at the heart of society.

Reflection: In what ways have retellings and imaginings of Mary's story been good news and not so good news?

Hopes for Liberation (Luke 1:57–80)

Listening to Luke

1:57 The time came for Elizabeth to have her baby, and she gave birth to a baby boy. **58** Her neighbors and family heard that the Lord had extended his compassion to her, and they shared her joy. **59** And it happened that on the eighth day they came to circumcise the child and they were going to call him by the name of his father, Zechariah, **60** but his mother said, "No. He's going to be called John." **61** They countered, "No one in your family has that name." **62** Then they motioned to the father to find out what he wanted the child to be called. **63** So, asking for something to write on, he wrote down: "His name is John." And everyone was amazed. **64** Then suddenly his ability to speak came back and he could talk, and he started praising God. **65** And all the neighbors were overawed, and these things were reported across the whole hill country of Judea. **66** Everyone who heard about it began to wonder, "What's this child going to become?" Because the hand of the Lord was with him.

67 Then Zechariah his father was filled with the Holy Spirit and uttered a prophecy, saying: **68** "Blessed is the Lord God of Israel, because he has come and brought liberation for his people, **69** and raised up an agent of salvation for us in the house of David his servant, **70** as he announced through the words of his holy prophets of old, **71** freedom from our enemies and the hands of those who hate us, **72** to show us the compassion he shared with our fathers and to remember his holy covenant, **73** the oath which he swore to Abraham our father, to grant us **74** that, liberated from our enemies, we might worship him **75** in holiness and uprightness before him all our days. **76** And you, child, will be called a prophet of the Most High; for you will go before the Lord to prepare his way, **77** to give knowledge of salvation to his people through the forgiveness of their sins, **78** by the deep compassion of our God, by which the dawn has shone upon us from on high, ⁷⁹ to bring light to those dwelling in darkness and the shadow of death, to set our feet upon the path of peace."

⁸⁰ The child grew and became strong in spirit, and he was in the outback until the day when he made his appearance to Israel.

Thinking About Luke

We now reach the climax of the story with which Luke's Gospel began, namely the story of John the Baptist's miraculous conception. Elizabeth has her baby. Luke continues the reference to her having felt ashamed at not being able to conceive and so frames the birth as, in part, God's saving her from such shame. This reflects values of Luke's world, which we no longer share.

No details are given of the birth, unlike what is to follow in the next chapter about Jesus. Instead, Luke takes us straight on to the child's circumcision on the eighth day, following biblical Law, and reported also of Jesus in Luke 2:21, where it is also associated with the naming. In John's case we have the little drama of the friends and family suggesting he be called after his father, which was common, but Elizabeth's objecting and saying it was to be "John" and Zechariah's having to confirm it in writing and then recovering his ability to speak.

That then leads to what is a poetic section, namely Zechariah's prophecy, widely known by its first word in Latin, the *Benedictus*, just as Mary's speech is known as the *Magnificat*. For both speeches Luke may well have been drawing on older tradition and adapting it for his story. These are liberation songs. In the *Magnificat* the beginning is specific to Mary, but halfway through the focus moves to hope of liberation in general. In the *Benedictus* we have the reverse. The first half focuses on hope in general and its fulfillment through the coming of the Messiah and the second half relates directly to his son, John the Baptist.

Mary's song looks very much like it has been composed on the basis of Hannah's song in 1 Sam 2:1–10. It portrays her as beginning with praise and thanksgiving to God and goes on to mention overcoming the powerful, lifting up the poor, and overcoming enemies. Indeed, much of its language echoes biblical passages. The same is true of the *Benedictus* of Zechariah. In the same way that Luke's style of storytelling in this chapter recalls the style of storytelling of the Old Testament, so the words he places on the lips of Elizabeth and especially Mary and Zechariah echo sacred stories of old.

Luke is telling sacred story. This is a way of saying that the story of Jesus continues the story of God and God's people and indeed brings it to a climax. The next chapter will similarly feature faithful and devout Jews. The message is clear. The coming of Jesus is not a departure from Israel's faith but its continuance and fulfillment. In the same way Luke will depict the beginning of the church in his second volume, the Acts of the Apostles, as a group of faithful devout Jews worshiping in the temple.

Like the *Magnificat*, Zechariah's prophecy uses the past tense: "Blessed is the Lord God of Israel, because he has come and brought liberation for his people" (Luke 1:68). It is similarly to be read not as a statement about the past but as a statement about what was to come. God has effectively done it, made it possible, by raising up the Messiah. In that sense, it is as good as done. If we ask what is to be done, it is "that, liberated from our enemies, we might worship him in holiness and uprightness before him all our days" (Luke 1:74–75). This is Jewish nationalism and reflects the aspirations of many Jewish movements of the time, but, as Luke will go on to show, it is also bigger than Israel, and means hope also for the non-Jewish world, to which the message of good news for the poor would also be proclaimed.

The Jewishness of this expectation is not to be denied or explained away. It meets us again in the following chapter, which hails Simeon as upright and devout and looking forward in hope and expectation for the relief to come for Israel (Luke 2:25), and hails Anna as also looking forward to Jerusalem being liberated (Luke 2:38). Luke will have Jesus himself tell the people of Jerusalem that the day will come when they will lift up their eyes to see him coming there to reign (Luke 21:28). Similarly, Luke hails Joseph of Arimathea who was "looking forward to the coming of the kingdom of God" (Luke 23:51) and has Jesus not quash the disciples' expression of hope on the Emmaus Road that he would liberate Israel (Luke 24:21) or when at his ascension they ask whether that was the time when he would restore the kingdom to Israel (Acts 1:6). His response is to tell them not to worry about the timing but in the meantime to go out into the wider world with his message of hope (Acts 1:7–8).

For many of Luke's hearers, who would have included Jews, former converts to Judaism, and gentiles now incorporated in the movement that claimed continuity with Israel's faith, these hopes would have been real. They reflect the belief that God would one day have Jesus return to rule the kingdom of God and be based in Jerusalem, at least for a period, in Revelation described as a thousand year reign, before the final transformation of all into a new form of creation, a common Jewish and early Christian hope. Imagining hope gave birth to many models, which could be elaborated in various ways. Imagination and fantasy abound, but the underlying reality beyond it all, inspiring the images, is the faith that in the end there is God, that God cares, and in God we have all we need for hope.

Luke's version of hope, envisioned within the framework of Jewish aspirations, is not to be watered down and treated simply as another way of saying that Jesus came to bring us forgiveness of sins, for instance. That is already contradicted in Zechariah's speech, which declares that his son John's role already includes declaring forgiveness of sins. Mark also makes clear that the offer to all of forgiveness of sins was central to John's message, something Jesus also offers during ministry. They also saw his death as like a sacrifice for sins, continuing this message, and not to be seen as replacing it or as the only point in time when forgiveness became possible, as some have seen it. But forgiveness was just the first step in the journey towards liberation in a broader sense. Luke portrays John as preparing the way for God's action in Jesus. That preparation included turning to God (repentance) and so opening oneself to forgiveness and renewal. That was and is preparation. There was something much more to come. Salvation/liberation is about much more, as Luke will tell us, and includes engagement in liberation also already in this age.

Luke has Zechariah frame John's role in a way which echoes what we find at the beginning of Mark's Gospel which Luke then picks up in Luke 3. John's is a subordinate role, but essential, and his historical mentorship of Jesus not to be denied. Luke hails his significance, but is careful to set Jesus above him. They are not to be seen as rivals. Rather, the focus of both is God and the hope of liberation, which God alone can bring and for which Jesus is the chief agent. Luke's imagining of what that will mean in the end, a reign based in Jerusalem, may not be a specific hope we would embrace. His depiction, however, of what it means at least in the interim invites us to hear the vision and aspirations expressed in Mary's *Magnificat* and Zechariah's *Benedictus* and embrace them as also our hope and agenda for living.

Reflection: What was the good news John the Baptist brought, and how was it similar yet different from the good news brought by Jesus? How does such good news speak to us today?

The Christmas Story (Luke 2:1–52)

Listening to Luke

2:1 In those days a decree went out from Emperor Augustus that the whole world be put on a register. **2** This first census took place when Quirinius was governor of Syria. **3** And all went off to be registered, each to their home city. **4** So Joseph, too, went up from the city of Nazareth in Galilee to Judea to the city of David called Bethlehem because he was of the house and lineage of David, **5** to be registered along with Mary who was betrothed to him, who was pregnant. **6** While they were there, her pregnancy reached full term, **7** and she gave birth to her baby boy, her first child, and she wrapped him up warm and laid him down in an animals' feeder box, because there wasn't any room for them in the guest shelter.

8 Now there were shepherds out in the field in that place and they were looking after their sheep overnight. **9** And an angel of the Lord appeared to them and the Lord's glory shone around them and they were very scared. **10** But the angel told them, "Don't be scared. For look, I've got good news for you that will bring a lot of happiness for all people, **11** because today someone to liberate you has been born, namely the Lord Messiah, in the city of David. **12** And this is the sign to indicate it: you'll find a baby all wrapped up warm and lying in a feeder box." **13** Then suddenly a crowd of the heavenly personnel appeared alongside the angel, praising God and saying, **14** "Glory to God in the highest and peace on earth to people who please him."

15 So when the angels left them and went back up into heaven, the shepherds said to each other, "Let's now go to Bethlehem and see this thing which the Lord has told us about." **16** And they rushed off down and found Mary and Joseph, and the baby lying in the feeder box. **17** When they saw them, they told them what had been said to them about this child. ⁱ⁸ And everyone hearing them was amazed at what had been told to them by the shepherds. ¹⁹ And Mary stored up the memory of all this, wondering about it in her thoughts. ²⁰ The shepherds meanwhile hived off back, glorifying and praising God for all they had heard and seen, just as it had been reported to them.

²¹ When eight days had passed, and it was time to circumcise him, he was given the name Jesus, as announced by the angel before his mother became pregnant with him. ²² And when the time came for their purification ritual in accordance with the Law of Moses, they brought him up to Jerusalem to present him to the Lord, ²³ as is required in the Law of the Lord, which states that every male baby which emerges from the womb is to be deemed holy before the Lord, ²⁴ and to offer a sacrifice in accordance with what is stated in the Law of the Lord, namely, a pair of doves or two young pigeons.

²⁵ Now there was a man in Jerusalem called Simeon, and he was upright and devout and was looking for relief to come for Israel, and the Holy Spirit was upon him. ²⁶ He had been assured by the Holy Spirit that he would not see death before he set eyes on the Lord's Messiah. ²⁷ Prompted by the Spirit, he came into the temple and, while the parents were bringing baby Jesus to do for him what was customary according to the Law, ²⁸ he took him into his arms and blessed God and said: ²⁹ "Now, my master, you're letting your servant go in peace in accordance with your word, ³⁰ because my eyes have seen your liberation, ³¹ which you prepared for us before all people, ³² a light to bring enlightenment to the gentiles and glory for your people, Israel."

³³ His father and mother were amazed at what was being said about him. ³⁴ And Simeon blessed them and said to Mary his mother, "Look, this boy will lead many in Israel to fall and others to rise and will be a controversial sign ³⁵ (and a sword will pierce your heart) so as to bring out into the open what's going on in the minds of many."

³⁶ Now there was also a female prophet, called Anna, daughter of Phanuel, of the tribe of Asher. She was very old and had once been married for seven years when she was a girl ³⁷ and was now at eighty-four years a widow. She never left the temple and engaged in worship by fasting and prayer day and night. ³⁸ And at that very time she came and stood there and was singing praise to God, and she started to tell all the people about him who were longing for Jerusalem's freedom.

⁳⁹ Now when they had completed all the requirements according to the Law of the Lord, they returned to Galilee to their town of Nazareth. ⁴⁰ And the child grew and became strong and filled with wisdom, and God's grace was upon him.

⁴¹ And his parents used to go up to Jerusalem every year for the Passover festival. ⁴² And it happened that when he was twelve and they had gone up to the festival, as was their custom, ⁴³ and the days came to an end and they set off to return back home, their boy, Jesus, stayed on in Jerusalem and they, his parents, were not aware of it.

⁴⁴ Assuming he was in the group they were in, they went on their way for a day and then looked for him among their family and acquaintances. ⁴⁵ When they didn't find him, they went back to Jerusalem to look for him. ⁴⁶ And it happened that they found him three days later in the temple sitting among teachers and listening to them and asking them questions. ⁴⁷ All who listened to him were astonished at his level of understanding and the way he responded.

⁴⁸ When they saw him, they were amazed, but his mother said to him, "My boy, why have you treated us like this? Look, your dad and I have been worried sick looking for you." ⁴⁹ He replied, "Why were you looking for me? Don't you know that I've got to be on about my Father's agenda?" ⁵⁰ And they didn't understand what he was saying to them. ⁵¹ So he went on down with them and entered Nazareth and was obedient to them. His mother stored up memory of all of this in her mind. ⁵² And Jesus grew in wisdom and maturity and in good standing with God and people.

Thinking About Luke

Luke is still in the mode of telling wondrous stories about Jesus' origins, replete with heavenly signs and angels. He places it initially in the context of a census, which eases the shift from Nazareth as the place where Jesus was apparently brought up to Bethlehem, which was richly symbolic, as the city of David.

Luke has assumed that his dating fits what he had already said, namely that John's and Jesus' births took place in the final years of Herod the Great's reign, who died in 4 BCE, but he may not have realized that the Quirinius he mentions was not governor of Syria until ten years later. We have no evidence of a census in 4 BCE, let alone one of all the world, and a Roman census would have been only of Roman citizens and Judea did not fall under direct Roman rule until 6 CE. Perhaps the fact that there were revolts against Rome both in 4 BCE and in 6 CE contributed to the confusion. These are inaccurate incidentals of no great significance.

There is much greater significance in the links between the story and what has been said thus far in Luke's Gospel, and such references to political realities evoke such reflection. For here we have the birth of the one announced to be the Messiah, the liberator. Luke's hearers would have been aware not only that Bethlehem was David's city but also that David was a shepherd. They would also very likely have been aware of Roman propaganda, which hailed the emperor as Son of God, used the language of "good news" to announce its achievements, and declared that one of those achievements was to bring peace. They had, after all, cleared the land and sea routes of rebels and bandits and made peaceful travel possible and through their powerful army had crushed dissent and brought stability.

By contrast, Luke subversively proclaims a very different Son of God, not on an imperial throne, but lying in a feeder box, being a bearer of very different good news and a very different kind of peace. He would ultimately be enthroned, but upon a cross. Luke's apparently harmless, almost romantic, Christmas story hides a challenge and embodies a call for change.

The theme of liberation continues in the account of Simeon and then Anna. Both are devout and upright and both embrace the expectation of change and both see Jesus as God's agent to bring change: "liberation" for Israel and enlightenment for the gentiles; freedom for Jerusalem! This further underlines that the underlying theme behind the celebrated Christmas story is also hope for change. In this way Luke's first two chapters set the scene for what follows in his gospel. It is about Jesus as the Messiah, the hope for Israel but also for the gentile wider world, and it is about liberation.

Luke imagines this as very soon to result in Jesus coming to rule God's kingdom from Jerusalem. That didn't happen. Imagining the shape of hope is never easy, but the notion that hope means liberation from oppression is not just about what one might imagine as the end of history. It is also the hope and agenda for the here and now and this is what Luke will go on to show in his gospel. It will be good news for the poor and bring about change. We prepare for it by following John in the sense of heeding the call to turn to God, receive forgiveness, and then be empowered by the Spirit to bring love and change into the world.

Luke ends what effectively is his long overture to his gospel with a story about the twelve-year-old Jesus. Nowhere in the four Gospels do we find any information about Jesus' life beyond his birth till when his ministry began. This passage is the only exception. The temptation to fill in the thirty-year gap was hard to resist, not least also because it was what those writing biographies of heroes did. Thus, in second-century gospels we find many wonder-boy stories about Jesus, who dazzles his playmates and others with his magical powers.

Is Luke one of the first to write one of these wonder-boy stories about Jesus, or is there some actual memory being reworked here? It would be a lot more impressive if Luke told us that the teachers in the temple sat around listening to Jesus teaching them. Was he interrogating them, testing them with questions? One way of hearing Luke's story is a lot more restrained: the twelve-year-old was asking questions, seeking information, and then showing a good deal of maturity in the way he responded.

One might also wonder about how those early listeners to Luke's story would have understood the story. "Sorry, mom; I should have been more considerate to you and dad." That isn't there, but nor does the story tell us that Mary apologized for confronting him. Did his response that he was about God's work justify his not telling them? Is his response in some way a foreshadowing of how his followers might have to treat their families? Was that really acceptable behavior?

Too many questions! This is a simple story designed to highlight Jesus' significance, credibly building on the assumption that he must have shown wisdom and intelligence as a young person. Luke shows little interest in speculation about what the boy asked about, or in how we are to evaluate Mary's interaction, and settles it all down with the note that they all went home and Jesus was a good boy who, like John, grew in wisdom, maturity, and acceptability. The real story of what happened roughly eighteen years later was yet to come.

Reflection: A harmless romantic story about baby Jesus—was it?

Getting Ready (Luke 3:1–38)

Listening to Luke

³:¹ In the fifteenth year of the reign of Emperor Tiberius, when Pontius Pilate was prefect of Judea, and Herod tetrarch of Galilee, and his brother Philip tetrarch of Ituraea and the region of Trachonitis, and Lysanias tetrarch of Abilene, ² and during the high priesthood of Annas and Caiaphas, the word of God came to John, son of Zechariah, in the outback. ³ And he went into all the area around the Jordan announcing a baptism in which people could represent their turning to God and having their sins forgiven, ⁴ as it is written in the book containing Isaiah the prophet's sayings: "A voice calling out in the wilderness, 'Prepare the way of the Lord; make his paths straight! ⁵ Every valley will be filled in and every mountain and hill made low and the crooked things will be straightened out and the rough places made into smooth paths; ⁶ and all flesh shall see God's liberating action.'"

⁷ For he would say to the crowds coming out to be baptized by him, "You nest of snakes, who warned you to escape from God's impending anger? ⁸ Produce fruit indicating you're turning yourselves back to God and don't start telling yourselves, 'We're children of Abraham,' because, I'm telling you, God can raise up children to Abraham from these stones. ⁹ The axe is already poised at the root of the trees, and every tree which doesn't produce good fruit will be cut down and thrown into the fire."

¹⁰ Then the crowds asked him, "What should we do?" ¹¹ He replied, "Anyone with two coats should give one to someone who has none and anyone who has food should do the same." ¹² Even some tax collectors came to be baptized, and they said to him, "Teacher, what should we do?" ¹³ He responded: "Don't take more than what is allocated for you to take."

¹⁴ And some soldiers also asked him, "What should we do?" He told them, "Don't exploit anyone or accuse them falsely, and be content with your wages."

¹⁵ People had great expectations and were all wondering about John, whether he might be the Messiah. ¹⁶ He responded to them all, "I baptize you with water. Someone more powerful than me is coming. I don't deserve even to undo the strap of his sandals. He's going to baptize you with the Holy Spirit and fire. ¹⁷ His winnowing fork is in his hand to get on to cleaning out his threshing floor and to bring the wheat into his silo, and he'll burn up the chaff with fire that never goes out."

¹⁸ In many other ways he addressed the people as he brought them good news. ¹⁹ But when Herod the tetrarch was accused by John of wrongdoing because of marrying Herodias, his brother's wife, and the many other bad things that Herod did, ²⁰ he topped the lot by putting John in prison.

²¹ Now it happened that while all the people were being baptized, Jesus also was baptized, and when he was praying the heaven opened up ²² and the Holy Spirit came down in bodily form like a dove and alighted on him and a voice came from heaven saying, "You are my beloved Son; I am very pleased with you."

²³ And Jesus, himself, started his ministry when he was around thirty years of age, being the son, as was assumed, of Joseph, who was son of Eli, ²⁴ son of Matthat, son of Levi, son of Melchi, son of Jannai, son of Joseph, ²⁵ son of Mattathias, son of Amos, son of Nahum, son of Esli, son of Nangai, ²⁶ son of Maath, son of Mattathias, son of Semein, son of Josech, son of Joda, ²⁷ son of Joanan, son of Rhesa, son of Zerubbabel, son of Shealtiel, son of Neri, ²⁸ son of Melchi, son of Addi, son of Cosam, son of Elmadam, son of Er, ²⁹ son of Joshua, son of Eliezer, son of Jorim, son of Matthat, son of Levi, ³⁰ son of Simeon, son of Judah, son of Joseph, son of Jonam, son of Eliakim, ³¹ son of Melea, son of Menna, son of Mattatha, son of Nathan, son of David, ³² son of Jesse, son of Obed, son of Boaz, son of Sala, son of Nahshon, ³³ son of Amminadab, son of Admin, son of Arni, son of Hezron, son of Perez, son of Judah, ³⁴ son of Jacob, son of Isaac, son of Abraham, son of Terah, son of Nahor, ³⁵ son of Serug, son of Reu, son of Peleg, son of Eber, son of Shelah, ³⁶ son of Cainan, son of Arphaxad, son of Shem, son of Noah, son of Lamech ³⁷ son of Methuselah, son of Enoch, son of Jared,

son of Mahalaleel, son of Cainan, son of Enoch, son of Seth, son of Adam, son of God.

Thinking About Luke

With chapter 3, Luke picks up Mark's story and makes it his own. Over two chapters at the beginning of his gospel, he has highlighted John the Baptist's significance and may even have used legendary material associated with his birth. Now he uses Mark, but also the material he had in common with Matthew, which provided some sayings of John, and in addition he brings material unique to his gospel.

He begins with detailed dating. This is at one level doing history. At another level it is implicitly placing the story in real time and real history. The message is: this is not myth; this is real. As in his previous references to dates in relation to who ruled at the time, his sources may not have been very reliable. The fifteenth year of Tiberius's reign would take us to ca. 29 CE, and this may well be the basis on which our calendar places Jesus' birth at the year zero, since Luke goes on to speak of Jesus at the time as thirty years old (Luke 3:23). As we have seen, Luke places John's and Jesus' births in the latter years of Herod the Great, who died in 4 BCE, a timing that matches Matthew's account. This is more likely. We also noted that in 2:1–2 Luke has even another date for Jesus' birth, ten years later, namely 6 CE, when we know Quirinius became governor of Syria.

More important is what he goes on to report of John's activity. He omits details about his dress and diet but, taking up Mark, he makes it very clear that John came to call people to turn their lives around (repent) and submit to God by allowing John to immerse them in the Jordan, symbolizing their being immersed in God's forgiving compassion. Usually people immersed themselves for purification or in relation to seeking forgiveness of sin. John's innovation of doing it to others gave him the reputation of being John the Baptizer or Baptist, perhaps originally a nickname, John the Dipper. Luke had already signaled this as John's key role in the words of Zechariah: "to give knowledge of salvation to his people through the forgiveness of their sins" (Luke 1:77). In this, John was offering divine forgiveness to all.

Frequently people have missed this when they have reduced the Christian gospel to just forgiveness of sins, often in a limited understanding of the gospel, as if it was merely about assuring people that they will go to heaven when they die. Instead, Luke makes it very clear that John offered forgiveness of sins in preparation for what the gospel would be about, the intervention of God to bring hope and change. John was giving radical expression to what was presupposed as part of Israel's faith, namely that God forgives sin, as part of preparing the way. The gospel also presupposes such forgiveness but is about much more. Indeed, John portrays forgiveness as part of getting ready for what was about to come.

As he follows Mark, Luke does not take up the first half of Mark's citation from Isaiah, "Look, I am sending my messenger ahead of you, who will prepare your way" (Mark 1:2), though he had used its wording in Zechariah's depiction of John's role: "And you, child, will be called a prophet of the Most High; for you will go before the Lord to prepare his way" (Luke 1:76). It is, in fact, a citation from Mal 3:1 (but also echoing Exod 23:20), not Isaiah, as Mark claims, and so both Luke and Matthew delete it. Instead, Luke cites the passage that Mark has from Isa 40:3 and then extends it to include also Isa 40:4–5. This has the advantage that Isa 40:5 refers to God's promised act of liberation, which all humanity would see, a key theme in Luke's portrait of Jesus.

It coheres with Luke's approach that he then brings exchanges, unique to his account, in which John challenges people coming for baptism to be serious about turning their lives around and to demonstrate it by engaging in generous and socially just behavior. For Luke, turning to God (repentance) had to mean embracing God's agenda, and that agenda is compassion and social justice. Elsewhere he speaks of it in terms of being good news for the poor. That is what counts, not one's claimed racial and religious status.

John's challenge is stark. Its assumption is not only that there will be liberation, but also that there will be accountability and judgment, which Luke depicts using sayings attributed to John in the source he shares with Matthew: about the axe and the burning up of chaff. This is more than a prediction of the impending action of God. It is also a prediction about the role of the Messiah, John's superior, as Luke has reinforced during the birth narratives.

Jesus as the Messiah is to be God's agent in baptizing with the Holy Spirit and fire. This version of John's prediction found in Matthew and Luke's source goes beyond Mark's by adding "fire." In Mark, Jesus' baptizing with the Spirit refers to what he would do through the Spirit in his ministry. This is likely also the case in Luke, though his second volume will relate it to the day of Pentecost, which celebrates the coming down of the Spirit upon believers (Acts 1:5), indeed, also using the imagery of fire. Both Luke and Matthew include the prediction that Jesus will baptize with fire, a clear allusion to his being God's agent in judgment. By this they were referring to the day of judgment to come at the end of time. They probably envisaged it as not too far away—and certainly not two millennia away!

It is very likely that the historical John the Baptist did point forward to an imminent intervention of God to bring both liberation and judgment. Such expectations were around at the time, and it is also clear that the first followers of Jesus shared the expectation that they were living at the climax of history. It did mean, however, that they had to give careful attention to John's predictions, not least because Jesus did not in fact fulfill them during his ministry.

There are indications that John and his disciples found this failure of fulfillment to be a problem, so the source that Matthew and Luke use reports that John sent to Jesus to enquire what was going on. Jesus' response was to say that the prediction would, indeed, be fulfilled, but that in the interim he was engaged in the task of already bringing liberation to people and John should not be disappointed. We will be discussing this when we come to it in Luke 7:18–23 (its parallel in Matthew is 11:2–6).

Luke does not, therefore, proceed to show Jesus wielding an axe or a winnowing fork. Instead, he will show Jesus embarking on a ministry that will be good news for the poor. Before Luke moves to his account of Jesus' baptism, he brings a summary of what happened to John, as is reported in detail in Mark 6:11–29, which he omits when he reproduces Mark at that point. Like Mark, Luke notes that John had offended Herod Antipas by criticizing him for marrying his brother's wife.

In fact, what happened was that Antipas had an affair with Herodias, the wife of his half-brother, Herod, whom Mark calls Philip (not the Philip he mentions in 3:1). Herodias then divorced Philip and Antipas divorced his wife and then Herodias and Antipas married. Marrying the divorced wife of one's half-brother breached incest laws in Lev 18, if interpreted very, very strictly. It would not be a breach of law in most societies today, at least in the Western world. Others might have objected to the divorces themselves and the affair, and Essenes and Sadducees to the fact that Herodias was Antipas's niece, something they opposed, whereas Pharisees did not.

Luke adds that Antipas did much else that was blameworthy, and this is closer to what the Jewish historian Josephus, writing about the same time as Luke, tells us, namely that the larger issue was that John called Antipas's rule into question.

Mark mentions John's arrest as the point after which Jesus began his ministry (Mark 1:14). Luke does not do so, but, having offered his summary, moves on to Jesus' baptism. Some see the fact that Luke mentions Jesus' baptism almost incidentally as something Jesus underwent along with everyone else was in order to play it down and ward off the embarrassment that Jesus in this way took the junior position, but this need not be so. Nor does Luke seem bothered that Jesus' undergoing baptism would suggest that he, too, needed forgiveness of sins. For Luke that seems not to have been an issue. Instead, he has Jesus, too, immersed in God's compassion, and that made sense.

More important is what then happened. Here Luke adapts Mark's story, adds, as he often did, that Jesus was praying, and supplements the scene to make it more vivid. For he has the Spirit alight on Jesus visibly in actual bodily form as a dove. Luke was fond of creating such artistic scenes and will do so when he paints the scene on the day of Pentecost and has flames descend from heaven and appear on people's heads (Acts 2:3). Such artistry belonged to a historian's repertoire to enhance a scene's importance. "You are my beloved Son" may recall for some listeners the way his twelve-year-old adventure ended when he spoke of God as his Father (Luke 2:49). More significantly it recalls the word that Ps 2:7 reports as addressed by God to a king at his coronation, "You are my Son; today I have begotten you," adopting the king as his vice-regent, and the words spoken to God's servant in Isaiah, "Here is my servant, whom I uphold, my chosen, in whom my soul delights; I have put my spirit upon him; he will bring forth justice to the nations" (Isa 42:1).

Luke has reached the point where Mark portrays Jesus retreating into the outback, but instead pauses to offer a genealogy, after initially identifying Jesus' age as thirty when he started his work. The most common pattern in both Jewish and Greco-Roman societies of the time was that men married around this age and started a family with a bride chosen for them by the wider family and usually half their age. Luke's listeners would have recognized the significance of the age as given. It indicated an unusual choice, a special calling.

Mostly, genealogies could be reconstructed from biblical lists, such as we find in the early chapters of 1 Chronicles. Matthew plays with his similar genealogy using numbers: three sets of roughly fourteen (= 6 x 7), emphasizing Davidic lineage. The Hebrew consonants of David's name, read as digits, added up to fourteen. He also adds the names of rather unusual women, fitting for the unusual values of the gospel. Luke, on the other hand, simply gives us a list, going all the way back, further than Matthew, to Adam, indeed to God, though not implying God fathered Adam. If anything, taking the genealogy back to what Jews of that period saw as the beginning of humanity was a way of saying that what follows has universal significance. This was their world and their understanding that the universe would have come into being only about four thousand years before their time—their science, not ours, but we can still appreciate the intended message.

Reflection: What is the overlap between John's message and Jesus' message, and what does Jesus add?

Facing the Options (Luke 4:1–13)

Listening to Luke

4:1 Filled with the Holy Spirit, Jesus returned from the River Jordan and was led by the Spirit into the outback, **2** where he was exposed to testing for forty days at the hands of the devil. And he didn't eat anything during that time and when it was up, he was hungry. **3** And the devil said to him, "If you are the Son of God, tell this rock to turn into bread." **4** Jesus replied, "It is written, 'People are not to live only by bread.'"

5 Then he took him up on high and showed him all the world's empires in a moment of time, **6** and the devil said to him, "I'll give you all this power and the glory that goes with it, because it's been given to me to grant to whomever I want to give it. **7** So, if you bow in submission to me, it's all yours!" **8** Jesus responded, "It is written, 'You shall bow in submission to the Lord your God and serve God alone.'"

9 Then he took him to Jerusalem and placed him on the high point of the temple and said to him, "If you are the Son of God, throw yourself down from here, **10** because it is written, 'He will instruct his angels about you to ensure they protect you' **11** and 'they will carry you in their hands, so you'll never dash your foot against a rock.'" **12** Then Jesus answered, "It has been said, 'You shall not put the Lord your God to the test.'" **13** And when the devil was done with testing him, he left until the next time he'd have a chance.

Thinking About Luke

The barren outback region to the east of the Jordan River held great significance for the story of Israel. It was their last staging post before they invaded the land of Canaan. The story of their liberation from Egypt has them spending forty years passing through the barren regions of Sinai and then these eastern parts.

This inspired those movements that sought to regain control of the land from the Romans to hold out there, not just to be safe but also to symbolize what they hoped would soon become reality, history repeating itself. For some it was envisaged as victory in battle, led by God's Messiah, the promised king of David's dynasty. Some fantasized that angels would join the fight to overthrow Rome's might. Others saw the triumph as largely an act of God without armed help. John the Baptist and then Jesus declared the coming of God's kingdom, God's empire, and called people to get ready by turning back to God in baptism.

By the time that the Gospels came to be written, history had moved on, but the outback continued to be seen as a place of renewal and preparation. Luke follows Mark in having Jesus sent immediately into the outback after his baptism. Already in Mark the scene takes on rich symbolism. Forty days recalls Israel's forty years in the outback regions. For Mark, an important aspect of Jesus' ministry would be liberating people at a personal level by expelling the demons that afflicted them with illness and suffering, reflecting a first-century science that personalized viruses and saw healing therefore primarily as exorcism. Mark's account has echoes of the garden of Eden. Jesus is with the animals, faces Satan's confrontation, but unlike Adam, does not fall. Head-to-head with the enemy of humanity he wins the first battle.

While Luke follows Mark in also having Jesus led into the outback for forty days to face the devil's wiles, he, like Matthew, also knows a different symbolic elaboration that reports a threefold challenge from the devil. There is some poetic license in the account, such as the conflict between saying that the testing took place over forty days but then having the first one take place after forty days. Artists don't have to be strictly accurate.

Matthew and Luke have the same story with some differences. The major one is in the order of the devil's challenges. Matthew has the offer of world dominion as the climax, whereas Luke makes the temple stunt the climax. We may not be able to recover what was in their source. Luke's, which finally has the devil quote Scripture, might seem more likely. Matthew's climax, which widens the scope, also makes good sense and fits neatly with the way his gospel ends where it is God who gives Jesus authority over all peoples (Matt 28:18–20). Then, of course, he has Jesus expound it not as achieving glory, but as spreading his teaching to every nation, not least the good news of God's love.

Luke's historical artistry expands on Mark's story, so repeats the image of forty days, far too long to be without food, of course, but this is symbolism. More important is the bad-dreamlike encounter that plays with the options that at a personal level may well have faced Jesus. The story assumes being Son of God would confer magical powers on Jesus to enable him to turn rock into bread. Wonderful. If we step for a moment into reality, we could certainly do with such magic when facing desperate human need, and there was plenty of need in Jesus' world, as there is in ours. This is not, however, reality, much as we would have loved to see Jesus creating food for the starving of his world.

Behind the fantasy of magic is a serious option. Was Jesus going to make meeting his immediate needs his highest priority? Was he going to abandon the moments of reflection, for which the discipline of a time of fasting helped focus the mind? Modern versions of not taking time to reflect and consider include always keeping the radio blaring, or remaining glued to screens, as well as, of course, doing lots of other things to distract us from sitting down and facing reality, being quiet, praying, reflecting. Such discipline is so important that even commercial industries, these days, will sometimes take staff away on a secular retreat to get back in touch with priorities. No, there's more to life than immediate sense gratification. Get the perspectives right!

Luke's next test is equally pertinent. The lust for power and glory seeks expression in every age and in every community. Sometimes it is a kind of desperate bid for compensation for what people have missed out on, gaps of love in their lives, often from the beginning, and the need ever since to make up for it and have the world compelled to say they love you or at least will let you have all the toys! Mostly, this option takes subtle and sophisticated forms, clothed in respectability. Luke's devil offers such rewards, such fulfillment. His story will cancel the fantasy with a cross, an assertion of love and lowliness, a redefinition of greatness and worth, also a rethinking of who God is and wants.

Finally, Luke's devil quotes Scripture (Ps 91:11–12)! Not the last to cite it in order to do harm, deliberately or otherwise. We remain in fantasy as Jesus is still in the outback but flown off, as it were, to be set up for the big jump. Just imagine the fame, the crowds of adoring fans. Isn't that what Jesus was about, some might ask. Indeed, we find evidence very early on that some parts of the Jesus movement started trying to win believers to the cause by highlighting genuine stories that they had about Jesus performing miracles. Soup them up and soon Jesus could win in the marketplace of those competing for fans, whether as teachers or emperors, because many did it.

Wow-propaganda was the way to go! Paul corrects it at Corinth by arguing that love was the best evidence of the Spirit. The Fourth Gospel strikingly says that many believed in Jesus because of his miracles but he didn't believe in them; they needed to undergo a radical change, be born again, if they were really to see (John 2:23—3:3). Luke is generally more open to emphasize the miraculous, but nevertheless makes it very clear that the wow option was not for Jesus, tempting as it was.

It is fitting that Luke ends with the temple in Jerusalem, because that is how his gospel ends, and it is where his story in Acts begins. Luke holds Jerusalem in high regard and, as we shall see, embraces grief at what would befall it, rather than seeing it as judgment.

Luke's reworking of Jesus facing the options in the outback belongs to storytelling and convention. It was not uncommon among such historians wanting to celebrate the significance of great heroes to depict them as undergoing some testing and trials before they embarked on their achievements. Jesus comes through unscathed and is now set to begin. In Luke he was faced with options that continue to confront would-be leaders. Matthew's emphasis, while similar, gives more emphasis to Jesus' obedience in contrast to Israel's failures and faithlessness in its wilderness wanderings. Luke now takes us in the next section straight to Jesus stating what he sees as his priority and mission.

Reflection: How do you see these options playing out in your world—or yourself?

Jesus' Mission Statement (Luke 4:14–44)

Listening to Luke

4:14 Empowered by the Spirit, Jesus returned to Galilee and his reputation spread through the whole region. **15** He was teaching in their synagogues, and everyone was giving him high praise. **16** Then he came to Nazareth where he was brought up, and went into the synagogue on the Sabbath as was his custom and stood up to do a reading. **17** The book of the prophet Isaiah was handed to him, and he unrolled it to find the place where the following is written: **18** "The Spirit of the Lord is upon me because he has anointed me to declare good news to the poor, he sent me to proclaim release for the captives, sight recovery for the blind, to let the oppressed be set free, **19** to proclaim the year of the Lord's favor."

20 And he rolled the scroll back up, handed it to the attendant, and sat down, and everyone in the synagogue was looking intently at him. **21** So he started to tell them that this scripture had reached fulfillment in the act of their listening to it. **22** And everyone started providing evidence about him and expressing amazement at the gracious words that issued from his lips, but some started saying, "Isn't this Joseph's boy?"

23 And he said to them, "I suppose you'll be confronting me with the quip, 'Doctor, heal yourself! Do here in your hometown what we've heard you did in Capernaum.'" **24** And he told them, "No prophet is accepted in his own hometown. **25** It's true, I'm telling you, there were many widows in Israel in Elijah's day when there was no rain for three and a half years and there was a great famine in the land, **26** and Elijah was sent to none of them except to the widow woman in Sarepta in Sidon. **27** And there were many lepers in Israel in the time of Elisha the prophet and none of them was healed except Naaman the Syrian."

²⁸ Hearing this, the people in the synagogue became really annoyed ²⁹ and got up and drove him out of town, bringing him to the edge of the cliff where the city had been built to throw him off, ³⁰ but he managed to make his way through them and went off on his way.

³¹ And he came down to Capernaum, a city in Galilee, and was teaching people in the synagogue, ³² and they were really taken with his teaching because he spoke very convincingly.

³³ Now there was a man there in the synagogue who had an unclean spirit, and it caused him to shout out loud, ³⁴ "Hey there, go away! What have you got to do with us, Jesus of Nazareth? Have you come to destroy us? I know who you are: you're God's holy one." ³⁵ Jesus shut him up, telling him, "Silence! Leave him!" And the demon convulsed him in front of them all and left him and did him no harm. ³⁶ So everyone was amazed and started saying to each other, "What is this all about? Because he's giving instructions to unclean spirits with authority and power and they're leaving people." ³⁷ And reports about him started spreading across the whole region.

³⁸ Then, leaving the synagogue, he came to Simon's house, and Simon's mother-in-law was sick with quite a fever and they asked him what he could do for her. ³⁹ He stood over her and rebuked the fever and it left her. Immediately she got up and started looking after them. ⁴⁰ At sunset everyone with various sick people brought them to him. He laid his hands on each one of them and healed them. ⁴¹ And demons, too, left many and would shout out, "You are the Son of God," but he told them off and told them not to say anything, because they knew he was the Messiah.

⁴² Next morning he set off and came to an isolated place. And the crowds were looking for him and approached him and tried to keep him from leaving them. ⁴³ He told them, "I need to preach the good news of the kingdom of God to other towns, because that's my commission." ⁴⁴ So he went on preaching in the synagogues of Judea.

Thinking About Luke

Mark follows the account of Jesus' stay in the outback with a report of John's arrest and then Jesus' beginning his ministry, including a summary of his preaching: "The time of fulfillment has arrived, and the kingdom of God has now come near. Turn to God and believe the good news!" (Mark 1:15). Luke has already referred to John's arrest and demise, so he simply moves straight to a summary statement of Jesus' ministry, but he does not include Mark's summary of Jesus' message just cited. He will refer to Jesus' message as being about the kingdom of God later, in 4:43. Luke's characteristic addition is that Jesus was "empowered by the Spirit," an emphasis he adds also in reporting of Jesus when he went into the testing encounter in the outback.

Luke's innovation at this point is to take what Mark reported later in his gospel, namely Jesus' encounter with his home synagogue (Mark 6:1–6), and transfer it to make it the first scene in his account of Jesus' ministry. In doing so he has also expanded it, so that it now functions as in many ways a summary of what Jesus was about, his mission statement. He has Jesus read Isa 61:1–2a, concluding with "to proclaim the year of the Lord's favor," but not "and the day of vengeance of our God." That would have fitted John the Baptist's role description given to Jesus, namely as judge to come, but, as we have seen, Luke separates the end time day of judgment from Jesus' mission in the interim.

That interim commission comes, therefore, to expression in the words of Isa 61, which fits well the report of Jesus' baptism when the Spirit, so emphasized by Luke, came upon Jesus, but it also fits the way Luke depicts Jesus' significance generally. As the "anointed," understood within a broader sense, as the Messiah, Jesus proclaimed good news to the poor—change will happen for them—but was also already engaged in actions that brought liberation, not least through healing and freeing people from the demonic powers that oppressed them.

This statement of Jesus' commission will be echoed when Luke has Jesus declare in 6:20, "Happy are you who are poor, because the kingdom of God is for you." It is echoed again in Jesus' answer to John the Baptist's worry about his role when Jesus declares: "Go and tell John what you've seen and heard: the blind have their sight restored; the lame are now walking about, lepers are healed and the deaf now hear, the dead are brought back to life and the poor have good news brought to them" (Luke 7:22). Indeed, Luke arranges his story so that by the time we get to chapter 7 all these acts of liberation have been illustrated.

The language of "good news" may well have come into the Jesus movement through Jesus himself applying such texts as Isa 61:1 and Isa 52:7 to what he was doing. (Isaiah 52:7 reads, "How beautiful upon the mountains are the feet of the messenger who announces peace, who brings good news, who announces salvation, who says to Zion, 'Your God reigns.'") The message of hope, of the coming reign of God, central to Jesus' preaching, was good news, the meaning of the word "gospel." When sayings and anecdotes were later put together as extended accounts of Jesus and his ministry, such accounts came themselves to be called "good news" accounts, namely "gospels." As noted in discussion of Luke's Christmas story, "good news" was also language used in Roman imperial propaganda.

Luke had already signaled that the story of Jesus would not end well when he has Simeon warn Mary of the grief she would face (Luke 2:35). Putting the encounter between Jesus and his home synagogue at the beginning of his account was also a way of foreshadowing what was to come. Luke offers more, however, than just foreshadowing here. He also gives some reasons for it. Elijah and Elisha healed outsiders, gentiles. At one level this foreshadows Jesus' reaching out to marginalized people during his ministry, the tax collectors and sinners, which brought him criticism, but at another level it foreshadows the church's mission to the non-Jewish world where Acts shows the gospel achieving greater acceptance than among Jesus' own people. In that sense this first scene encapsulates all that is to come in Luke's two-volume work.

While Luke has expanded the story as he found it in Mark, he has also edited out what might have been problematic for his story, namely Mark's report that Jesus spoke of prophets facing lack of acceptance not just in their own hometown but also in their own family: "A prophet is not without honor except in his hometown, and among his kin and in his family home" (Mark 6:4). Mark had illustrated this well in Mark 3:20–21, where he reports that Jesus' family is worried that he has gone mad or worried that others think so. Luke deletes that report and retains only its sequel in Mark 3:31–36, where Jesus explains what being his true family means (Luke 8:19–21). Similarly, here in the saying about prophets not being accepted (Luke 4:24), Luke deletes the reference to a prophet not being accepted "among his kin and in his family home" (Mark 6:4), which might imply Jesus was rejected by his, hardly conceivable given Luke's account of his birth. The closest Luke comes to it is when he tells the story of the twelve-year-old Jesus being growled at by his mother (Luke 2:48).

Having brought this opening scene, Luke returns to Mark's order, but leaves out Mark's account of Jesus calling disciples (Mark 1:16–20), because he has taken up elements of it in the story about the miraculous catch of fish with which the next chapter begins (Luke 5:1–11). Instead, he goes straight to the exorcism Jesus performs in the synagogue in Capernaum (Mark 1:21–28; Luke 4:31–37). Within the thought world of Luke and his hearers it would make sense to imagine that demons, beings of the spirit world, would recognize who Jesus was, as here in Luke 4:34 and also later in Luke 4:41.

In some forms of mental illness we do meet the phenomenon of people hearing voices and speaking in strange ways, so that it is no surprise that the ancient world's pathology would attribute such phenomena to people being inhabited by demons. We understand the complexities of mental illness differently, but reading the stories within their frame of thought we see that the underlying thought is that Jesus was able somehow to heal people of their illnesses, to liberate them from the state they were in and give them back their control.

We encounter the ancient world's pathology also in Luke's rendering of the story of the healing of Peter's mother-in-law that follows (Luke 4:38–40), where he rewrites the account of Jesus' act of healing, as described in Mark, to portray it, too, as an exorcism, unlike in Mark: for Jesus here rebukes the fever (Luke 4:39; Mark 1:29–31).

Behind this framework of thought is the myth of lusty angels who breached the created order by descending from heaven and sleeping with women. We know the story best from the Jewish writing known as 1 Enoch, which incorporates an account of the story reaching back probably as far as the fourth century BCE. A brief version of the story appears also in Gen 6:1–2. Chaos ensued. The women gave birth to giants—that's where giants came from! The giants then fought among themselves, and all died, but out of their corpses came half human, half divine spirits, evil or unclean spirits, to plague humanity ever since. Indeed, some accounts give them the names of illnesses. Their medical assumptions were informed by this myth, and hence healings were seen as a form of exorcism.

It is in part against this background that Luke, like Mark before him, saw Jesus' ministry in terms of liberation, freeing people from whatever oppressed them, and in that ministry, exorcism—liberating them from demons—played a major role. While this is a worldview far from our own, what we have in common is the notion of liberation and healing. Good news is about liberating people from whatever oppresses them, whether that takes the form of personal illness or social justice. They also recognized political powers as often oppressive and explained such oppression as the work of demonic forces. The reign of God would replace the reign of such demonic powers and their political agents. While far from our understanding, we, too, can recognize the reality that liberation is about more than personal freedom and change; it has political and social justice implications, a systemic dimension.

Luke follows Mark in reporting crowds coming to Jesus with their sick. Where Mark indicates that Jesus healed many, Luke and Matthew both change "many" to "all," an understandable embellishment, and typical of a trend to heighten impact. We are not the only ones prone to some embellishment and exaggeration for effect. Luke was human, too. These opening scenes lay open what Luke sees as the good news that Jesus brings. It is then not surprising that only after these scenes does he turn to the issue of recruiting others to be involved.

Reflection: Our understanding of what constitutes human need in individuals and in society is very different from theirs. Is there any continuity between their understanding of what constitutes good news and ours?

2

Hope in Action

What Are God's Priorities? (Luke 5:1—6:11)

Listening to Luke

^{5:1} One time when the crowd was pressing in on him to listen to his message while he was standing on the edge of Lake Gennesaret, ² he saw two boats anchored near the shore. The fishermen had disembarked and were mending their nets. ³ He got into one of the boats, the one belonging to Simon, and asked him to push out for a bit, and so he sat down and was teaching the crowds from on board the boat.

⁴ When he'd finished speaking, he said to Simon, "Push out into deeper water and let down your nets for a catch." ⁵ In response Simon said, "Master, we've been at it all night and haven't caught a thing, but if you say so, I'll let down the nets." ⁶ They did so and netted a huge haul of fish, so that the nets started to rip. ⁷ They beckoned to their colleagues in the other boat to come and give them a hand. They did and they filled both boats so much so that they started to sink.

⁸ When Simon Peter saw what was happening, he fell at Jesus' knees and pleaded with him, "Go away from me, because I'm a sinful man, master!" ⁹ For he was so amazed and so were all those with him at the catch of fish they'd taken, ¹⁰ as were similarly James and John, sons of Zebedee, who were Simon's colleagues. So Jesus said to Simon,

"Don't be scared. From now on you'll be catching human beings." ¹¹ Getting out of the boat onto dry land, they left all this and followed him.

¹² And it happened once that he was in one of their towns and there was a man there covered with leprosy. When he saw Jesus, he fell down before him and begged him, "Master, if you decide to, you can heal me." ¹³ Jesus then reached out his hand and touched him and said, "I'm happy to do so. Be healed!" And straightaway the leprosy left him. ¹⁴ And Jesus told him, "Tell no one, but go off and show yourself to the priest and offer what Moses directed for cleansing, as evidence for them." ¹⁵ And the report of what Jesus had done spread even more and many crowds of people started gathering to listen to him and to be healed of their illnesses, ¹⁶ but, for his part, he used to withdraw into the outback areas and pray.

¹⁷ One day he was teaching, and Pharisees and teachers of the Law were sitting there. They had come from all the villages of Galilee and Judea and from Jerusalem. The Lord's power was with Jesus enabling him to heal. ¹⁸ And then, lo and behold, some men came carrying a paralyzed man on a stretcher and they endeavored to bring him before Jesus, ¹⁹ but, not finding a way through to him because of the crowd, they got up onto the roof of the house and let him down through the roofing tiles right into the middle in front of Jesus.

²⁰ When he saw their faith, he said, "My man, your sins are forgiven."

²¹ Then the scribes and the Pharisees began to discuss among themselves, "Who is this guy who's blaspheming like this? Who can forgive sins? Surely only God." ²² Jesus recognized that they were having this discussion and so said to them, "Why are you bothered about this? ²³ What is easier, to say, 'Your sins are forgiven' or to say, 'Get up and walk!'? ²⁴ But so you can know that the Son of Man has authority on earth to forgive sins," he said to the paralyzed man, "I'm telling you, get up and pick up your stretcher and go home!" ²⁵ And he got up in front of them straightaway, picked up what he was lying on, and went off home glorifying God. ²⁶ Everyone was amazed and started glorifying God, and they were filled with awe, saying, "We've seen something extraordinary today!"

²⁷ After this he went off and happened to see a customs agent, called Levi, sitting at his customs desk. And he said to him, "Follow me!" ²⁸ He left it all behind, got up, and started following him. ²⁹ And the fellow put on a special meal for him in his house, and there was a big crowd of customs agents and others who were reclining along with them. ³⁰ The Pharisees and their scribes started saying to his disciples, "Why is he eating and drinking with customs agents and sinners?" ³¹ In response Jesus said to them, "Those who are well don't need a doctor; the sick do. ³² I didn't come to call the upright but sinners to turn their lives around."

³³ Then they said to him. "John the Baptist's disciples often fast and pray, as do the disciples of the Pharisees, but yours are eating and drinking." ³⁴ Jesus responded, "Can you really imagine wedding guests fasting while the bridegroom is with them? ³⁵ The time will come when the bridegroom will be taken from them and then in those days they'll fast."

³⁶ And he started telling them a parable, saying, "No one tears a patch from a new garment and sews it onto an old garment, because otherwise the patch from the new would rip away, because the patch from the new garment is not compatible with the old. ³⁷ And no one pours new wine into old wineskins, because otherwise the new wine will split open the wineskins and the wine will be spilled and the wineskins ruined. ³⁸ New wine is to be put into new wineskins. ³⁹ No one drinking the old wine wants the new, because, they say, the old is better."

⁶:¹ Once he was making his way through a field of wheat and his disciples started plucking heads of wheat, rubbing them in their hands to get the wheat kernels, and then eating them. ² Some Pharisees said, "Why are you doing what is forbidden on the Sabbath?"

³ In response Jesus said, "Haven't you read what David did when he and his men were hungry, ⁴ how he entered the house of God and ate the offering bread and gave some to those with him, which was forbidden to anyone except priests?" ⁵ And he told them, "The Son of Man is lord of the Sabbath."

⁶ On another Sabbath he went to the synagogue and was teaching and there was a man there with a shriveled right hand. ⁷ The scribes and the Pharisees were keeping an eye on him to see if he would heal him on the Sabbath, so that they could find grounds to prosecute him. ⁸ He knew what they were thinking, and said to the man with the shriveled

hand, "Get up and stand here!" So, he got up and stood there. ⁹ Jesus then said to them, "I ask you, is it lawful to do good or do harm on the Sabbath, to save life or to destroy it?" ¹⁰ Then looking around at all of them, he told him, "Stretch out your hand!" He did so and his hand was restored. ¹¹ They were furious and discussed with one another just what they were going to do to Jesus.

Thinking About Luke

Luke has been rewriting the first chapter of Mark's Gospel. As noted in the previous section, Luke made some major changes and rearrangements in using Mark's material. He brings the summary of Jesus' activity, as in Mark 1:14 (Luke 4:14), but not Mark's summary of Jesus' message in Mark 1:15. Instead, he inserts in 4:16–30 an expanded version of Jesus' visit to his home synagogue which he found in Mark 6:1–6. He then also omits the story of Jesus calling Simon and Andrew and James and John to follow him (Mark 1:16–20) and moves straight on to what came next in Mark, namely the exorcism in the synagogue (Luke 4:31–37; Mark 1:21–28) and the healing of Simon's mother-in-law (Luke 4:38–40; Mark 1:29–31).

He then inserts in Luke 5:1–11 a story that appears to draw on various sources. It begins with Jesus under crowd pressure and coping with it by getting into a boat (Luke 5:1–3). Luke has lifted this from the beginning of Mark 4, where Mark tells us that Jesus got into a boat and went on to tell the famous parables about the sower and seeds. Accordingly, when Luke gets to Mark 4, he leaves out the detail about Jesus getting into a boat because he has brought it here. The fact that Jesus takes the initiative of getting into Simon's boat matches what appears to be the case already when Jesus and the disciples enter Simon's house, namely, that they are already well acquainted.

Luke then continues his story by having Jesus initiate a miraculous catch of fish (Luke 5:4–11). We find this miracle story also in John's Gospel (John 21:5–11). It must have circulated among stories about Simon Peter and his calling and so appears independently in two places, here and in John 21. In John, the encounter at the lake is also after a night of having caught no fish, but it is with the risen Jesus. Similar to what we find in Luke's story, Jesus suggests they try again, and in both stories there is a huge catch, which John's Gospel gives as 153 fish, perhaps symbolic of all kinds of fish and so symbolic of all the various peoples who would turn to the faith. It is in this context that Jesus rehabilitates Peter, who had denied him three times, by asking him three times if he loved him and then commissioning him to feed his sheep (John 21:15–19).

In Luke's story, Peter is overawed by the miracle and tells Jesus to go away, a typical response of the time when people felt they were being confronted with supernatural powers at work. Instead, Jesus reassures Peter, and here Luke picks up what Mark had reported when speaking of Peter's call to be a disciple: now he is to go fishing for human beings (Luke 5:10; Mark 1:17)!

The miracle story clearly relates to the commission given Peter to help win followers for Jesus. We are in the dark about its origin. Did it begin as an Easter story, as John suggests? Or was it originally about Peter's initial call to be a disciple? Luke has incorporated into his account a reference to James and John as colleagues, the two other disciples that Mark has Jesus call (Mark 1:18–20). The end effect is that we hear that all three left their fishing and followed Jesus. In the process of rearrangement and retelling, Luke has left out Peter's brother, Andrew. In the very different account of the call of the first disciples in John's Gospel, Andrew, in fact, is the one who summons his brother Peter and brings him to Jesus (John 1:40–42).

Such stories have legendary character and render any attempt to harmonize them into a historical account a fruitless endeavor. In their various ways their message is that Peter is to have a leadership role and that the task is to engage others in embracing the message of Jesus, a task foundational for the church's self-understanding.

After the account of this significant encounter by the lakeside, Luke returns to Mark and reports the healing of a leper (Luke 5:12–16; Mark 1:40–45). Luke often heightens the miraculous and so changes Mark's description of the man as "a leper" to a man "covered with leprosy." There are two conflicting readings in manuscripts of Mark about Jesus' response in Mark 1:41. One has him moved with compassion. The other has him moved with anger. Perhaps anger was replaced at some stage by compassion. Anger would relate to the fact that lepers should keep their distance from people, something we may recall from restrictions about people with Covid in the pandemic of 2020. Mark has Jesus also virtually growl at him when sending him off to the priest to certify his healing. Luke omits both references to Jesus' feeling responses, something he often does.

Both Mark and Luke portray Jesus as observing the Law and expecting others to do so. Luke will go even further and have Jesus insist that every stroke of the Law is to be upheld until or unless God indicates otherwise (Luke 16:17). Mark has the leper not heed Jesus' instruction to keep quiet about the healing, as a result of which Jesus had to avoid entering the towns because of the crowds and so tended to stay in remote areas (Mark 1:45). Luke does not indicate the leper disregarded the instruction but does mention Jesus' growing popularity, though not as a problem. For, according to Luke, it was Jesus' choice to stay in remote areas and, he adds, it was to pray (Luke 5:16), another detail Luke often adds.

In the dramatic story of the healing of the paralytic let down through the roof, Luke stays close to Mark and so retains Jesus' two-liner quip about whether it was easier to say your sins are forgiven or tell a paralyzed person to get up and walk (Mark 2:1–12; Luke 5:21–26). Its effect is to expose the objection of his religious critics as absurd. Luke also retains the defense against the accusation of blasphemy. Jesus was not forgiving sins of his own accord, but was declaring God's forgiveness and had been authorized to do so as Son of Man. "Son of Man" was a title given in some Jewish sources to the man whom God would appoint to act as judge at the end of time, sometimes also seen as the role of the Messiah to come. Thus Luke, like Mark before him, portrays Jesus as exercising this role already during his ministry when he declares people's sins forgiven. John the Baptist, as Luke told us earlier, also had such authority.

Linking paralysis to guilt was common, and we may sometimes recognize a connection, though mostly this is not our understanding. Similarly, we do not attribute sickness to demons as they did. This means that we need to acknowledge our distance from their diagnoses. We no longer share their medical assumptions. What we do and can share is the notion that we, too, remain committed to healing and health as a primary priority, which we, too, see as God's priority.

As Luke follows Mark, the next scene is the call of Levi (Mark 2:13–17; Luke 5:27–32), whom Matthew knows as Matthew (Matt 9:9–13), a fact that may have inspired why his gospel was attributed to this Matthew, on the assumption of inside knowledge, although other factors may have played a role. Like Luke, the author of Matthew's Gospel is dependent on Mark's story, not on personal memory. The tax collectors referred to in this story are likely to be collectors of customs taxes charging people bringing goods across borders, such as between Herod Antipas's territory of Galilee and Philip's territory to the east.

Some had a bad reputation because of overcharging, and they were known for making enough money to engage in an indulgent lifestyle, such as having special dinner gatherings, as in our story. The "sinners" mentioned along with them might well have been entertainers, including female entertainers. It is not unexpected that people committed to living upright lives would be expected to avoid such company. Hence the criticism here of Jesus, who gives another neat two-liner answer along the lines that the sick, not the well, need a doctor. This response reflects the fact that Jesus' highest priority was not to protect himself from moral or ritual contamination, let alone from getting a bad reputation, but to bring healing and hope. Luke adds to Mark's version of Jesus' response the words "to turn their lives around" ("to repentance"), perhaps to underline the legitimacy of Jesus' stance. Other people and their needs matter most, not protecting oneself from moral danger, important as that can also be.

Following Mark, Luke then reports the questioning of Jesus about why his disciple did not fast like others (Mark 2:18–20; Luke 5:33–35). Jesus' response is again simple but implies a claim, namely that what people looked forward to as hope is already coming into reality. They are no longer praying and fasting as people do who are awaiting change. They are involved already now in change. This is an emphasis that characterized Jesus' ministry and Luke highlights it throughout: change now; good news for the poor now.

One of the common images of hope was a great feast, reflecting the rarity of such occasions in everyday life. You could expect such a feast when there was a wedding, hence the imagery here, which is effectively saying: your hope, symbolized by a wedding, is happening already to some degree. Luke follows Mark in then having Jesus develop the image to say that there would come a time when the bridegroom would leave them and then fasting and hoping would be appropriate. For the Gospel writers, that was their time, and their hope was for Jesus to return, but they could still affirm the reality that hope could also be realized in their own time and setting.

The sense of conflict between Jesus and his critics returns when Luke moves on in Mark to record two images that depict the conflict between old and new priorities (Mark 2:21–22; Luke 5:36–38). Don't use new cloth to patch up old cloth. It won't work. And don't pour new wine into old wine containers of the kind they used, because they would burst. Luke's closing comment about people preferring old wine to new (Luke 5:39) appears not to be a complaint about the old, but a claim that indeed what Jesus brought was the old's true meaning. It is a slightly awkward addition, given that originally the "new" had been a reference to Jesus' approach in Mark (Mark 1:27).

The two sayings may have us thinking that Jesus and traditional Judaism are incompatible, but no such generalization is intended. The contrast is between the two different approaches to what they saw as God's priorities: keeping oneself safe from potential danger and contamination or engaging in love and renewal.

The contrast comes again into focus as Luke continues to follow Mark in the two stories that come in Luke 6. Both depict conflict over the importance of Sabbath law. The first depicts an extremist view that would forbid even such a minor thing as rubbing a head of wheat to release the kernel so you could eat it (Mark 2:23–28; Luke 6:1–5). Luke follows Mark in having Jesus cite David's action once of getting food for himself and his men (1 Sam 21:1–7), but, like Matthew, omits Mark's error of dating it to the time of Abiathar the high priest. Abiathar was not the high priest at the time. Human need must come first, but neither Mark's nor Luke's description says Jesus and his disciples were hungry. They were just casually plucking heads of wheat. Like Matthew, Luke omits Jesus' main and probably original response: "the Sabbath was made for people, not people for the Sabbath" (Mark 2:27), perhaps sensing it as too radical, but does bring the reference to Jesus' authority as Son of Man to interpret Sabbath law. The story implies that the objection is absurd and inappropriate.

Similarly in the synagogue, the story exposes the critics as taking an absurd position from the storyteller's perspective, which clearly implies that responding to human need matters most, and that means: matters more to God (Mark 3:1–6; Luke 6:6–11). A halfway position might have been to suggest that Jesus come back the next day when there would not be a problem, but that, too, would be deemed absurd. Mark heightens the irony by concluding with the report that the Pharisees and Herodians got together as a result and plotted Jesus' death. Luke reduces the response to their thinking about what to do about Jesus.

Mark has five stories in which Jesus finds himself under fire from critics, and Luke has repeated them with minor changes. Mark's are neatly arranged. The first and fifth are about paralysis (Mark 2:1–12; 3:1–6). The second and fourth are about food (Mark 2:13–17; 2:23–28). The third is about fasting (Mark 2:18–22). These stories will have been told and retold before Mark, but most of them probably go right back to Jesus with his typical two-liner responses in each. They would have been retold and supplemented in the broader context of conflict with fellow Jews in the early days of the church over attitudes towards the Law. We see further such supplementing in Matthew's reworking of the scene where he has Jesus offer further arguments to justify overriding the Sabbath and cite Hos 6:6, "I desire compassion, not sacrifice" (Matt 12:1–8). This was not to oppose sacrifice, but to put compassion at the heart of interpreting the Law. You uphold the Law in full. Not a stroke is to be set aside as Luke will tell us in Luke 16:17 (and Matthew does in Matt 5:18), but you apply the Law on the basis of what makes most sense in terms of love and caring.

Such stories were valuable in teaching. Their depiction of Jesus' opponents serves to bring out two different approaches to biblical Law and so two contrasting understandings of God. In that sense, the opponents serve as stereotypes. If read in a generalizing way, however, these stereotypes scarcely do justice to all Jews and Jewish teachers of the day and can generate stereotypical, even anti-Semitic, attitudes. These are unwarranted. What comes through clearly in all five stories is not an abandonment of biblical Law but an approach to its application that puts human need at the center rather than worries about offending God, based on an understanding of God as concerned more with laws and rules than with people.

Reflection: The conflict is not over whether to uphold the Law but how to do so. What were the options and how do you see them playing out as options in our world?

Jesus' Teaching (Luke 6:12–49)

Listening to Luke

6:12 And it happened in those days that Jesus went off up a mountain to pray and spent the night in prayer to God. **13** In the morning he gathered his disciples and chose twelve of them, whom he designated as his envoys: **14** Simon, whom he named Peter, his brother Andrew, James and John, Philip, Bartholomew, **15** Matthew, Thomas, James son of Alphaeus, Simon called the Zealot, **16** Judas son of James, and Judas Iscariot who became a betrayer.

17 And he went down and stood with them on a flat area, along with a big crowd of his disciples and a large crowd of people from all over Judea and Jerusalem and the coastal region of Tyre and Sidon. **18** They had come to hear him and to be cured of their illnesses, and people plagued by unclean spirits were being healed. **19** And the whole crowd was wanting to touch him because power went out from him and healed everyone.

20 And he lifted his gaze towards his disciples and said, "Happy are you who are poor, because the kingdom of God is for you. **21** Happy are you who face hunger now, because you're going to have enough to eat. Happy are you who are in grief now, because you're going to have laughter. **22** Happy are you when people hate you and exclude and abuse you and bring your name into disrepute because of the Son of Man. **23** Count yourselves fortunate on that day and jump for joy, because your reward in heaven will be substantial, for our ancestors treated the prophets in the same way.

24 "And woe betide those of you who are wealthy, because you've already had your benefits. **25** And woe betide those who are chock full of food now, because you're going to be hungry. And woe betide those who are now laughing, because you're going to have grief and sorrow.

²⁶ And woe betide when everyone speaks well of you, because our ancestors did that in relation to the false prophets.

²⁷ "But I'm telling you, if you're willing to listen: Love your enemies. Do good to those who hate you. ²⁸ Bless those who curse you. Pray for those who maltreat you. ²⁹ And if someone slaps you on your cheek, expose the other one to them, and if someone steals your coat, don't stop them also taking your inner garment. ³⁰ Give to those asking things of you and don't ask those who are robbing you of your property to return it.

³¹ "And as you'd like people to treat you, treat them in the same way. ³² If you love those who love you, what's so special about that? For even wicked people love those who love them. ³³ And if you do good only to those who do good to you, what's so special about that? Even wicked people do that. ³⁴ And if you lend expecting to have it repaid, what's so special about that? Wicked people lend to wicked people expecting to get it back. ³⁵ But love your enemies and do good to them and lend not expecting repayment, because your reward will be great and you will be truly children of the Most High, because he is generous also to the ungrateful and wicked. ³⁶ Be compassionate as your Father is compassionate. ³⁷ And don't judge and you won't be judged, and don't condemn and you won't be condemned. Forgive and you'll be forgiven. ³⁸ Give and it will be given to you, they'll place abundance in your lap, pressed down, shaken up, poured out. The measure you apply will be applied to you."

³⁹ He also used this image: "You don't think the blind can lead the blind, do you? Won't both end up falling into the ditch? ⁴⁰ Disciples are not superior to their teacher, but everyone who learns well will end up like their teacher. ⁴¹ Why do you look for the speck in the eye of your fellow human being and not notice the log in your own? ⁴² How can you tell your fellow, 'Dear colleague, let me remove the speck from your eye' while you yourself don't see the log in your own? Hypocrite, get rid of the log from your own eye and then you'll see clearly to be able to remove the speck from your colleague's eye.

⁴³ "For a good tree won't produce bad fruit; nor will a bad tree produce good fruit. ⁴⁴ For every tree is recognized by the fruit it bears; for you don't harvest figs from thorn bushes nor get grapes from prickly shrubs. ⁴⁵ The good person produces goodness from the treasure of

goodness in their inner self and the evil person produces evil from the evil in their inner self. The way people speak is a product of who they really are.

⁴⁶ "Why do you call me, 'Lord, Lord' and not do what I tell you? ⁴⁷ Anyone coming to me and listening to my words and doing them, I'll tell you what they're like. ⁴⁸ They're like a person building a house who digs really deep and lays a foundation on solid rock. When there's a flood and the torrent of water hits that house, it can't be shaken because it's well-built. ⁴⁹ Anyone hearing what I teach and not following it is like someone having built his house just on the ground without a foundation, which the torrent will vibrate, and it will collapse, and that house will face great devastation."

Thinking About Luke

Luke skips the summary that Mark brings about Jesus' activity following the set of five conflict episodes (Mark 3:7–12) and instead goes straight on to what follows in Mark, namely the appointing of the twelve (Mark 3:13–19; Luke 6:13–16). Luke rewrites it slightly to have Jesus first withdraw up a mountain to pray. Luke often inserts references to Jesus praying. Here he has him spend the night doing so. Luke thereby reflects the wisdom that for making big decisions about leadership there needs to be prayer and reflection and so he imagines it must have happened, and therefore adds it.

Only then does Jesus gather those who were following him—literally and figuratively, because there were also some who were his followers but stayed home. From among those gathered he appoints twelve. The traditional translation calls them "apostles." I have given the literal translation "envoy," in part to bring out what "apostle" actually meant. It meant someone who could be sent to act on someone else's behalf, an essential function in days without our modern forms of telecommunication. They were in that sense to represent Jesus in his leadership role.

Luke's hearers would have been very aware that twelve was a symbolic number: there were twelve sons of Jacob and so twelve tribes of Israel. Appointing twelve such envoys reflects the belief that they, along with Jesus, were to lead Israel and all who joined Israel. Luke does not tell us when Jesus gave Simon the name Peter (which means a Rock and in Aramaic is Cephas). John's Gospel suggests it was when he first called him to be a disciple (John 1:42). Matthew suggests it was in a conversation about the church for which Peter would be the foundation member (Matt 16:16–18). Finally, Andrew, his brother, appears here in Luke 6:14, after being omitted in the scene by the lake (Luke 5:1–11). Aside from James and John and Judas Iscariot, the others do not feature by name in the rest of Luke's story.

The section Luke 6:20–48 brings the first major speech that Jesus gives in Luke. It has the same basic outline as the better known Sermon on the Mount in Matthew (Matt 5–7), which is much longer because Matthew has a version that had been significantly supplemented and expanded. Luke introduces it by having Jesus turn his attention to the disciples. It is likely that he is portraying it as advice being given to them, and this would make sense of references to the likelihood that they would face persecution. At the same time, however, Luke has the crowds present, so they hear it too.

Matthew's creative innovation was to have it delivered on a mountain (Matt 5:1). He took the reference to Jesus going up a mountain from Mark's account of Jesus doing so to appoint the twelve (Mark 3:13) and uses it for the location of the address. That fitted a symbolism that recalled Moses receiving the Law on a mountain, Mount Sinai, and Matthew depicts the sermon as an exposition of the Law. From a practical point of view, Luke locates the event in a place where there would be lots of room for everyone, namely a flat area.

The speech begins with a promise to the poor. The disciples who had left everything were certainly poor and so it certainly applied to them. Being poor would also have applied to many others present. The promise was that this situation was to be reversed. This is the good news for the poor that Luke has Jesus describe as central to his message (Luke 4:18). The same applies to the promise to the hungry and those who were hurting or grieving. There will be change. This is central to how Luke portrays Jesus and his message. It is a message not just for the disciples but for all who in effect become disciples by believing it.

The traditional description of these promises is that they are "beatitudes," promises of blessing. The word that begins each promise simply means happy. Matthew's more familiar version (Matt 5:3–12) has "poor in spirit," which people can misread to mean people who keep putting themselves down and trying to be humble (Matt 5:3). Its real meaning is dispirited and is language we also find elsewhere to describe people facing need, for instance, in writings found among the Dead Sea Scrolls. Matthew's version has thus expanded the meaning of "poor" and has similarly expanded the meaning of hungry and so it reads "those who hunger and thirst for justice." That broadens its application to include not only those who seek justice for themselves but also those who seek justice for others.

On the lips of Jesus this would have been addressed to the people of his day in their need. Prophets sometimes used "the poor" as a description of Israel in its state of need. The promise to the hurting and grieving also belongs to the promise of change, a change from sorrow to joy. Pronouncing the poor and hungry happy is not therefore about saying they should stop complaining and be happy with their plight, but quite the opposite. Rather, they can be happy at the prospect of change.

The fourth promise takes a different shape, is longer, with more detail, and seems clearly related specifically to followers of Jesus and what they might face. It is likely to be an early supplement added in the time of the church to address their situation. Matthew brings it as the eighth promise and adds a ninth, which expands even further on the issue. Matthew's additional promises, to the compassionate, the meek, the pure in heart, the peacemakers, are all about encouraging behavior rather than identifying need and are probably additions made for the purpose of faith education like much of the rest of Matthew's sermon.

Only Luke has a matching set of threats against those who choose the opposite path. These may well be an expansion developed in Luke's context or perhaps even by Luke himself, who lays great emphasis on proper use of resources and attacks greed. They echo the words he places on Mary's lips in the *Magnificat* about reversal, sending the rich empty away and dethroning the powerful (Luke 1:51–53). The fourth threat addresses another theme, familiar in all ages, namely the obsession with popularity at the expense of truth and justice.

It is very clear that Luke is not portraying Jesus as divisive, teaching that his audience should secure their identity by knowing who their enemies are and so who to write off and hate, such as the rich, because he goes straight on to have Jesus encourage people to love their enemies, offering some striking images of what rejecting hate means. His teachings here are not meant to be a new set of rules to be adhered to literally, but they all illustrate that hate is not the answer. Love sometimes means we need to resist harm being done to others and so we need a legal system. However, it is not there to be an instrument of hate, but an instrument of fairness and protection of the worth and dignity of all.

The basic principle of treating others the way you, yourself, want to be treated echoes a widely attested insight already in the world of Jesus, which Luke has Jesus affirm and Matthew describes as the basic principle behind the Law and the Prophets, the so-called golden rule (Matt 7:12). Why embrace this approach? Luke has Jesus make clear: because it is how God is, and so Luke has Jesus declare: be compassionate because that is how God is. That was already evident in the conflicts that Luke reported in the stories leading up to this speech. Nonjudgmental generosity is to be the norm.

Luke has Jesus point out that when you learn from him as a teacher, the goal is to become like him. Part of that learning is to attend to one's own development, and certainly not to be obsessed with criticizing others. The reference to trees and fruit also reflects the importance of dealing with one's inner being, because when that is healthy, our responses will be healthy. Paul talks about the fruit of the Spirit as love, namely the outcome of opening oneself to love and to being freed from guilt and fear and preoccupation with oneself (Gal 5:22–23).

Luke's and Matthew's sermon concludes with the house-building metaphor, which is making a similar point. Their source had clearly shaped the collection of Jesus' sayings so that they would address followers of Jesus of a later time, hence the saying about calling Jesus "Lord," but the sayings in the broader context clearly have universal relevance and would have been spoken by Jesus originally to his own people in general. The message is clear: make the teachings of Jesus about God and love the foundation for your life and living. That will bring the reward of stability, security, and peace, and also enable you to do the things and have the attitude the sermon advocates.

Reflection: What personal and social values do you see in this body of teaching? How do they relate to Luke's image of Jesus as a messenger of hope?

Jesus and John (Luke 7:1–34)

Listening to Luke

⁷:¹ When he had finished saying all this to the people, he went to Capernaum. ² A centurion who lived there had a slave who was very unwell and at the point of death. He meant a lot to him. ³ So when he heard about Jesus, he sent some of the Jewish elders to him to ask if he wouldn't mind coming to heal his slave. ⁴ Those who went to Jesus urged him to come, saying, "He's very deserving to have you do this for him, ⁵ because he cares about our people, and he got the synagogue built for us."

⁶ Jesus went off with them. When he was already nearly there, the centurion sent some of his friends from his place to say, "Sir, don't trouble yourself, because I am not worthy to have you come under my roof, ⁷ which is why I didn't consider myself worthy to come to you, but just issue a command, and let my boy be cured. ⁸ I'm a person placed in a position of authority, too, and have soldiers under me and I tell one of them, 'Go!' and he goes and another, 'Come!' and he comes and I tell my slave, 'Do this!' and he does it." ⁹ When Jesus heard this, he admired him, and, turning to the crowd following him, said, "I tell you, in Israel I haven't found such faith." ¹⁰ When those who had been sent returned to the house, they found the slave well again.

¹¹ Next day he went to the city called Nain, and his disciples went with him along with a big crowd. ¹² As he approached the city gate, the only son of a woman who was a widow was being carried out, accompanied by a big crowd of city people. ¹³ When the Lord saw it, he was moved with compassion for her and told her, "Don't cry!" ¹⁴ And then he went and touched the coffin. Those carrying it came to a stop, and he said, "Young man, I'm telling you, get up!" ¹⁵ And the dead man sat up and started to talk. And Jesus handed him over to his mother.

¹⁶ Everyone was filled with awe and started to glorify God, saying, "A great prophet has arisen among us and God is looking to the needs of his people." ¹⁷ The news about him spread like wildfire right through Judea and the surrounding area.

¹⁸ John's disciples told him about all this, so, summoning two of his disciples, John ¹⁹ sent them to the Lord, saying, "Are you the one to come or should we be expecting someone else?" ²⁰ These men came to Jesus and said, "John the Baptist sent us to you to ask, 'Are you the coming one or should we be expecting someone else?'" ²¹ Just at that moment he was healing many of their diseases and afflictions and liberating people from evil spirits and helping blind people to see. ²² So he replied saying, "Go and tell John what you've seen and heard. Blind people are being made to see, lame to walk, lepers are being cleansed and deaf are being enabled to hear, the dead are being raised to life, and the poor are being given good news. ²³ And happy is anyone who isn't offended over me."

²⁴ After those sent from John went off, he began to speak to the crowd about John. "What did you go out into the outback to see? A reed being blown by the wind? ²⁵ No; really, what did you go out to see? A man dressed in lovely fine clothes? You'll find those dressed in glorious luxurious attire in royal courts. ²⁶ But really, what did you go out to see? A prophet? Yes, I tell you, and more than a prophet. ²⁷ This is the one of whom it was written, 'Look, I'm sending my messenger ahead of you, who will prepare your way.' ²⁸ I tell you, there's no one greater than John among all born of women, but the one who is least in the kingdom of God is greater than he is." ²⁹ The whole crowd along with the customs agents who had been baptized with John's baptism acclaimed God's goodness, ³⁰ but the Pharisees and Law specialists rejected what was God's intent also for them by refusing to be baptized by him.

³¹ "To what can I compare the people of this generation and what are they really like? ³² They're like kids sitting in the market square and calling out to each other, 'We played music on the flute and you didn't dance, and we started a dirge and you didn't cry.' ³³ For John the Baptist came not eating bread or drinking wine and you say, 'He's mad.' ³⁴ And the Son of Man came eating and drinking and you say, 'Look, the guy's a glutton and on the booze, a friend of crooked customs agents and sinners.' ³⁵ But wisdom gets shown up to be right by all her children."

Thinking About Luke

Luke tells the story of the healing of the centurion's slave directly after the account of Jesus' teaching. The source that Matthew and Luke have in common must have done the same, because in Matthew, too, it follows the great Sermon on the Mount (Matt 8:5–13). Matthew, however, tended to weave his sources together more, rather than use them in blocks like Luke, so has another short episode from Mark inserted in between, the healing of the leper, which Luke has in any case already told (Luke 5:12–16; Matt 8:1–4; Mark 1:40–45).

Both Luke and Matthew use the story of the centurion to highlight the positive response of someone who was not a Jew but a gentile. Matthew even appends a saying to it that came from their common source and that Luke has elsewhere. It has Jesus declare: "Many will come from east and west and will sit down and share a meal with Abraham, Isaac, and Jacob in the kingdom of heaven and the folk of [Israel's] kingdom will be thrown out into outer darkness" (Matt 8:11–12; Luke 13:29). Luke's expanded account of Jesus' hostile reception in his own hometown synagogue similarly goes on to point to positive engagement with non-Israelites (Luke 4:25–27). Luke's second volume, the book of Acts, will put great emphasis on the success of outreach beyond Israel.

Matthew's version of the centurion story has nothing about local Jews making the first approach and affirming the good character of the centurion. Luke may have added this. Why? To add justification for Jesus' response? Perhaps he was doing the same when he told the story of the centurion Cornelius in Acts 10, and called him upright and supportive of the Jewish nation. Perhaps it was not part of the story in the source.

On the other hand, both Luke and Matthew cite what the centurion himself says about not expecting Jesus as a Jew to come under his roof. It reflects the widespread assumption that, normally, observant Jews would not enter gentile houses, especially because of the danger of being exposed to impurities, above all, in relation to foods. The story about the centurion in Acts 10 also reflects this, where Peter had to be persuaded by a divine vision to set such concerns aside and set aside his reluctance to go to Cornelius' house. The same concerns lie behind the incident that Paul tells us about in Galatians, according to which strict fellow Jewish Christ-followers sent from James' church in Jerusalem persuaded Peter and Paul's companion, Barnabas, to stop sharing meals regularly with gentiles in Antioch (Gal 2:11–14). It also explains why we have stories of Jesus healing gentiles at a distance, such as here and also in the healing of the Syrophoenician woman's daughter (Mark 7:24–30), a story Luke omits.

That concern with impurities sets up the special character of this miracle as happening at a distance. John's Gospel also knows a version of this story that makes much more of the distance and has Jesus do the healing not within Capernaum but from the neighboring town of Cana, and gives much space to emphasizing that the healing took place at the exact moment when Jesus spoke his words (John 4:46–54). Clearly this was an impressive miracle story and Luke, who is fond of emphasizing Jesus' miraculous powers, shows no hesitation in affirming it, unlike John. For John has Jesus express frustration that people were wanting signs and wonders ("You're just not going to believe, are you, unless you see signs and wonders!" John 4:48) and that they were therefore missing the point of his message, like Nicodemus. Like him they needed to be reborn if they were ever to see what it was all about (John 2:23—3:3).

Luke has no qualms about the credibility of the story. He was a person of his age. Nor should we wonder if he ever questioned why someone with the power to heal people at a distance by word of mouth would not, on grounds of compassion, have exercised that ability much more widely given the suffering of the time. These stories arise within the realm of adulation not as scientific reports of medical phenomena. Their lasting value lies rather in how they have been used, namely, to affirm inclusivity.

In recent years when same-sex relations have become an issue of dispute, some have used this story to argue that the slave must have been a slave boy lover, something not unknown in that world, and to argue that absence of disapproval could mean approval. Nothing, however, indicates that those who told the story saw homosexuality here, which would in any case have been pederasty. Those retelling these stories would have shared the widespread assumption that all human beings are heterosexual so would have been most unlikely to let a reference to same-sex relations go by without judgmental comment, let alone what would have in any case been sexual abuse. To affirm, as we know, that not all people are heterosexual and that therefore healthy same-sex relations are for some natural, we do not need to try to read it into biblical texts where it is clearly not assumed or approved.

Only Luke brings the story about Jesus raising a young man, a widow's son, back to life. It recalls the miracles attributed to Elijah (1 Kgs 17:17–24) and Elisha (2 Kgs 4:32–37), figures to whom Luke already drew attention in the story of his reception at Nazareth (Luke 4:25-27) and whose stories may have inspired the story. It claims a massive miracle, which raises all the same questions about credibility and ethics. Retelling it here enables Luke to have Jesus refer to raising the dead in the account of Jesus' response to John the Baptist, which he goes on to relate.

The problem that Luke then addresses in Luke 7:18-20 was that John the Baptist had announced that the one to come would execute judgment, expressed as wielding an axe and a winnowing fork and burning up chaff (Luke 3:9, 17). Jesus, however, was doing nothing of the kind. Behind the problem, historically, is the reality that Jesus and John were closely connected and that John baptized Jesus, which for some would have made him John's junior. The baptism is likely to be a historical fact because it would be scarcely something you would make up if you were wanting to assert Jesus' superiority.

Our data in the Gospels already reflects attempts to explain this relationship. The indications are that Jesus was first a disciple of John, but then set out on his own, also probably baptizing like John and sharing the same call to people to turn their lives around and turn to God, to repent, and to do so in the light of God's impending intervention to bring restoration and change. That much is clearly shared, but Jesus does take a different tack within that framework of thought and so makes the claim that already in the present signs of God's intervention are to be seen. So, instead of remaining at the symbolic place of waiting and expectation, at the Jordan River, with John, he entered the land, symbolizing his claim that indeed expectations were beginning to be fulfilled.

Historically, the degree to which John actually identified Jesus as God's agent to enact God's intervention is not clear, despite the claims made in the Gospels. The continuing existence of the John the Baptist movement, which has survived right through to the present day, might suggest that he did not. There was in any case the problem that when he did speak of God having an agent to execute judgment (if he did, rather than just referring to God as coming), the figure and the actions depict a very different picture from the one we have of Jesus. This meant that the claim that Jesus was God's agent had to come to terms with that difference, and this is what we see happening here in the passage where John questions Jesus, a story found also in Matthew and drawn from their common source (Matt 11:2-6). For attentive readers of the Gospel, too, this needed to be clarified.

John is perplexed because if Jesus is the one he predicted to be God's agent, Jesus is not doing what John had said he would do. The story has Jesus reply by effectively portraying his role in two stages and putting the emphasis on the first stage, which John clearly did not have in mind. Thus, Jesus' response points to his activities, which match what the prophet Isaiah had predicted might happen sometime in the future when God intervenes in history. Isaiah had spoken of a day when the blind would see, the deaf hear, the lame walk (Isa 29:18; 35:5–6), and the dead would be raised (Isa 26:19) and, as in the words that Jesus had already cited at Nazareth, the poor would be given good news (Isa 61:1; Luke 4:18). The latter reference to the poor was reinforced in the promise, "Happy are you who are poor, for yours is the kingdom of God" (Luke 6:20).

The import of Jesus' response is certainly to turn the focus to renewal and healing as well as to claim that he was indeed doing what was predicted. It did not eliminate the notion that he would one day be God's agent of judgment, but it shifts the focus more towards the positive side, including that that event would be good news because it would bring radical change.

The comment that hopefully this would not cause offense may possibly reflect tensions with the John the Baptist community in Luke's day. John was significant and at this point the story brings the citation from Mal 3:1 about God sending a messenger in advance to prepare his way, which Mark had used to introduce John and incorrectly cited as coming from Isaiah (Mark 1:2). As in Mark's use of the citation, Luke and Matthew, reproducing their source, have it spoken as if to Jesus, so that the messenger, John the Baptist, is to prepare the way for Jesus.

Strikingly, Jesus goes on to hail John as the greatest person ever born, but then quickly puts him in his place. The one least in the kingdom of God may just be any disciple, even the lowest. It would signal a demarcation between the Jesus movement and its claim to represent the kingdom of God and the movement of John the Baptist, reflecting tensions between the two as both movements developed after the death of their founders. Alternatively, but less likely, is that Jesus might be understood as making a reference to himself.

Next, Luke and Matthew's source has Jesus speak of the negative response each evoked, John as an ascetic and Jesus engaging with crooked customs agents and their sinner associates, only to assert that wisdom will prove itself right by its outcomes (Luke 7:31–35; Matt 11:16–19). The image of children playing a game leaves us to imagine what game it might have been. We do not know, but the meaning is clear. John and Jesus are, in fact, quite different in their approach, while both being God's agents. John saw himself as being in the time of waiting and expectation. Jesus is depicted as being in the time when that expectation was beginning to be fulfilled.

Luke had Jesus announce his mandate when he read from Isa 61:1 in his hometown synagogue (Luke 4:18–21). That was about hope for the future for the poor and hungry, and he repeated it in declaring them happy because of the prospect of relief (Luke 6:20) and here in response to John's worries he repeats the assertion of hope of good news for the poor (Luke 7:22).

The passage from Isaiah was about more than announcing future change. It was also about liberation in the present. That comes through also in Jesus' response to John's disciples, which, in taking up images from Isaiah, lists miraculous healings, which Luke has illustrated in his story in the interim since his announcement in the synagogue at Nazareth. That liberation was also not just healing, as if Jesus' significance could be reduced to being a miracle worker and so a good competitor for those who also promoted themselves with such tales, but included reaching out to crooks and sinners, and, as Luke will go on to show, bringing about real change through restoring people's relationships with God and each other.

Reflection: How were John the Baptist and Jesus similar and yet different, and how does Luke use this difference to highlight Jesus' role?

Jesus and Women (Luke 7:36—8:3)

Listening to Luke

7:36 Now a Pharisee invited him one day to come for a meal with him, so he went to the Pharisee's house and took his place reclining at the table. **37** And, lo and behold, a woman from the town, a wayward woman, found out that he was dining at the Pharisee's place, and brought a jar of myrrh **38** and standing behind him near his feet weeping, started shedding tears onto his feet and wiping them away with her hair. And she kept kissing his feet and smearing them with the myrrh.

39 When the Pharisee who had invited him saw this, he began to say to himself, "If he were a prophet, he'd have recognized just who this is who's touching him and the sort of woman she is; she's a bad lot."

40 In response Jesus said, "Simon, I've got something I want to tell you."

He said, "Teacher, tell me!"

He said, **41** "There were two people owing money to a certain money lender. One owed five hundred denarii; the other, fifty. **42** When they were unable to pay him back, he canceled both their debts. Which of the two will love him more?"

43 Simon replied, "I suppose the one with the biggest canceled debt."

He said, "You're right."

44 Then turning to the woman he said to Simon, "You see this woman here? I came to your place and you didn't give me any water to wash my feet; but she has rained tears on my feet and dried them with her hair. **45** You didn't greet me with a kiss, but she's not stopped kissing my feet ever since she got here. **46** You didn't anoint my head with oil, but she anointed my feet with myrrh. **47** Let me tell you, her many sins are forgiven and that's why she is so loving. People forgiven little, love little."

⁴⁸ And he said to her, "Your sins are forgiven."

⁴⁹ Those dining together at the meal started saying among themselves, "Who is this who forgives sins?"

⁵⁰ He said to the woman, "Your faith has saved you. Go in peace!"

⁸:¹ And after this he traveled around the towns and villages preaching and proclaiming the good news of the kingdom of God. The twelve were with him ² and so were certain women whom he had cured from their evil spirits and illnesses, including Mary, called Magdalene, from whom seven demons had come out, ³ and Joanna, the wife of Chuza, one of Herod's officials, and Susanna, and many other women, who tended to their needs from the resources they had.

Thinking About Luke

There is much in the final episode in Luke 7 that needs explanation, particularly the cultural norms that are so different from what most of us assume. To begin with, houses were very unlike ours. A reasonably sized house would have private quarters at the back but be largely open to the public at the front. People on the street could often see what was going on there, and that included when people were having a meal with friends.

Dining was usually around a very low table with guests reclining, lying sideways around the table. What I translate as "took his place reclining at the table" is a word meaning simply "reclined." Such low tables for reclining can still be seen today in some cultures. I remember seeing them in a restaurant in Kerala, India. If you are reclining on your side leaning on one elbow, your feet would usually be away from the table, otherwise you would be taking up too much space. This makes sense of the woman standing behind Jesus and touching his feet.

Given the structure of the house, the woman would simply have come in off the street, not have knocked on a front door or rung a bell, as in our contexts. When Luke describes her as a "sinner," which I have translated as "wayward," men hearing the story would very likely read this in sexual terms, so have often assumed she was a prostitute. Perfumed oil of myrrh for massage, made from the sap of the myrrh tree, could belong to the tools of the trade. The account does not describe her as a prostitute, but the likely assumption of men listening to Luke's story would be that her waywardness would include sexual wrongdoing.

Jesus' complaint also reflects what are for us unfamiliar cultural practices. When you came in off the unpaved, often dirty or dusty, streets into someone's house, you would normally be helped to wash your feet. The closest we come to this is when some people prefer to have people leave their shoes at the door. Another unfamiliar practice is anointing or putting oil on someone's hair. I can remember when men widely used hair cream. For a man to look swish in public he would normally have oiled hair. Greeting people with a kiss was and is still widely practiced in many cultures.

If we turn to the story itself, Luke contrasts two different approaches to people who were considered to be sinners, like this woman. This contrast comes through frequently in Luke's story of Jesus. Jesus shows them compassion and offers God's forgiveness. His critics disapprove, on the assumption that he should have nothing to do with them. This is why they criticized his dining with Levi and his friends, crooked tax agents and other sinners, as we saw in Luke 5:27–31, and he has just addressed such criticism in the image of children playing games in the marketplace. Luke introduces the parables of the lost coin, the lost sheep, and the prodigal son by reporting such disapproval (Luke 15:1–2).

Jesus' behavior in reaching out to such people would have courted criticism from some, while others may well have approved if he was reaching out in order to tell them to repent and turn to God. The issue appears to have been that some assumed that such people were not worth bothering about and should therefore be seen as basically bad people to be avoided and written off.

Our story could be read as though the woman is now seeking forgiveness and as though Jesus in response declares her sins forgiven, as he does in 7:48. That, however, contradicts the initial response of Jesus, which defends her behavior on the grounds that it expresses gratitude for having her sins already forgiven, as he states in 7:47. Jesus' words about forgiveness in 7:48 are best understood as restating what had already been declared and for which she shows such affection. Male imagination will have speculated about the "much" for which she has been forgiven, but Luke's interest lies elsewhere. Jesus offered God's forgiveness, and in response people loved him for it.

Luke's story appears to be a variant of a story we know from Mark, repeated in Matthew, and with more variation in John (Mark 14:3–9; Matt

26:6–13; John 12:1–8). Unlike Luke, they all locate it in Jesus' last days and at Bethany. The host, according to Mark's story, is also called Simon, as in Luke. They also tell of a woman who shows affection to Jesus with a jar of myrrh, as in Luke. They also tell of objections from those present, including that it is wasteful to use such costly perfume in this way. There are variations: in Mark and Matthew she anoints Jesus' head, possibly a play on anointing him as the Messiah, the anointed. In John she anoints Jesus' feet, as in Luke. Unlike in Luke, these other accounts play with the notion of myrrh being used also in attending to corpses and see her act as foreshadowing Jesus' death.

Behind all these stories is very likely an occasion during Jesus' ministry when such a woman came to where Jesus was with others in a meal situation and expressed affection using myrrh. The norm would have been for Jesus not to have allowed this to happen. The fact that he allowed it posed problems. John, in part, solves it by identifying her as Mary, Martha's sister, a respectable woman and friend, so that it becomes a simple and acceptable show of affection by a friend. Luke's story also offers a solution by depicting her as a forgiven sinner.

Probably, she was neither a friend nor a forgiven sinner but simply a woman who in her own way was expressing faith and affection towards Jesus, not in a sexual way but in the way she could. Jesus did not turn her away for fear of risking his reputation and contracting religious impurity. This woman, and similar women, were not a danger, not to be shunned, nor exploited. As Mark has Jesus say, the story would circulate in remembrance of her (Mark 14:9). She would not be shown the door, as it were, but remain as a symbol of Jesus' openness towards women and his refusal to embrace the prejudice against her shown by the men.

It is not difficult to imagine that the story in some sense developed a life of its own over the four or so decades before it was written down. Was Luke right that it was something that happened earlier in Jesus' ministry? Did Mark and those who followed him place it at the end because of the meaning that could be read into the anointing, as a foretaste of burial or symbol of messiahship? We may never know. The variations in the accounts do seem to reflect various attempts to come to terms with what many must have felt ran contrary to their cultural norms.

When we move straight from this scene to Luke's account of Jesus proclaiming the kingdom of God in the towns and village round about in Luke 8:1–4, we see another reflection of positive values in relation to women. Luke still, however, sees them primarily as catering for the needs of male disciples with the resources available to them (Luke 8:3), some of whom must have had some wealth. Nevertheless, Luke has preserved mention of these women who were part of the movement and may well have been more than just ancillary supporters as he describes them. Elsewhere, we hear of them taking leadership roles, such as in Paul's list of greetings in Rom 16, where he incidentally provides such evidence, when he describes Junia as an apostle (Rom 16:7) and others: Mary as a very hard worker (Rom 16:6), and Tryphaena and Tryphosa as "workers in the Lord" (Rom 16:12).

Speculation surrounds Mary Magdalene. John's Gospel has her, indeed, the first to see the risen Jesus, implying very high status (John 20:1), and in other versions she was at least one of the women both at the cross and at the empty tomb (Mark 15:47—16:1; Matt 27:56, 61; 28:1; Luke 24:10). The largely male memories that passed on traditions may have left behind detail of what she did and the role she played. Many speculate about her possible roles, including fantasies, with no basis in fact, that she became Jesus' wife. By contrast, some in the past have identified her with the woman who anointed Jesus' feet, but nothing in Luke indicates that.

If the initial group Jesus gathered around him was in fact stepping outside the norms of their social system with its hierarchies of rich and poor, we can understand that this might well have extended to treating women differently, at least as affirming women, despite some of the cultural assumptions still showing in the initial choice of twelve men to be apostles.

There would have been enormous pressure over time to impose what were seen as respectable norms on members of the Jesus movement as it grew. You needed to show to fellow citizens in the wider Roman Empire that followers of Jesus were upright, good citizens and upheld the best household norms, which saw men as the head of families, responsible for public engagement, and women as responsible for household management (Col 3:18–25; Eph 5:21–33).

The fact that in both Jewish and Greco-Roman cultures men married around thirty and married wives usually half their age reinforced for men the belief that their wives were not only younger and less experienced, but were also inferior to them in control of feelings and intelligence. Already in Paul, who affirms women in Christ (Gal 3:28), we see this assumption of inferiority (1 Cor 11:3, 7), and ultimately it would lead to creating a male-dominated religion and society from which we are still in the process of recovery.

Reflection: What were the issues about women, as men saw them (and how might women have seen them), and how did they play out then and still to some extent play out?

Hope and Reality (Luke 8:4–21)

Listening to Luke

⁸:⁴ When a big crowd gathered and people were converging on him from all the towns around about, he addressed them using a parable. ⁵ "A farmer went out to sow wheat. In the process some wheat fell along the path and got walked on, and birds came and ate it. ⁶ And other wheat fell on rocky ground, and when it sprouted, it soon shriveled up because it had no moisture. ⁷ And some fell where there were thorn bushes, and their seeds sprouted and choked them. ⁸ And some fell into good soil, and it sprouted and produced heads of wheat with a hundred seeds." Saying this, he called out, "Anyone with ears, listen to this!"

⁹ His disciples started to ask him what this parable was about. ¹⁰ He said to them, "It's given to you to know the mysteries of the kingdom of God, but as for the rest, it's given to them in parables, so that seeing they may not see and hearing they may not understand.

¹¹ "This is what the parable is about: the seed is the word of God. ¹² Those falling along the path are those who hear, but then the devil comes and takes it from their mind, lest they believe and be saved. ¹³ And those falling on rocky ground are the ones who, when they hear, are happy to take it on board, but they don't have any roots and so for a while they believe, but then the moment they face trouble they give up. ¹⁴ And with regard to what falls among thornbushes, these are the ones who hear, but then when worries and money matters and life's pleasures come along, they're choked and fail to end up producing ripe grain. ¹⁵ And as for what falls into good soil, those are the ones who listen to the word with a healthy, wholesome mind and hold onto it, and they produce grain and keep on doing so.

¹⁶ "No one lights a lamp and then puts a cover over it or puts it under a bed, but they put it on a lampstand so that everyone coming

in can see the light. ¹⁷ There's nothing hidden that won't be exposed, nor anything secreted away that won't be made known and brought to light. ¹⁸ Watch how you listen. For whoever has got the point, will be given more, and whoever doesn't get it, even what they seem to have will be taken away from them."

¹⁹ One day his mother and his brothers came to him but couldn't get close to him because of the crowd. ²⁰ People told him, "Your mom and your brothers are standing outside wanting to see you." ²¹ In response he said, "My mother and my brothers are those who listen to God's word and act accordingly."

Thinking About Luke

Luke has just mentioned Jesus' activity in summary and told us about the importance of women in the movement. Now he presents Jesus' teaching. He did something similar back in Luke 6 where he told us about the twelve apostles before going on to present Jesus' teaching.

To do so, he returns to using Mark. He had left using Mark back midway through Luke 6. Now he goes back to Mark 4, where Mark brings a cluster of Jesus' parables. Mark's chapter begins with Jesus getting into a boat and positioning himself just offshore so he could teach from there. Luke had already used that scene at the beginning of Luke 5, so now goes straight on to the first parable that Mark brings.

Traditionally called the parable of the sower, it picks up the very familiar and uses it to make people think. Jesus will have told it in the region of Galilee, which was known for its wheat farms. There were probably local farmers listening to Jesus. Of course, some of the wheat you scatter is not going to produce anything. But some will. So you go ahead. Very likely people wondered about the hope Jesus spoke about. Would there really be change? There was so much that suggested otherwise and, of course, opposition would escalate, and execution would eventually follow.

Jesus picked up the familiar image of harvest to speak about hope. His was a message of good news, good news for the poor, which was most of them, when the kingdom of God, God's empire, replaced Rome's. Mark's version of the parable brings it to a climax with the claim that the one seed would multiply itself forty, sixty, even a hundredfold! Luke keeps it simple: a hundredfold.

Already when the story came to Mark it had undergone further reflection, especially in a church setting where the fate of the various seeds could be applied to what they observed was happening in their congregations. Some people simply never joined, but, among those who did, there were the enthusiastic ones who came but then went again, because they really had no depth. There were also those who got distracted with wealth and self-indulgence. But some, a good many, stayed. This would have been just as relevant for Luke and his listeners as for Mark and his . . . and for us!

This application of the parable to what it means to hear and receive the message of Jesus puts the focus not so much on hope in the future as on bearing fruit in the present. That will include showing in one's life the kind of love and compassion Jesus showed during his ministry.

Luke keeps the parable and its interpretation very brief compared with Mark. As in Mark, he has a conversation placed between the parable and its interpretation, but here, too, he trims it to a minimum. The disciples as insiders are given the secrets of the kingdom of God. Mark had written secret in the singular, but Luke clearly understands this as referring to inside information. Luke then repeats Mark's citation of Isa 6:9 and the suggestion that outsiders would be told parables to keep them from getting the message.

That is quite counterintuitive. Parables serve to communicate, not to block communication. Was this a desperate attempt to come to terms with why some people did not accept the gospel: it was meant to be? This is hardly the case. On the other hand, parables, like metaphors, are suggestive, and minds open to the possibility that they mean more than they say will "get it." The penny will drop, as we used to say. When someone says, "She's an encyclopedia," it will be just nonsense for some people, but others will make the jump and get the intended meaning. That is how parables work. Something of this sense probably lies behind what seems a rather exclusive and contradictory statement which Mark and Luke bring us about parables. Matthew sensed the potential problem and changed the saying from explaining that parables are to cause people not to see, to explaining that parables are given because people do not see (and need to be helped to see) (Matt 13:13).

Luke continues to follow Mark 4 in bringing the sayings about the lamp and nothing being hidden. Jesus was lighting a lamp of hope and change and there was no way he was going to hide it. Future change is also in mind in the saying about nothing being hidden. Judgment day will come, and people will have to face up to reality.

The command to be careful how you listen reinforces the point being made in the interpretation of the parable. The more you let the message in, the more you will get from it, and the opposite is true. This saying also belongs to the threats about judgment day.

Mark goes on to bring more parables, including the parable of the seed growing secretly, and the parable of the mustard seed, concluding with an observation about the purpose of parables which echoes what was said between the sower parable and its interpretation. Luke bypasses this material. He has a second source for the parable of the mustard seed and prefers to use it when he is drawing from that source (Luke 13:18–19).

The theme of hearing and responding to the message, hearing God's word, continues in Luke's account of Jesus' mother and his brothers wanting to come to him. Luke is heavily abbreviating what he found in Mark 3:20–35. He leaves out much of it, including the detail that his family wanted to get to him because they thought he had gone out of his mind, or at least others did (Mark 3:20–21). Between their resolve to come and their arrival to get Jesus, Mark inserts an account of religious leaders claiming he was indeed mad and in league with Beelzebul. Luke has a second source also for these accusations and so leaves it out here. Luke therefore brings only the detail that the family turns up wanting to see Jesus.

Mark mentions his sisters as well as his brothers. Luke mentions only his brothers and his mother. Sadly, sometimes women were overlooked. There is no mention here of Joseph, neither in Mark nor in Luke. But, given that men married around the age of thirty and Jesus was thirty when his ministry started, it is not surprising to find no mention of Joseph. Given the average age of death of those days he is likely to have already died.

Jesus' statement that his true family are those hearing and doing God's will reinforces the message Luke has been presenting, but it does imply some distancing from his family, reminiscent of his behavior as Luke portrays it as a twelve-year-old. In an age when families exercised enormous power, it is perhaps not surprising that Luke takes over at least this detail from Mark. Care and regard for family never meant letting family usurp the role of God, an insight Mark and Luke have preserved for every age.

Reflection: In what ways did the parable tie hope to reality, in Jesus' ministry, in the early church, and how might this apply today?

Worlds Apart (Luke 8:22–56)

Listening to Luke

8:22 One day he got into a boat with his disciples and told them, "Let's go across to the other side of the lake," and they sailed off. **23** As they were sailing along, he took a nap. And a strong wind sprang up on the lake and they were beginning to get swamped and faced danger. **24** So they went to him and woke him up, saying, "Master, master, we're gonna drown!"

He then woke up, and firmly told the wind and wild swell to stop it, and they stopped, and things calmed down. **25** Then he said to them, "Where's your faith?" They were flabbergasted and said to one another in amazement, "Who is this man, that he can tell the wind and waves what to do and they obey him?"

26 And they sailed to Gerasene territory, which is on the opposite side to the Galilee region. **27** And there, a man from the town approached him when he disembarked. He was possessed by demons and for a long time hadn't worn any clothes and didn't stay in a house but lived among the tombstones. **28** So when he saw Jesus, he shouted out loud and fell at his feet and in a loud voice said, "What's your business with me, Jesus, Son of the Most High God? Are you going to torment me?" **29** For he had told the unclean spirit to get out of the man. For it often used to take control of him; and he used to be tied up under guard with chains and shackles, but he would break his bonds and was driven off by the demon into the outback regions.

30 So Jesus asked him, "What's your name?" He said "Legion," because many demons had entered him. **31** And they were pleading with him not to order them to return to the depths of the sea. **32** Now there was a herd of big fat pigs grazing on that hill and so they (the demons) asked him to let them enter them. So he did **33** and the demons left the man and entered the pigs and the herd charged off down the cliff into the lake and drowned.

⁳⁴ When the pig farmers saw what had happened, they fled for their lives and told people about it in the city and the region. ³⁵ People came out to see what had happened and when they got to Jesus, they found the man from whom Jesus had expelled the demons sitting down at Jesus' feet, clothed and making sense, and they were scared. ³⁶ And those who had seen how the demon possessed man had been liberated told them about it. ³⁷ Then the whole crowd from the region of the Gerasenes asked Jesus to go away, because they were really scared. He got into the boat and sailed off back. ³⁸ The man whom the demons had left asked if he could hang out with Jesus, but he sent him off, saying, ³⁹ "Go back home to your place and tell people all that God has done for you." So off he went proclaiming right through the whole town what Jesus had done for him.

⁴⁰ When Jesus got back, the crowd welcomed him because many had been waiting for him. ⁴¹ And there was a man named Jairus, a leading person in the synagogue, who approached Jesus. He fell at his feet and pleaded with him to come to his place, ⁴² because his only daughter, twelve years old, was at the point of death.

As Jesus went, the crowds pressed in on him. ⁴³ Now there was woman with a hemorrhage, which she'd had for twelve years. [Despite having spent all her life savings on doctors] she hadn't been able to be healed by anyone. ⁴⁴ Coming up behind Jesus, she touched the edge of his coat and immediately the flow of blood stopped. ⁴⁵ Then Jesus said, "Who just touched me?" When everyone said it wasn't them, Peter said, "Master, there's crowds all around you and they're pressing in on you." ⁴⁶ But Jesus said, "Someone touched me, because I sensed that power had gone out from me." ⁴⁷ When the woman saw that she wouldn't get away with it, she came to Jesus very scared and fell at his feet and told him in front of everyone why she touched him and how she was immediately healed. ⁴⁸ He said to her, "My daughter, your faith has healed you. Go in peace!"

⁴⁹ While he was still speaking, someone from the chief of the synagogue's place came, saying, "Your daughter has died. Don't bother the teacher." ⁵⁰ Jesus heard and replied, "Don't worry, just trust and she'll be made well again." ⁵¹ When he got to the house, he didn't let

anyone else in with him except Peter and John and James along with the father of the girl and her mother. [52] Everyone was weeping and mourning over her. He said, "Don't mourn. She hasn't died; she's just asleep." [53] Some laughed in his face knowing that she had died. [54] But he took her by the hand and called out, "My child, get up!" [55] And her spirit came back, and she immediately got up, and he instructed that she be given something to eat. [56] Her parents were beside themselves, but he told them not to tell anyone what had happened.

Thinking About Luke

To understand these three stories we need to enter Luke's world. Already when he retold the story of the healing of Peter's mother-in-law, we observed that Luke described the healing as an exorcism. Jesus firmly told the fever off, and it went. The assumption was that a demon caused the fever. Luke understands not only illnesses but also natural phenomena as caused by demons. When he tells the wind and waves to stop doing what they were doing, he was addressing the evil spirits that controlled them.

This is not how we understand the weather. Nor is it how we understand what people at one with God might do. Were it possible, it would, of course, be of huge value to be able to relieve the suffering and disaster caused sometimes by weather events, whether floods, tornadoes, or wildfires. The problem is not solved by saying that only Jesus had such power, and that this power did not pass on to Jesus' disciples and the church.

We inevitably approach such stories informed by what we as human beings have learned so far about weather and about sickness, and it does not accord with first-century science. It happens quite regularly that a sea breeze sweeps in over the Sea of Galilee. I have experienced it, myself. So the image of suddenly finding that a boat gets itself into trouble is realistic. Whether such an actual event lies behind the story, it came to be told as an occasion where Jesus demonstrated his powers over the forces of the deep. It was a wonder story designed to evoke adulation of Jesus.

Such stories then develop a life of their own. Not viewed as repeatable, they come to serve as symbolic of help when facing life's storms and turbulence. That can inspire individual faith and trust, but the story can also come to symbolize the church or congregation facing distress. The boat came to be seen as a symbol of the church, and we still see it used in this way, for instance, in the emblems of the World Council of Churches or in Australia of the Uniting Church in Australia.

Luke will have seen the event as a miracle demonstrating Jesus' power over the powers of evil forces, which cause danger. He is following Mark, who has the stilling of the storm follow Jesus' teaching by parables. As in Mark, Luke then brings two more stories of wonder and they, too, need to be read within the cultural assumptions of their world.

People explained mental illness as demon possession, the invasion of a person by powers from the spirit world. This explains why such powers could recognize someone significant from that world, in this case, Jesus. The assumption is also that they recognize that Jesus is to be God's agent on the day of judgment when such demons will finally be disempowered and sent to everlasting punishment. Such is the assumption here, but there is more.

Gerasa is understood as gentile territory, not holy land, and so a place where one would be likely to encounter the demonic and the unclean. Tombs and cemeteries were seen as dark places where spirits may abound, especially at night, an understanding that was widespread and continued to be assumed right through to the present day in many cultures. Engagement with such powers was scary, and so it is not at all surprising that the locals want Jesus to go away.

Pigs were also unclean animals, according to biblical tradition. There is even more. Many saw the depths of the sea as a place of demons, so to have the demon-possessed pigs rushing down into the sea fits these assumptions. The name, "Legion," alludes to military occupation forces of the empire, Rome and its legions. Many saw political powers as also ruled and controlled by demons.

Gerasa was some thirty-seven miles/sixty kilometers from the Sea of Galilee, perhaps something Mark and then Luke did not realize. Matthew brings the location nearer by placing the event at Gadara just five to six miles/eight to nine kilometers from the lake. Even so, the story assumes that the herd of pigs was near the sea, and this cannot have been the case. It is a story, after all, and perhaps its origin was simply an exorcism near Gerasa which was supplemented by storytellers with the symbolism of the unclean pigs and their fate.

For listeners to Luke's Gospel, many of whom would be Jews or, as converts, people sharing Jewish presuppositions, this event would be rich in meaning. It celebrated liberation coming not only to this man but also generally to non-Jews, gentiles. Jesus tells the man to go and relate to people how God had liberated him, a model for gentiles. Luke has largely reproduced Mark's story with little variation.

Luke, following Mark, next brings the story of the healing of the woman with the hemorrhage and the restoring back to life of Jairus' daughter. In Mark, the story at Gerasa and this one form a two-part panel celebrating the gospel coming to gentiles and to Jews. For this story takes place in Jewish territory, and its symbolism is underlined by the detail that the woman's hemorrhage had been going on for twelve years and that the girl was twelve years of age, twelve recalling the twelve tribes of Israel.

While this appears to have been Mark's intent in juxtaposing the stories, it is not clear that Luke is doing the same, especially because he does not take up Mark's next attempt to symbolize the gospel going to Jews and gentiles through his accounts of the feeding of the five thousand and the four thousand. Luke simply repeats Mark's story, trimming it somewhat. The detail about the woman's expenditure on doctors—preserved in some but not all Greek manuscripts, hence in brackets in the translation—may reflect someone's early attempt to restore detail that Luke omitted.

Again, we encounter cultural presuppositions. Biblical laws deemed bodily excretions, including bleeding, as rendering people ritually unclean, which then required acts of purification, and required them not to come into touch with others. Having permanent bleeding was therefore a problem, both ritually and socially, because the woman would have to keep apart from others who, should they be touched by her, would be rendered unclean. Her act therefore potentially rendered Jesus unclean, but those who first told the story would probably reckon him immune from such contamination. It would have been an offense for her in her state to touch Jesus, but already as Mark retells the story, that is no longer in focus. Rather, the issue is the power that it claims Jesus sensed as having gone out of him.

Both the Gerasa story and this story will have first been told among people sharing Jewish purity assumptions. They are no longer Mark's concern and may not be Luke's either. Touching a corpse would also render a person unclean, so that Jesus' doing so with the girl would also have been a problem, except that the storyteller assumes that Jesus with his holy power was immune.

Luke does not indicate what else he might have seen in these stories other than that Jesus had the power by the Spirit to heal and to bring the dead back to life. Would he have reflected on the fact that both stories related to women's issues, vaginal bleeding and a girl at the age when menstruation might be beginning? Whatever Luke may have intended, the stories do have a life of their own and connect us in that sense to realities of human existence, even if we no longer can share their cultural and demonological assumptions.

Reflection: In such stories we encounter assumptions that most of us no longer share, about the weather, about mental illness, about pigs, about blood, about corpses, but what remained as cultural contexts changed, and what remains as we read such stories in ours?

3

Following the Way of the Son of Man

The Way of the Son of Man (Luke 9:1–27)

Listening to Luke

⁹:¹ Calling the twelve together, he gave them power and authority over all demons and to heal sicknesses ² and sent them off to proclaim the kingdom of God and to heal [the sick], ³ and told them, "Don't take anything with you on the way, neither a staff nor a money bag nor food nor money, nor have two tunics. ⁴ And when you get to someone's house, stay there and leave from there. ⁵ And whoever does not welcome you, head off from that town and shake the dust off your feet as a testimony against them." ⁶ So off they went traveling around village by village preaching the good news and performing acts of healing everywhere.

⁷ Now Herod the tetrarch heard that all this was happening and was puzzled because some were saying that John had been raised up from the dead, ⁸ and others that Elijah had appeared, and others that one of the prophets of old had come back to life. ⁹ Herod said, "I decapitated John, so who's this that I'm hearing such reports about?" and he was wanting to see him.

¹⁰ When the apostles returned, they told Jesus what they'd done. Then taking them with him he went off just with them to a town called

Bethsaida. ¹¹ Crowds, however, found out and followed him. He then welcomed them and spoke with them about the kingdom of God and cured those in need of healing.

¹² When it got late in the day, the twelve came to him and said, "Send the crowd off to go into the villages roundabout and the countryside to find somewhere to stay and get themselves something to eat, because we're stuck in the outback here with nothing."

¹³ He told them, "You give them something to eat!" They replied, "All we've got are five loaves of bread and a couple of dried fish, unless we, ourselves, were to go off and buy food for all these people." ¹⁴ There were around five thousand men.

So he told his disciples, "Get them to sit down in groups of fifties." ¹⁵ They did so, and sat them all down. ¹⁶ Then taking the loaves of bread and the two fish he looked up into heaven and blessed them and broke up the loaves and gave them to his disciples to distribute to the crowd. ¹⁷ They ate and all were satisfied and what was left over from the pieces of bread was collected up, twelve baskets full.

¹⁸ And once when he was praying alone and his disciples were with him, he asked them, "Who do people reckon I am?" ¹⁹ They replied, "John the Baptist, others say Elijah, others, one of the prophets of old who's come back to life." ²⁰ He said to them, "And who do you say I am?" Peter answered, "God's Messiah." ²¹ He told them firmly not to tell anyone this was so, ²² adding, "The Son of Man must undergo a lot of suffering and be rejected by the elders and chief priests and scribes and be put to death and be raised again on the third day."

²³ And he started telling them all, "If anyone wants to follow me, let them deny themselves and take up their cross daily and follow me. ²⁴ Whoever wants to keep their life will lose it, and whoever loses their life for my sake will save it. ²⁵ What does a person profit by gaining the whole world, only to lose their real self and end up in emptiness? ²⁶ For whoever is ashamed of me and my words, the Son of Man will be ashamed of them, when he comes in his glory and that of the Father and the holy angels. ²⁷ I'm telling you truly, there are some standing here who will not taste death before they see the kingdom of God."

Thinking About Luke

As Luke was following Mark, he came to the end of Mark 5, which told the stories of Gerasa and Jairus. He then omitted what he found at the beginning of Mark 6, namely Jesus' visit to his hometown synagogue (Mark 6:1-6), because he had already used it. He had made it the opening scene of Jesus' ministry in Luke 4. So he goes straight on to what follows in Mark, namely the sending out of the twelve (Mark 6:7-13; Luke 9:1-6).

Matthew and Luke knew another account of this sending. Matthew's solution was to merge the two accounts into one (Matt 10:5-15). Luke instead brings both accounts: in Luke 9:1-6 the one he found in Mark and in Luke 10:1-12 the one he found in the source he shared in common with Matthew, but turns it into a sending out of seventy. We shall return to this below.

The two accounts, Mark's and the one from Matthew and Luke's other source, are very close, with only minor differences in the instructions. Mark's account has Jesus allow them to take a staff. The other version does not, so Luke has Jesus forbid it in both his accounts. It is likely that these are two different accounts of one occasion when Jesus sent the twelve out to do what he was doing, namely, to perform exorcisms, heal people, and proclaim Jesus' message of hope about the coming kingdom of God.

The rule that they were to be totally dependent on others for their support probably goes back to Jesus. It matches the discipline he imposed on himself, but we know that it was certainly seen as the rule once the movement expanded after Jesus' death. Keeping up connections was important; so apostles, envoys, would visit faith communities in various towns and villages and be put up by the locals during their visit. This reproduced what will have happened during Jesus' own ministry. His was an itinerant group dependent on locals for support as they went from town to town.

Luke suggests in chapter 10 that they were sent out in pairs (Luke 10:1) and this is the pattern he reports in Acts, when he mentions such pairs as Paul and Barnabas, or Paul and Silas. There were always going to be difficulties as people exercised this itinerant role. How would the locals know the person was genuine and not an imposter? Concern about itinerants surfaces, for instance, in 2 John 10 and 3 John 9-10, and over time became a major problem.

Already in Paul's time, he had to grapple with competing claims (2 Cor 3:1), especially from those who sought to undermine his influence. In addition, for practical reasons, Paul sometimes decided to work to support himself instead of being totally dependent on locals, as the mission instructions required. This laid him open to the charge that he was breaking the rule and showing he did not have faith that God would support him. Paul argued that the only significant rule was to do what was most considerate and caring and this was his way of doing it (1 Cor 9). Those who took a fundamentalist attitude towards Jesus' instructions—unlike, for instance, Jesus' own approach to biblical law—plagued Paul throughout his ministry.

Usually houses were very accessible, so we can imagine such itinerants arriving and hoping to be put up. If they were not, instead of arguing and insisting, they were simply to leave, but then indicate that the lack of hospitality would be one day punished on the day of judgment and symbolize that by shaking the dirt from their shoes as they left. Those who passed on these accounts clearly saw such threats of judgment as acceptable, where we might see them as potentially problematic.

The modern equivalent of the itinerant code is the ministerial stipend, which in most churches is a standard amount independent of years of service, skill level, and seniority, designed to enable people to be free to function effectively in ministry. Our age, too, has examples of exploitative profiteering by populist preachers.

Mark's account goes on to report the story of John the Baptist's dramatic demise (Mark 6:14–29), but Luke had already summarized it back in Luke 3:19–20, so brings only the account of Herod Antipas pondering who Jesus might be. He corrects Mark, who called Herod a "king," labeling him properly as "tetrarch." Luke then brings the story of the apostles' return and of Jesus' taking them off to Bethsaida for an appropriate rest, and there to be confronted again by crowds, among whom Jesus spoke of the kingdom of God and healed the sick.

There follows the account of the feeding of the five thousand men, to which only Matthew adds that there were in addition also women and children. Luke tells the story much as in Mark, but clearly not with Mark's intent. For Mark uses the feeding of the five thousand (Jews) in Mark 6:32–44 and the four thousand (gentiles) in Mark 8:1–9 to celebrate the good news coming to both Israel and to gentiles. The numbers reinforce this. The five loaves and the five thousand suggests the five books of Moses, and twelve reflects the twelve tribes of Israel. In addition, Mark describes the five thousand Jews as like sheep without a shepherd, echoing the prophet Micaiah's words about Israel (1 Chr 18:16; Num 27:17) and has them seated in hundreds and fifties like Israel in the wilderness (Exod 18:25; Deut 1:15).

Mark then locates the feeding of four thousand in gentile territory, has seven loaves and seven baskets full, reflecting seven as a universal symbol. Between the two feedings he has the episode where Jesus declares all foods clean (Mark 7:1–23), so removing the contentious issue of whether Jews and gentiles should share meals, which evoked the crisis in Antioch that Paul tells us about in Galatians (Gal 2:12–15). It is one of Mark's finest compositions.

Luke, however, will not deal with openness to gentiles until Acts 10 in his second volume, so does not take up Mark's stories, leaving out the entire section, Mark 6:45—8:26. Instead, he jumps right across to Mark 8:27 where Jesus asks his disciples about who they think he is. He may well also have been unhappy with Mark's story, which he uses to justify disregard of food laws, because it would have stood in tension with the saying that he and Matthew found in their common sources, according to which Jesus declared that not a stroke of biblical law was to be set aside (Luke 16:17; Matt 5:18). Only God could do so by direct intervention, which he then shows happening in Acts 10.

Because of the way Luke made his choices in using Mark, the accounts of Herod's pondering about Jesus' identity and Jesus' questioning the disciples about his identity come quite close together (Luke 9:7–9 and 9:18–20). As in Mark, Peter gives the right answer in declaring Jesus the Messiah. Telling them not to tell anyone made sense in a world where being Messiah often meant wanting to lead revolts against the Romans. That was not how Jesus saw his role, and so he effectively quashes such sentiment by speaking of his impending rejection as Son of Man by the religious authorities and execution, before then on the third day being raised from the dead (Luke 9:22). Son of Man was the title for God's agent of future judgment. There is, therefore, some irony when here the judge himself is to be condemned. Son of Man was sometimes used as a title for the hoped for Messiah, especially as people re-used Daniel's imagery of the human figure, the "one like a son of man," in Dan 7:13, who would follow the collapse of evil empires depicted as ruled by animal figures.

Missing from Luke's account is the somewhat shocking exchange that follows in Mark, according to which Peter, based on his understanding of his hope for what the Messiah would achieve, rejected Jesus' prediction as inappropriate. It evokes the stern rebuke of Jesus, who calls him Satan and declares that he's embracing not God's but popular human priorities (Mark 8:32–33).

For Mark this is the first of three scenes in which Jesus' prediction of his fate is contrasted with the opposite values expressed by the disciples (Mark 9:30–37; 10:35–45), leading to the climax in which Jesus declares, "The Son of Man came not to be served but to serve and give his life a ransom for many" (Mark 10:45). Again, Luke abandons Mark's striking composition, by omitting the first of these, the exchange with Peter, and the third, also because he uses parts of the second and third in his depiction of Jesus' closing words to his disciples in Luke 22:25–27. He retains only the second as Mark had it, in Luke 9:46–48.

Luke, therefore, goes straight on after Jesus' prediction to Mark's account of Jesus' teaching about what is really in a person's best interest (Mark 8:34—9:1; Luke 9:23–27). Contrary to how it might seem, one's best interest is not served by making oneself the main agenda, but by embracing love for others, even when that means facing execution, as Jesus would. Greed and profit-seeking are not the way to life. Applied to Jesus' followers, Luke brings Mark's climax where Jesus the Son of Man, judge to come, declares that he will be ashamed of anyone ashamed of him.

Taken out of their broader context these verses could sound like the typical demands of a cult leader bent on demanding absolute loyalty, a very dangerous move but one our world has seen all too often in both religion and in politics. Such leaders want followers, admirers, people to adore them. Some people at times portray Jesus like this, and even God as someone whose main focus is being the center of adoration, as though masking a deep sense of neediness.

Jesus' passion, according to Luke, lies elsewhere. It is to bring hope and change. The challenge is not to grab for oneself and save and protect the self, which one fears will otherwise miss out, but to see that the way to life is to embrace and share love. Nor was Jesus asking his followers to do one thing, while harboring the opposite ambition for himself. On the contrary, as Luke has just told us, his passion as God's Messiah was to give and to love, including when it meant facing suffering and death. He is not the counter example but the actual example, and Mark brings this out even more strongly when he reports Jesus' confronting Peter with harboring typical human priorities and not God's (Mark 8:33). The best theology does not see Jesus as an exception in the life of God, an interim adventure of generosity, but the way God really is. Our ways are to be Jesus' way and Jesus' way is God's way.

These verses have also sometimes led people to believe that to follow Jesus and deny ourselves means we should always put ourselves down and indeed not love ourselves. On the contrary, they are in fact an appeal to do what is also best for us, so to care about ourselves. Don't embrace an image of yourself where you can't afford to love others and need to be constantly occupied with seeking others' adoration. Instead, recognize that God loves you, and love and accept yourself, and you will then be free from being preoccupied with trying to win other's love and see yourself in competition with them, but will have space and freedom to love others. Love for God, love for self, and love for others are then not in competition but belong together in mutual nourishment.

To reinforce the urgency that Luke still shares with Mark, Luke finally reports Jesus as saying that he would come as judge and the kingdom of God would be established in the lifetime of some of those listening (Luke 9:27; Mark 9:1). Luke reports a similar prediction in Luke 21:32. It did not happen. This could have caused the whole movement to collapse, but it didn't, because the ultimate focus of faith was not an event in the future, however near or far, but God. The Jesus movement began in circles that expected history would soon be sorted, and, in a way, Jesus' innovation was to say that this was already beginning to happen. Paul thought it would occur in his lifetime (1 Thess 4:15; 1 Cor 15:51–52) and others kept the expectation alive until late in the first century. What mattered most was knowing God's goodness already in the here and now and being willing to accept the invitation to partner with God.

Reflection: How can we hold together love for self, love for God, and love for others? How does that work?

Priorities and Projections (Luke 9:28–62)

Listening to Luke

9:28 Having said this, around eight days later, Jesus took Peter and John and James with him and went up a mountain to pray. **29** And while he was praying the appearance of his face changed and his clothes became glistening white. **30** Then, lo and behold, two men were there speaking with him, namely, Moses and Elijah. **31** Having appeared also in such glory, they were talking with him about his exit from this life, which was about to take place in Jerusalem. **32** Peter and his companions were very tired, but managed to stay awake, and they saw his glory and the two men standing beside him.

33 And when they were in the process of taking their leave of Jesus, Peter said, "Master, it's great that we can be here. Let's erect three tents, one for you, one for Moses, and one for Elijah," not really knowing what he was saying. **34** As he was saying this, a cloud came and overshadowed them, and they were scared as they entered the cloud. **35** And a voice came from the cloud, "This is my chosen Son, listen to him!" **36** When the voice finished saying this, there was Jesus on his own. And they kept quiet about this and told no one those days what they had seen.

37 Next day, when they had come down from the mountain, a large crowd met him. **38** And a man called out from the crowd, "Teacher, I beg you to have a look at my son, my only child. **39** All of a sudden, a spirit overtakes him and immediately he shrieks out loud and it convulses him, and he foams at the mouth, and it hardly leaves him alone, but makes him shake. **40** And I asked your disciples to expel it, but they couldn't." **41** Jesus responded, "O faithless and twisted generation, how long must I hang around and put up with you? Bring your boy here."

⁴² While he was still being brought, the demon attacked him and convulsed him. Jesus then rebuked the unclean spirit and healed the boy and gave him back to his father. ⁴³ Everyone was amazed at the greatness of God. While everyone was stunned at all that he was doing, he said to his disciples, ⁴⁴ "Let these words sink in: the Son of Man is going to be delivered over to [the sons of] men." ⁴⁵ They had no idea what this meant and it was kept a mystery from them, so they didn't get it and were scared to ask him what the saying meant.

⁴⁶ They started having a debate about who among them was the greatest. ⁴⁷ When Jesus picked up what their debate was about, he took a young child and placed the little one next to him ⁴⁸ and said to them, "Whoever welcomes this child in my name, welcomes me. And whoever welcomes me, welcomes the one who sent me. For the one who is least of all among you will be great."

⁴⁹ John responded to Jesus, saying, "Master, we saw someone casting out demons in your name and we tried to stop him, because he's not one of us, your followers." ⁵⁰ Jesus said to him, "Don't stop him; whoever is not against you is for you."

⁵¹ When the time came for him to be taken from this life, he set his mind firmly on going to Jerusalem. ⁵² And he sent messengers ahead of him. So they went off and came to a Samaritan village to get things ready for him. ⁵³ But they did not welcome him, because his mind was set on going to Jerusalem. ⁵⁴ When his disciples, James and John, saw this, they said, "Lord, do you want us to call down fire from heaven to destroy them?" ⁵⁵ Turning to them, Jesus told them off ⁵⁶ and went on to another village.

⁵⁷ As they were going along the road, someone said to him, "I will follow you wherever you go." ⁵⁸ Jesus told him, "Foxes have holes and birds have nests, but the Son of Man has nowhere to put his head down for a sleep." ⁵⁹ He said to another person, "Follow me!" But he said, "[Lord] Let me first bury my father." ⁶⁰ He said to him, "Let the dead bury their dead, but as for you, take your leave and start proclaiming the kingdom of God." ⁶¹ Another person said to him, "I will follow you. But first let me say goodbye to my household." ⁶² Jesus said to him, "No one putting his hand to the plough and looking back is fit for the kingdom of God."

Thinking About Luke

Luke follows Mark in going on to report the highly symbolic image of Jesus meeting with Elijah and Moses on a mountain, but with some variations. As he often does (e.g., Luke 3:21; 5:16; 6:12), he adds a reference to Jesus praying. Jesus went there to pray. Luke's assumption was surely not wide of the mark that Jesus was a person of prayer, but he wants to emphasize it.

Mountains were often seen as places of prayer or of being close to God and frequently serve that role symbolically. One of the best-known scenes is Moses on Mount Sinai receiving the Law. Another of Luke's additions was to mention that Jesus went up the mountain after eight days, just as Moses went up Mount Sinai after eight days, reinforcing that connection.

In addition, he tells us what Moses and Elijah were discussing with Jesus, namely his impending departure from this life. Perhaps he was aware that curiosity would want to ask what they were talking about, which Mark and Matthew do not tell us. So Luke seeks to satisfy that curiosity and, in doing so, brings the focus back from the far future to Jesus' impending death. In Mark their presence is the important thing, not what they are saying or doing, because their presence symbolized that the climax of history is being reached when, according to some traditions, Moses and Elijah would appear.

To understand the scene, we need to see that it foreshadows what was expected at the climax of history. Already twice earlier in the chapter we have had reference to Elijah and one of the prophets (usually identified as Moses or like Moses), because there was a widespread expectation that they would return at the end of time. This partly went back to the story of Elijah not dying but being taken up into heaven in a chariot where he remained alive waiting to return. There was a similar belief about Moses ascending to heaven. Mark's description refers to Elijah with Moses, reflecting the normally greater emphasis on Elijah, but Luke, like Matthew, puts them in sequence: Moses and Elijah. Perhaps they are also suggesting fulfillment of the biblical hope, the Books of Moses and the Prophets, although that would be secondary at most.

At the end of time there would be resurrection, and one of the ways of understanding this was that people would come back to life with shiny, renewed bodies, sometimes with glistening clothes. The vision that the disciples see is of all three, with Jesus looking the way they believed he would appear at the end of time. Another of Luke's additions is to refer to glory (Luke 9:32), echoing Jesus' saying just a few verses earlier about Jesus' return in glory (Luke 9:26).

The scene reaches its climax when the cloud surrounds them and the disciples hear the voice of God, just like it was heard at Jesus' baptism (Luke 3:22), but this time telling them, as in Mark, that Jesus is God's chosen Son and he is to be listened to. And as in Mark, Peter proposes erecting tents to house them, a suggestion depicted as arising from his being in a state of consternation at what had happened. One might see him pioneering the initiatives of those who see church buildings as such a priority. Another of Luke's modifications was to depict the disciples as being very sleepy, perhaps suggestive of their sleepiness in Gethsemane. They are human.

Mark brings the scene to a close with Jesus telling them to keep quiet about it. Luke simply notes they said nothing about it. Instead of then going on to have Jesus say that they could in fact see John the Baptist as Elijah having come again, as in Mark (Mark 9:11–13), Luke leaves that out and goes straight to the encounter with the crowd. Perhaps he sensed that it could be confusing to speak of Elijah in this way.

Such symbolic narratives, like the baptism of Jesus with the descending dove, and the various stories of angelic interventions, belong to the storyteller's art and often feature in stories of great people back in those days. We need to read them not as reporting history but as coloring it so that we can recognize its deeper meaning. It is a little like visiting a gallery and seeing a painted scene that has so much more in it through the artist's hand than a mere photograph would have. Connection to God and connection to hope is what is being celebrated here.

Luke trims the encounter with the father concerned about his son, which follows in Mark (Mark 9:14–29), from sixteen verses to six, but keeps its central focus: Jesus' exorcism of a demon possessed boy. We would see the behaviors of the boy within the framework of our understanding of mental illness, or in this instance, epilepsy. Within Luke's worldview, liberation mean liberation from demons and ultimately that would mean liberation for all, a vision we might also espouse, though understand quite differently. Jesus is depicted as frustrated that his disciples failed to meet the need. Luke omits Mark's final comment to them that such exorcism works only through prayer.

Luke connects this episode more closely with what follows than Mark, who simply moves on. For Luke has Jesus address his disciples in the context of people being stunned by his exorcism. He has Jesus speak again to his disciples about his impending fate in that context of everyone admiring him and adds a striking introduction, as if to say, "Now, get this into your head!" (Luke 9:44). Luke then trims it simply to the prediction that as Son of Man he would be delivered up to men, summarizing his fate. The Greek original allows us to hear a play on the title Son of Man and those to whom Jesus is to be delivered up. I have tried to indicate that in the translation: "the Son of Man is going to be delivered over to [the sons of] men." Luke makes more of the disciples' failure to understand what he meant than Mark, emphasizing that they really had no idea.

Then Luke, again, trims Mark's account, which reports the disciples arriving in Capernaum and arguing among themselves about who was the greatest (Mark 9:33–37). Mark has Jesus confront them with the claim that anyone wanting to be first needs to be last, challenging their obsession with being great. His then putting a small child in front of them was enough to say: go back to before you felt you had to compete for worth with others and be like this child. Luke reverses Mark's order by first bringing the saying that equates welcoming such a child in his name with welcoming him, and welcoming him with welcoming God. Only then does he make the statement about true greatness, that one among them who is least would be greatest.

Luke continues with Mark, reporting more briefly on John's concern about someone else performing exorcisms in Jesus' name, which Jesus saw as no problem (Mark 9:38–41; Luke 9:49–50). At this point Luke departs from Mark and brings material he will have found elsewhere. He introduces it with the image of Jesus setting his focus on going to Jerusalem (Luke 9:51). It echoes his addition to the transfiguration story about Moses and Elijah talking with Jesus about his departure from this life (Luke 9:31). Luke reflects what we see also elsewhere in accounts of Jesus' life, that Jesus saw going to Jerusalem as bringing his mission to a head. Jerusalem was, after all, the seat of power, the location of Jewish authorities and the temple, which also had significance as being effectively the bank, and also as the city firmly in Roman imperial control.

Luke then pictures Jesus setting off through Samaritan territory and, as was the pattern with itinerants, expecting to be put up along the way, but facing rejection. James and John want to call down fire on the village that refused him, but Jesus tells them off for their attitude. He had instructed them to move on from unwelcoming villages and shake off the dust from their feet (Luke 9:5). This sits well beside the story just told from Mark about John's worry about the other exorcist. In that story Jesus tones down John's response and here Luke has Jesus tell off both brothers, John and James.

The disciples' call for vengeance on those who refused Jesus' hospitality should not be all too surprising. In their world vengeance was considered a legitimate aspect of the justice system. When they thought about God's justice, they apparently had no qualms about seeing God as being vengeful against sinners, indeed, not just writing them off, but inflicting them forever with excruciating pain with no relief. If God, as they understood God, is going to be like that, then such approaches to justice are warranted, and indeed some people have justified vengeance on the basis that God, in their view, clearly sanctions it.

Our thinking about the justice system has matured over the years. Hatred has no place in the justice system. We have also rejected the idea of capital punishment and have no tolerance for permanent infliction of pain. Justice means bringing people to face up to what they have done, to engage in restitution, and where punishment is imposed it is never to be a dead end but rather serves partly as a deterrent and also as something from which people can learn and be rehabilitated.

Imagining God as, in effect, turning from love to hate is a projection of human hate and stands in conflict with the notion of God as loving, confronting, and restoring. As often, we find such tensions within our tradition, which has made it difficult for love and compassion to survive. They could contemplate love as temporary and could project their hate onto God who would exercise it on their behalf. Our choice is between: in the end hate or in the end love. That is not about love as not caring and not confronting, but about love caring enough to confront and bring people to face the consequences of what they have done and then getting them back up onto their feet again. That is what a justice system does at its best, and often our theology still needs to catch up with these insights and understandings.

The final section of Luke 9 draws on the source Luke shares with Matthew (Matt 8:19–22; Luke 9:57–62). Its focus is on what should have priority. It is not about Jesus claiming priority for himself, as if needing to satisfy his ego, but ultimately about aligning oneself with God's priorities. The first exchange picks up in part the refusal of hospitality in the previous section. Jesus as Son of Man finds himself an outsider. Those with him need to be willing also to be outsiders.

The second exchange is very confronting, especially given the unwritten rules of family priorities, not least in dealing with the death of loved ones. In that sense, it is deliberately shocking and provocative. Family power was very strong. People needed to be willing to see that family power must not rule everything. The third encounter also addresses the issue of family power. Commitment to the vision of the kingdom of God and its priorities—which in effect means upholding oneness with God, with love, justice, and liberation—needs to matter most. You'll make a mess of ploughing if you don't keep your eyes on the job.

These are not anti-family statements. On the contrary, one could argue that putting God and God's love at the heart of our priorities is surely the best thing we can do for our families. Meaningful and fulfilling life, according to such teaching, is to share what were also Jesus' and God's priorities, namely, to embrace love and engage in love. It stands in contrast to what many then and now would think of as the more sensible option, namely, to focus on yourself and your interests and try to ensure others serve them. Frequently such narrowed self-obsession is a response to sensing that you have not had enough love and so have needed to compete for it with others and forever try to compensate for the missing love. Helping people open themselves to be loved can transform that and deal with the fear and anxiety that generates it, opening the way for true self love, which is at one with, rather than in conflict with, loving others.

Reflection: Human priorities and projections and divine priorities sometimes conflict. How can we resolve them?

Liberating Mission (Luke 10:1–24)

Listening to Luke

10:1 After this, the Lord appointed another seventy and sent them off ahead of him two by two to every town and place he was going to visit. **2** And he was telling them, "The harvest is great, but the workers are few. Pray to the Lord of the harvest to send workers for his harvest. **3** Go! And look, I'm sending you like lambs among wolves. **4** Don't take a moneybag, nor a backpack, nor sandals, and don't say hello to anyone on the road. **5** And whatever house you go into, first of all say, 'Peace be upon this house!' **6** And if a person of peace is there, let your peace rest upon them, but if not, it will return to you. **7** Stay in the house eating and drinking what they offer, for a worker deserves his wages. Don't go from house to house. **8** And if you go into a town and they welcome you, eat what they put in front of you. **9** And heal any sick folk in it and tell them, 'The kingdom of God has come to you.' **10** And whatever town you enter that doesn't welcome you, go out onto their streets and say, **11** 'We're wiping the dust off our feet at you, but be assured of this, that the kingdom of God has come near.' **12** And I'm telling you it will be more bearable for the people of Sodom on that day than it will for that town.

13 "Woe to you, Chorazin, woe to you Bethsaida! Because, had the miracles done among you been done in Tyre and Sidon, they would have repented with sackcloth and ashes. **14** So now it will be more bearable for Tyre and Sidon on judgment day than for you. **15** And you, Capernaum, don't elevate yourself up to heaven, because you'll be going down to Hades. **16** Anyone who listens to you is listening to me and anyone rejecting you is rejecting me; and anyone rejecting me is rejecting the one who sent me."

¹⁷ The seventy came back very happy, saying, "Lord, in your name even the demons submit to us." ¹⁸ He said, "I saw Satan falling from heaven like lightning. ¹⁹ I have given you authority to tread on snakes and scorpions, and on every enemy force, and nothing will hurt you. ²⁰ But don't be so happy about the fact that spirits submit to you, but rather be glad that your names have been written down in heaven."

²¹ At that moment he was filled with joy through the Holy Spirit and said, "I thank you, Father, Lord of heaven and earth, that you have hidden these things from the wise and learned and have revealed them to little children; yes, Father, because that's how you wanted it to be. ²² All has been granted me by my Father, and no one knows who the Son is but the Father and who the Father is except the Son and those to whom the Son decides to reveal him." ²³ Then turning just to his disciples, he said, "Happy the eyes that see what you are seeing! ²⁴ For I tell you, many prophets and kings longed to see what you are seeing and didn't see it, and to hear what you are hearing and didn't hear it."

Thinking About Luke

Luke had two accounts of Jesus sending out disciples, one in Mark and one in the source he shared with Matthew. Whereas Matthew merges the two together in his much-elaborated account of the sending out of the twelve apostles in Matt 10, Luke chose to bring both accounts separately. It is likely that he was responsible for portraying the second account as a sending out of seventy (some manuscripts say seventy-two). In Luke's world people would recognize the symbolism, for there was a widespread belief that there were seventy (or seventy-two) nations in the world. As often, Luke is being suggestive of the wider mission to follow.

The rules are stricter than in Mark, who allows them to wear sandals and have a staff. Matthew adjusts Mark's account to bring it into line with this stricter version. Sending them out two by two may well have been in Luke's source. It is what we see among apostles and missionaries in Acts and appears assumed as the pattern in Paul's writings. As in the sending out of the twelve in Luke 9, so here the assumption is that those sent will expect to be put up by locals. As we noted in discussing Luke 9, this was treated very strictly by some who therefore criticized Paul for sometimes working part time.

The addition to the instruction to expect hospitality is to eat and drink whatever they would be offered. That would be especially relevant in contexts where they might enter gentile homes. Food laws and concerns about potential impurities are to take second place to accepting hospitality and building relationships.

These instructions, like those of Luke 9, must have been guidelines from very early times, perhaps even going back to Jesus, if he really did employ some of his disciples to act on his behalf in this way. It certainly seems that they very early understood their agency as authorized by Jesus, whether the earthly or the risen Jesus. The word "apostle," which became a technical church term, simply meant "sent one" or "envoy" and reflected the notion that they were sent to act on Jesus' behalf. Envoys authorized to act on behalf of their sender were an essential part of communication in the ancient world. The sayings also reflect responses to rejection, sounding perhaps more like John the Baptist than Jesus in warning the unresponsive of judgment at the last day, which they assumed was near at hand.

In essence the commission is as in Luke 9, namely, to proclaim the coming reign of God, the kingdom of God. In Luke 10 this is related in particular to acts of liberation where they set people free from demons. Such liberation was a sign that the hope of God's reign was already being realized. As noted previously, theirs was a world quite foreign to us and imagining what actually might have happened is challenging. Were these people, presumably suffering from mental illness, really brought back to health through the work of Jesus and his disciples? Did they really trigger a change somehow through what they saw as exorcism? We are left wondering. Our point of connection is the notion of healing as belonging to what God wants us to help make possible, even if our framework for understanding the need is informed by a differently grounded analysis of human need.

Imagination will have played a role in their way of telling the story. There were popular stories of heroes untouched by snake bites and scorpion stings, and these likely fed the imagination in such accounts. Similarly, we can appreciate the imagery of seeing Satan fall from the sky in a flash of lightning. One of the ways of speaking of future hope was to envisage that one day Satan, understood as the personal power of evil, and his angels would be disempowered at the climax of history. This a mythological way of describing hope and so when Luke portrays Jesus as seeing Satan already falling, this was another way of saying that God's reign was already breaking in when people were being freed from what oppressed them. At its simplest, God's will is to see healing and restoration.

Appreciating what we affirm as central to God's will, namely love and liberation, is to embrace true wisdom, greater than all other learning. That is the point of Jesus' prayer of thanksgiving. It speaks of revelation, but that revelation is not about special secrets and complex analyses, but simply about love and knowing who God is.

Luke and Matthew cite a saying found in their common source, which has Jesus speak of himself as God's Son entrusted with this special relationship. God knows who Jesus is and Jesus knows who God is. The formulation is exclusive and could be read as denying that anyone else knows God or knows who God is, which would stand in contradiction to what is assumed in Jesus' teaching elsewhere. It is best taken in the context of future expectation, as the following verses suggest, and so refer to Jesus' distinctive role as God's agent in bringing about God's reign. Prophets longed to see such change, and the disciples are now seeing it and following Jesus as the one to lead it.

This first half of Luke 10 spells out who the disciples were to be. Over two millennia we can stand in continuity with them and him in also embracing the mission to bring change, also to be partners and agents in what God wants, even if ours is not a flat earth plagued by demons, but a broader sphere where freedom and liberation confront us in a more informed way but with equal urgency.

Reflection: Why was the notion of agency and envoys so significant in their society and in their understanding of what following Jesus entailed? What might it mean in our world and our understanding of mission?

Beyond Prejudices (Luke 10:25–42)

Listening to Luke

10:25 Now, one time, a specialist in the Law turned up to test Jesus out. He said, "Teacher, what do I have to do to inherit eternal life?" **26** Jesus responded: "What is written in the Law? How do you read it?" **27** He answered, "You shall love the Lord your God with all your mind and all your existence and with all your strength and with all your intelligence, and you shall love your neighbor as you love yourself." **28** Jesus said to him, "You're right. Do this and you'll have life." **29** But the Law specialist, wanting to justify himself, said to Jesus, "And who is my neighbor?"

30 Taking this up, Jesus replied, "There was once a fellow who was on his way down to Jericho from Jerusalem and he landed up with bandits who stripped him of his clothes, beat him up, and went off leaving him half dead. **31** Now by chance a priest was heading down that way and he saw him but went on down on the other side. **32** And similarly a Levite also came to that place and seeing him went on down on the other side. **33** Now a Samaritan came to the same place on his journey and, when he saw him, took pity on him. **34** He went over to him, dressed his wounds, applying oil and wine to them, and, lifting him up onto his own animal, took him to an inn and looked after him. **35** Then the next day he took out two denarii and gave them to the innkeeper and told him, 'Look after him and whatever more you spend, I'll fix you up for it when I come back.' **36** Which of these three men do you reckon was a neighbor to the man who got done over by the bandits?" **37** He said, "The one who took pity on him." Jesus told him, "Go and do the same!"

38 As they continued on their journey, he came into one of the villages, and a woman called Martha was there who welcomed him in. **39** She had a sister called Mary, who then took her place sitting at the feet of the Lord listening to his teaching. [40] Now Martha was distracted with attending to their needs, so she went up to Jesus and said, "Master, doesn't it bother you that my sister has left me all on my own to look after things? What about telling her to help me." [41] In response the Lord said to her, "Martha, Martha, you're fussing around about so many things. [42] There's only one thing that matters. For Mary has chosen the right option and she's not going to be deprived of it."

Thinking About Luke

These are two of the best-known stories in the New Testament. The parable has a sharp edge. Samaritans were Jews, descendants of the northern kingdom that resulted from the splitting of Israel into two regimes after the time of Solomon in the tenth century. The northern regime was then devastated and all but wiped out in the late eighth century by Assyrian invaders. Those who survived down to the time of Jesus lived in the area called Samaria, hence being labeled Samaritans. Samaritans have survived right through to present times.

They remained worshipers of the God of Israel and their Scriptures were the first five books of the Hebrew Scriptures. They differed from other Jews in believing that the center of their worship was not Mount Zion in Jerusalem, but Mount Gerizim in Samaria. Many among the other Jews looked down on them and treated them as not belonging and as having a status similar to foreigners.

It was therefore very confronting that Jesus told a parable that highlighted a Samaritan as exemplary. This is subversive on the part of Jesus, not least because he set the Samaritan in contrast to a serving priest and a Levite (support staff) of the Jerusalem temple. It fits Jesus' confrontations elsewhere of what he saw as abuses on the part of the temple establishment.

Luke introduces the parable with material he found later on in Mark where an interpreter of the Law asked Jesus which was the greatest commandment, to which Jesus gives the answer, to love God and one's neighbor (Mark 12:28–34). It fits well as an introduction to the parable because it illustrates the meaning of loving one's neighbor. Luke's creativity is also to be seen in the fact that he changes the question that the interpreter of the Law asks to the question that the rich man who approached Jesus asks, a story Luke found in Mark 10, and which he reuses in Luke 18:18–25: "Teacher, what do I have to do to inherit eternal life?" (Luke 10:25; 18:18; Mark 10:17). By doing this, Luke turns this passage into a major statement about the gospel. What is eternal life? What is salvation? What does it mean to share the life of God? In this way he highlights the heart of Jesus' teaching, which is also the heart of Jewish teaching. You love God and you love your neighbor. Some would see neighbor as meaning only those close to you and your group. Clearly this is not how Luke saw it, nor how Jesus saw it. It means your fellow human being.

It is fascinating that this is the very issue that the Law specialist then poses: "Who is my neighbor?" One might expect that the parable would go on to answer that question, but it doesn't. Instead, it ends with Jesus posing the question, "Which of these three men do you reckon was a neighbor to the man who got done over by the bandits?" (Luke 10:36). This refocuses the Law specialist's question, so that it can no longer be about being selective about whom you'll love. It is about whether you, yourself, are a loving person, a caring neighbor.

Excuses, excuses! If these temple personnel were on their way to the temple to take up their duties, then they may have feared the man was dead and that they would contract corpse impurity. That would mean they would have to wait for a period and undergo purification before starting their shift. But they were apparently on their way home, having finished their shift.

Other excuses? We can always find excuses not to care when we are faced with people in need. Mass media frequently confronts us with need, which almost has the effect of making us immune to compassion. The opposite is to be overwhelmed by it. Self-care means acknowledging our limitations and being prepared, genuinely, to do what we can without carrying the world on our shoulders or being crushed by guilt.

It is instructive to note the core meaning of this passage. Faith means full openness to God, loving God and being loved by God, and full openness to loving others. It is something ongoing, not a status gained by making a decision in the past, any more than a wedding makes a marriage.

The next also famous story reflects the pattern of Jesus and his itinerant group receiving hospitality by locals, in this instance, by Martha and Mary. It is highly likely that the issue it addresses would have happened from time to time. Traditionally, in their cultures, the woman of the house cared for the guests. That is what Peter's mother-in-law did after she recovered from her fever (Luke 4:39). It is also reflected in Luke's description in 8:1–4 of the role of the women. The issue must also have come up as the movement spread and church life took the form of congregations meeting in people's houses. Women were normally the managers of domestic affairs. Do they also have a place with the men at the seat of learning?

Mary sits with the men. Should she? At one level, that is the issue. Can women also belong in the same way as men, or should they just be part of the support infrastructure? The story has Jesus give an unambiguous answer: yes, they can! To sit and learn; that is the higher priority. Don't take that right away from them! A strong message for men as well as for women.

The other issue is the very practical one. Martha raises a valid question. The Greek is somewhat ambiguous in describing her activities. Was she overly fussing about? Jesus' comments to her suggest that she was getting too fussed, literally, "You are worrying and getting bothered about many things" (Luke 10:41). This suggests excess rather than that Jesus places no value on people providing hospitality. Elsewhere, Luke clearly values such care and clearly sees it as appropriate. It is a question of priorities, and these days we have learned to share roles and not to put any at a disadvantage when it comes to spiritual nourishment . . . or we are learning.

Such stories are designed to provoke reflection rather than establish rules. Where the two great commandments are more than rules and become attitudes and orientations, then love leaves no one on the side of the road or in the kitchen.

Reflection: Why did Jesus not answer the Law specialist's question about who a neighbor is but, instead, turn it around? How does the Mary and Martha story reflect issues of their day, and our day?

"May your kingdom come!" (Luke 11:1–26)

Listening to Luke

^{11:1} Once he was in a certain place praying and when he'd finished, one of his disciples said to him, "Lord, teach us to pray, like John taught his disciples." ² He said, "When you pray say,

'Father,

may your name be hallowed!

may your kingdom come!

³ Give us the sustenance we need for today;

⁴ and forgive our sins, for we ourselves forgive anyone sinning against us.

And don't lead us into testing times.'"

⁵ And he said to them, "Imagine you've got a friend and you go to him at midnight asking him, 'Hey mate, can you lend me three loaves of bread, please, ⁶ because a friend of mine has just turned up from a trip and I don't have anything to give him'? ⁷ And imagine that that friend would answer from inside, 'Don't be a nuisance! The door's locked and the kids with me have gone to bed, so I can't get up and give you anything'? ⁸ I'm telling you, even if being a friend doesn't lead him to get up and give him something, the sheer cheek of his asking will have him get up and give him whatever he needs.

⁹ "So, I tell you, ask, and what you ask for will be given to you; and look for it and you'll find it; knock and the door will be opened for you. ¹⁰ For everyone who asks will get what they want and whoever looks for something will find it and whoever knocks, the door will be opened. ¹¹ Which of you, if your son asks you for a fish, instead of a fish would give him a snake? ¹² or would ask you for an egg and you'd give him a scorpion? ¹³ If you who are evil know it's right to give good

things to your kids, how much more is your Father in heaven likely to give the Holy Spirit to those who ask him for it?"

¹⁴ And he was exorcising a demon from someone that stopped him being able to speak, and when it left him, the mute man spoke again, and the crowds were amazed. ¹⁵ Some of them said, "He's exorcising demons with the help of Beelzebul the chief of demons." ¹⁶ Others were wanting a sign from heaven from him to test him out.

¹⁷ Realizing what they were thinking, he told them, "Every kingdom which is divided against itself will end up a wasteland and a house divided against itself will similarly collapse. ¹⁸ So if Satan is in conflict with himself, how can his kingdom survive? I say this because you are saying that I am performing exorcisms with the help of Beelzebul. ¹⁹ If I perform exorcisms of demons with the help of Beelzebul, whose help are your people getting when they perform exorcisms? That's why they will be your judges. ²⁰ But if I by the finger of God perform exorcism of demons, then the kingdom of God has landed among you. ²¹ When a well-armed strong man guards his foyer, his property will be safe. ²² If a stronger man comes and overpowers him, he'll take away his armor which he depends on and divide up his loot. ²³ Whoever is not with me is against me, and whoever doesn't join me in getting things together, scatters them. ²⁴ When an unclean spirit leaves a person and wanders across parched land looking for a resting place and doesn't find one, it says, 'I'll go back to the house I left.' ²⁵ And coming back, it finds it swept and tidied up. ²⁶ Then it comes and brings seven other spirits along with it, more wicked than itself, and goes in and takes up residence again, and the last state of that person is worse that it was before."

Thinking About Luke

Luke often adds into his sources a reference to Jesus praying and so may well have done so also here (Luke 11:1). It is fascinating that he has the comment about John the Baptist teaching his disciples to pray, because we have no actual record of it elsewhere, but it is certainly something we may assume. Given John's focus, too, on hope for God's action, we might imagine that an element in what he would have taught would have included the prayer that finally God's kingdom might come.

For the prayer, which we traditionally label "the Lord's Prayer," Luke is drawing on the same source as Matthew, except that, as we have seen elsewhere, Matthew is using a version of that common source that had received further elaboration than the version we find in Luke. We know and use Matthew's more elaborate version, which sounds more like something rendered suitable for use in corporate worship. Luke's is simpler.

Not "Our Father in heaven" but just "Father." Probably the original was simply "Abba," a term so characteristic of Jesus and the movement that we sometimes find it used untranslated, as in Gal 4:6 and Rom 8:15. In family contexts it could mean something like "daddy" or "dad," but in the context of prayer this simple form is best translated "Father," but with a sense of intimacy and closeness such as one would find in close family relations between children, including grown up children and their parents. This is another reflection of the understanding of God that keeps coming through in Jesus' teachings, namely that God is loving, compassionate, and approachable. "Father" often did not convey kindness but the opposite: harsh discipline and even brutality. That's not how Jesus sees it. These days we would want to be more inclusive and use both female and male parenting images.

When people spoke of a person's "name," it was another way of speaking of them as a person. So it is not about giving special honor to whatever name we might give to God. It is hallowing God. That means treating God as holy, acknowledging who God is. There is a sense in which relationships work best when we let the other be who they are for us and honor and accept that, instead of seeing them in ways limited to our personal interests. Let God be God for me and let me be in awe and openness to God and God's being.

This is not to picture God as remote and primarily looking for adoration, as in various ways we can see those in power wanting the world to center around them. That is not what it means to speak of God as loving and engaged, and the next part of the prayer makes very clear that God is the one to whom we look in hope. That hope is for God and God's will, God's way of love, to rule. "May your kingdom come!" Praying and hoping for the change that this will bring, expressed as the kingdom or reign of God, is a standard element in Jesus' teaching and at the center of his mission. It is hope for future change but also engagement in enabling and participating in that change already in the present, as the passage will later go on to emphasize. It means liberation already now.

Matthew's version expands on that idea to speak of God's will and purpose. The simpler and probably more original form goes on simply to identify basic human need for daily sustenance. We could read it in a literal kind of way as though God is being reminded and persuaded to intervene to feed us, but that is surely not the meaning. The prayer is a simple cry for existence and survival, a wish, which we need to hear and to which we also need to respond and become part of the prayer's answer.

Forgiveness of sins belongs not only to our facing up to ourselves before God—it is okay to acknowledge our limitations, our failures, and our guilt—but also to our having healthy relations with others. We don't need to pretend, sweep things under the carpet, engage in denial of our own reality or that of others. Love creates space for openness and in such openness there can be appropriation of forgiveness, therefore also forgiveness of ourselves. This is not about ticking off guilt, but engaging in ongoing transformation in ourselves and in our relationships. To forgive is to give up holding something against someone.

The final part of this brief version of the Lord's Prayer in Luke, like the basic human cry for sustenance, is the simple human cry not to have to face hard times. It is not about temptations, though there is a sense in which hard times can bring with it a temptation to give up. Again, it is not as though God sets up a program for people that includes a dose of suffering now and again. That is not what this is about. It brings to expression the fundamental hope not to have to face situations where we might be tempted to give up. That is a very natural, healthy human response, even if sometimes facing up to rough times is what we need to do, the path of Jesus himself being a good example.

The illustration that Jesus then brings about a friend is typical of his pointing to everyday life experience in order to teach people what God is like. If a friend can be persuaded to help even after being initially reluctant, can't you believe God will help? The sayings that then follow about asking and receiving can sometimes be read as a guarantee that I will get what I want for myself, which might be anything from wealth to health. It then comes as a surprise when we hear what will be given: the Holy Spirit. "How much more is your Father in heaven likely to give the Holy Spirit to those who ask him for it" (Luke 11:13).

The prayer requests are in the context of the work to be done. That becomes clear also in what immediately follows where attention turns to an exorcism. Their science told them that sickness and disability were regularly caused by demons, so that healing requires exorcism and you can perform exorcisms using the power of the Spirit. Within their world of thought we can understand the allegation that Jesus might have been allying with Beelzebul, the chief demon, and getting his cooperation to expel demons from people. Remaining within their world of thought we can then understand Jesus' counterargument that this would not make sense. Beelzebul would hardly cooperate against one of his own. Luke's hearers know that Jesus acts not in cooperation with the chief of demons but with the Holy Spirit, with God.

When Jesus declares that he performs exorcisms by the finger of God, he is making the claim that the great hope for liberation, the coming of God's reign, the kingdom of God, is at that point already breaking into reality. Matthew's variant of the same saying has Jesus say, not "If I by the finger of God" but "If I by the Spirit of God." The meaning is the same. It is in partnership with God that Jesus already in the present brings change and hope.

The added observation that demons can return even in greater numbers and create greater chaos in all probability has as its message: make sure you replace such expelled spirits with the Spirit of God.

The science of sickness and disability based on belief in demons is not ours. We understand illness and disability very differently. The distance between them and us, which we often meet in reading the Gospels, is significant and not to be explained away, but also not to be seen as a reason to give up faith altogether. It belongs in the same category as our different beliefs about creation and the world. It is not, as they thought, just six thousand years old and nor is the earth flat.

Acknowledging such distance does not prevent us from acknowledging the proximity to them that we can also find. That includes the faith and confidence that God calls us into partnership in bringing hope and healing in our world. Liberation is the agenda. Love is the way. When we, too, pray, "May your kingdom come," we share their vision, even though we do not share their science.

Reflection: What did it mean for them to pray, "May your kingdom come!" and what might it mean for us?

Confrontations (Luke 11:27–54)

Listening to Luke

11:27 While he was saying all this, a woman raised her voice from among the crowd and said to him, "Blessed is the womb that bore you and the breasts that nourished you!" **28** He responded, "Yes, but blessed more are those who hear the word of God and keep it."

29 As the crowds were starting to become larger, he began saying, "This generation is a bad lot; it wants a sign but it's not getting any sign except the sign of Jonah. **30** For as Jonah was a sign for the Ninevites, so will the Son of Man be for this generation. **31** The queen of the south will rise up on judgment day along with the men of this generation and she will condemn them, because she came from the ends of the earth to listen to Solomon's wisdom, and look, there's something much better than Solomon here. **32** And the men of Nineveh will rise up on the day of judgment along with this generation and condemn it, because they repented in response to Jonah's preaching, and look, something better than Jonah is here.

33 "No one lights a lamp and puts it in a crypt [or under a bed] but on the lampstand so that everyone coming in can see the light. **34** The lamp of the body is your eye. When your eye is in good order, your whole body has light; but if it's not in good order, then your body, too, will be in darkness. **35** Make sure the light in you isn't darkness. **36** If your body is fully in the light, not having any part of it in darkness, it will be fully in the light as when a lamp's shining gives you light."

37 While he was talking a Pharisee asked him to come and have a meal with him, so he went and took his place at the meal table. **38** The Pharisee, watching him, was surprised that he didn't first wash before the meal. **39** The Lord said to him, "Now you Pharisees purify the outside of the cup and the plate, but inside you're just brim full of greed and wickedness. ⁴⁰ You fools, didn't the one who made the outside also make the inside? ⁴¹ Turn your inside into generosity and then you'll find everything about you will be pure. ⁴² But woe to you Pharisees, because you tithe mint and rue and all kinds of herbs while at the same time neglecting justice and the love of God; these are what you need to be doing, without of course neglecting those other matters. ⁴³ Woe to you Pharisees, because you love to have the front seats in the synagogues and to be greeted in the marketplaces. ⁴⁴ Woe to you, because you are like unmarked graves which people simply walk over without noticing."

⁴⁵ In response one of the Law specialists said to him, "Teacher, by saying this you're insulting us." ⁴⁶ He replied, "And woe to you Law specialists, too, because you load people up with heavy burdens but you yourselves don't lift a finger to help them with their burdens. ⁴⁷ And woe to you because you erect tombstones to honor the prophets, yet it was your forebears who killed them. ⁴⁸ You bear witness to and hail your forebears' deeds, even though they killed the very ones for whom you now erect tombstones. ⁴⁹ That's why the wisdom of God said, 'I'll send them prophets and apostles, and some of them they'll kill and persecute, ⁵⁰ so that the blood of all the prophets shed since the world began will be laid at the feet of this generation, ⁵¹ from the blood of Abel to the blood of Zechariah killed between the incense altar and the sanctuary; it will all be laid at the feet of this generation.' ⁵² Woe to you Law specialists because you have taken away the key to knowledge but have yourselves not used it to open the door to knowledge for yourselves and have also prevented others from entering." ⁵³ When he went outside, the scribes and Pharisees started to attack him for what he said and to contradict much of what he said, ⁵⁴ and were on the alert to catch him out for saying such things.

Thinking About Luke

In the second half of Luke 11, Luke draws upon traditions that depict Jesus confronting the people of his time. Mostly they are drawn from the source he shares with Matthew. They begin with an exchange with a woman who says as much as, "Your mom must be very proud to have produced a boy like you." There is nothing incorrect in her observation, but seeing people within the limited framework of proud and blessed parents can mean we miss the main point. Admiring and congratulating Jesus' parents or even Jesus himself, which many people do, is not nearly as important as taking seriously what he says, and in particular what he tells us is God's will for us to follow.

The material that follows is very confrontational and framed within the perspective of judgment day, as a day when people will have to face up to who they are and what they have done. In a world of thought where Luke's listeners, familiar with biblical stories, will know of Jonah and the people of Nineveh and of Solomon and the queen of Sheba, the queen of the south, the confrontation is telling.

These accounts of confrontation may have originated when Jesus faced rejection or may have developed in situations of rejection faced in the early decades of the church. We see signs of the latter, especially in Matthew when what we read in Matt 23 appears to reflect tensions that developed in the late first century as Judaism revived after the catastrophe of the destruction of the temple in 70 CE. It is also reflected in Luke in the saying about wisdom sending "apostles" (Luke 11:49).

Before continuing with instances of confrontation Luke slips in the image of the healthy or unhealthy eye. He starts with what he found in Mark's parable chapter about why it would be nonsense to light a lamp and then not let it shine (Mark 4:21). Luke abbreviated it, but some manuscripts insert what Luke omitted. I have included it in square brackets. He then connects that saying to others about sight and light which he found in the source he shared with Matthew (Luke 11:34–36; Matt 6:22–23). The assumption is that health of the eye affects the whole body and the message is clear: let there be light! Light here is very much about God's light and love. That is what was missing in the kind of religious behavior that Jesus was confronting.

There follows then, a series of criticisms made against the failures of many Pharisees. Matthew brings them together in Matt 23, adding to each the charge of hypocrisy. Ritual purification of your hands before eating was not a biblical law, but one that cohered nevertheless with biblical concerns about what was ritually clean or unclean. Luke had omitted the large block of material across Mark 6–8, which includes the story of the controversy that arose when Jesus' disciples were criticized for not purifying their hands by washing them before eating (Mark 7:1–23), but the issue reappears here.

We rightly see washing our hands before eating as making good sense on grounds of hygiene, but the focus here is not hygiene. We could have had a conversation with Jesus and his disciples about the fact that there are good reasons from the point of view of good health.

The confrontation is not about hygiene but about the hypocrisy of being so focused on external ritual purity issues while at the same time neglecting the weightier issues of purity within, by which Jesus meant: love and justice and generosity in contrast to the greed and exploitative attitudes that he was confronting in them. The saying about tithing reflects these same priorities. It is about getting the priorities right. You take tithing seriously, but you give much more emphasis to love, justice, and generosity.

Like Matthew, Luke brings a saying in Luke 16:17 that has Jesus declare that he in no way came to set biblical laws, even about tithing, aside (Matt 5:17–18). Not a stroke of the Law is to be set aside, but within the Law, seeing where the priorities lie was essential. A fundamentalism that blindly sees all laws as infallible and fails to see that some need at times to override others can lead to abandoning what Scripture is basically about, namely love and compassion.

The confrontations that follow highlight how among would-be religious people things can often go wrong. That includes when the focus turns to being first and being admired, reflecting a sad failure to take love on board, for love would meet the deep inner need for acceptance and free people from making the pursuit of admiration their manipulative life agenda. Yes, they will be seen, but not as bearers of light and love, but like unmarked graves that people simply walk past without noticing them.

The confrontation with Law specialists again exposes a failure to see that the purpose of biblical Law is not to be an imposition, a burden, but to enable people to live in oneness with God. A perspective of compassion would of course mean that such teachers would offer help where people found such life difficult rather than being demanding overseers.

The challenge about honoring prophets with decorated tombstones but in fact having more in common with those who opposed them is strong. Luke cites a saying of Wisdom which Matthew converts to be a saying of Jesus, himself (Matt 23:34). It is likely to have emerged from after the time of Jesus, since it refers to apostles having been sent, unless Luke means us to see an allusion to those already sent in the previous two chapters.

It may seem unusual to have a reference to Wisdom speaking like a person, but this reflects an interesting development that reaches back to the book of Proverbs. It portrays God's Wisdom as like God's companion and as a woman calling out to men on the street. This is in part the creative invention of a teacher who is warning men about prostitutes soliciting clients on the streets of a city. They should listen instead to Wisdom's calls.

Proverbs speaks of God's Wisdom as like a person beside God (Prov 8:1–31). Wisdom came to be seen as God's agent in creation, in making God's will known through the Law, and in sending prophets, as here. God's Wisdom could also be called God's Word. Eventually, people came to portray Jesus as the embodiment of God's Wisdom, God's Word, such as we see in the Gospel of John, which hails Jesus as the Word, a powerful way of presenting his significance (John 1:1–18).

Blaming all such rejection of God's agents on one generation seems overly harsh and unfair, if we are to take it literally. Conflict and hurt in the early years of the Jesus movement did sometimes result in excessive claims and this may be what we see here.

Confronting teachers of the biblical Law with blocking rather than opening out biblical truth and wisdom is something relevant to every generation and the Christian movement has certainly had its history of being bad news like this. The sharp confrontations in this passage expose what has been just as possible within Christian history and so remain challenges to faith in every age. It is also important not to generalize from them in such a way as to attribute such abuses to all Pharisees and all Law specialists in Jesus' time and the time of the early church because we know of many who were not like that. Generalizing the comments foments anti-Semitism, which is the opposite of what Jesus' teaching clearly intended.

Reflection: What was behind the contrast between Jesus and the stance of these Pharisees and Law specialists whom Jesus confronts?

A Call to Trust (Luke 12:1–34)

Listening to Luke

12:1 When a crowd of such huge numbers was drawn to him that people were trampling on one another, Jesus started first of all speaking to his disciples, saying, "Beware of the leaven which is the hypocrisy of the Pharisees. **2** Nothing will stay covered up which will not be uncovered or hidden which will not become known. **3** What you said in the dark will be heard when the light comes and what you whispered in enclosed spaces will be announced from the roof tops.

4 "I'm telling you, my friends, don't be scared of those who might kill your body and after that have nothing more they can do. **5** I'll show you whom you need to fear. Fear the one who, after you die, has the right to throw you into hell. Yes, I'm telling you, fear him.

6 "Can't you buy five sparrows for just a couple of copper coins? Yet not one of them is lost sight of before God. **7** Even more, the hairs of your head are all counted. So don't be anxious. You're worth more than a few sparrows.

8 "I tell you, whoever acknowledges me before men, the Son of Man will acknowledge before the angels of God. **9** And whoever disowns me before men will be disowned before the angels of God. **10** Anyone who speaks a word against the Son of Man will be forgiven, but anyone repudiating the Holy Spirit will not be forgiven. **11** When they haul you up before their synagogue gatherings and their leaders and authorities, don't worry about how you should respond or what you should say, **12** because the Holy Spirit will teach you at the time what you need to say."

13 Someone in the crowd said to him, "Teacher, tell my brother to share the family inheritance with me." **14** He responded, "Look, mate, who made me judge or arbitrator for you?" **15** Then he said to them,

"Watch out and protect yourself against all greediness, because a person's life doesn't find fulfillment by accumulating lots of possessions."

¹⁶ He went on to tell them a parable. "There was this rich fellow who had lots of land. ¹⁷ And he was wondering, 'What should I do, because I don't have a place to store my harvest?' ¹⁸ And he decided, 'This is what I'll do. I'll pull down my barns and build bigger ones so I can store my crops and possessions in them. ¹⁹ And I'll say to myself, see, you've got lots of possessions stored up there for many years to come. Relax! Eat, drink, and be merry!' ²⁰ But God said to him, 'You're a fool, because this very night they'll take your life away. Who's, then, going to get what you stored up?' ²¹ That's the way it is for people who store up assets for themselves but have no credit with God."

²² And he said to his disciples, "This is what I'm telling you. Don't worry about your lives, what you're going to eat nor about what you're going to wear. ²³ Life's more than food and clothing. ²⁴ Look at the ravens. They don't sow or harvest, and don't have barns or storehouses, but God feeds them. Aren't you worth much more than the birds? ²⁵ Can any of you add extra to your life by worrying about it? ²⁶ If you can't do such a little thing, why worry about the rest? ²⁷ Look at how lilies grow; they don't work hard at it nor engage in weaving. Yet I tell you, not even Solomon arrayed in all his glory was a patch on one of them. ²⁸ If in this way God clothes the grass in the field, which is there today and tomorrow gets thrown into the furnace, surely, he'll all the more look after you, you who have such limited faith.

²⁹ "So don't focus your attention on what you should eat or what you should drink and don't get all het up. ³⁰ Foreign nations of this world obsess about all these things, but I'm telling you, your Father knows you need them. ³¹ Rather make his kingdom the focus of your concerns and all these things will come your way. ³² Don't be worriers, little flock, because it's your Father's pleasure to give you his kingdom. ³³ Sell up your possessions and give help to those in need. Make the kind of moneybags for yourselves that won't wear out, namely lasting treasure in heaven, where no robbers will come nor moths to eat holes in your bags. ³⁴ For your mind will be where your treasure is."

Thinking About Luke

Chapter 11 had concluded with warnings about hypocrisy. This chapter picks up that theme to begin with as Jesus turns his attention to the disciples. It broadens the focus by stating that one day the truth will come out, the truth about everything. The imagery of secrets in the dark being brought to light and private conversations being made public is a way of encouraging openness and honesty. Authenticity matters. Focusing on the traditional expectation of the day of judgment is one way of reinforcing that message.

The shift from such warnings to talking about sparrows and strands of human hair seems sudden. The implication is that things go wrong when people embrace fear. For fear people lie or create false impressions or become busy making themselves out to be what they are not, such as in hypocrisy. Luke has Jesus meet such fear with the assurance that God cares. If God cares about sparrows and even the hairs of a person's head, then surely, we can trust God and believe God. That then means believing God cares about us. As we take that on board, we learn to give up the manipulations of trying to persuade others and ourselves that we are of worth.

Trust, trusting love, sets people free to see things in perspective, from God's perspective, from eternity's perspective. Luke then has Jesus apply this even to situations of potential danger, including where loyalty to Jesus and his message might expose us to rejection and sometimes suffering. There is a play between "Son of Man" and "men," as I have translated Luke 12:8, which is lost if we use an otherwise more acceptable inclusive word.

Again, the focus moves to judgment day and the consequences of acknowledgment or denial. Ultimately, Luke has Jesus declare that it is not primarily about him as Son of Man, but about God. To repudiate or deny that Jesus' mission is an expression of God's way, expressed as the work of God's Spirit, is to reject God.

The theme of trust rather than fear returns when Luke has Jesus address the fear that many Jews who embraced Jesus' message will have faced, namely of being disciplined by their local Jewish community for embracing Jesus and his teaching. This will have been the experience of many, especially as the church grew. Paul is an early example of such persecution, both as its agent and then as its victim. The call to trust rather than fear seeks to encourage people not to be overanxious but simply to be present in openness to the Spirit and feel free to speak the truth.

The idea in that sense that the Spirit would help people charged with offenses gave rise to the notion of the Spirit as an advocate, an image used in John's Gospel (John 14:16). This then enables the author to present his version of the story of Jesus as inspired by the Spirit, making the case for Jesus.

The shift from such anxiety to anxiety about possessions follows as someone in the crowd seeks Jesus' help over a dispute about an inheritance, which Jesus refuses. Luke does, however, use it to bring further teaching about everyday anxiety. Some of the sayings that follow about food and clothing will doubtless go back to instructions given by Jesus to his disciples when he sent them out to go from village to village in Galilee. The guidelines, which Luke has brought in Luke 9 and 10, suggest that they take nothing with them, but expect hospitality to be given to them by sympathizers. It became a pattern for envoys of ministry and persisted into the early decades of the church. Some insisted it should be a rule. Others, like Paul, suggested new situations might require different strategies, such as when he defended his decisions at times to work part time (1 Cor 9).

What worked well in the relatively confined area of Galilee would not work well in the wider world, but the underlying message remained and remains pertinent. Even if we do need to buy clothes and purchase food, there is a big difference between making our immediate needs the primary focus of our attention and looking at life from a broader perspective. We know many modern variants of this, including the appeal through advertising that we should engage in short-term gratification. Worse still is greed for possessions, which ultimately means depriving others of what they need.

We are not in Galilee, in walking distance from all our destinations. Nor were Paul and the early church. Good self-care and care for others must entail planning for daily necessities, which do not automatically come our way even when we have abundance around us and certainly do not come the way of the impoverished. Good news for the poor is about all need, including saving people from starvation. The vision of the kingdom is radically inclusive. To make it central is to trust and to commit. A narrowed focus on immediate needs and on an agenda based on achieving contentment by accumulation is a different path, not the path Jesus advocates.

Luke preserves Jesus' sayings which we know also from Matthew's Sermon on the Mount, where Matthew has made them part of the wider collection of sayings that he has brought together there (Matt 6:25–33). They remained pertinent for their times and they remain so for ours. We see that their origin was in a Jewish setting when we hear Jesus refer to the values alleged of "foreign nations of this world" (Luke 12:30). It is a generalization about gentile nations, which like all generalizations will be both true and untrue. Jesus' message was a challenge to all whose values derive from the power of fear and from the greed of accumulation at others' expense.

Moths and thieves bring our passage to a conclusion. What is real treasure? It is possible to convert one form of greed into another and so portray the gospel as just another way of satisfying greed. Follow Jesus so that you will get a heavenly reward! Any concern for others would then be a seeking to qualify for the reward and not genuine love. To be on the receiving end of someone's help who is helping you for their sake and reward not for your sake is to be used, and, in a sense, abused.

The invitation to be partners with God and to follow Jesus is clearly not, according to Luke, just another form of acting solely in one's own interest for reward. It is, nevertheless, still to act in one's interests. In Luke and in all the Gospels Jesus is portrayed as appealing to what is in people's interests and that includes suggesting that his is the way to find life rewarding. The invitation is to embrace love for and from God, love for others and love for self, and in this way to find life and fulfillment. Jesus' call is to open oneself to the love perspective, because that is to share God's life, whose being is love and generosity. Moths won't eat holes in it and no one will take it away from you.

Reflection: In what ways does Luke have Jesus deal with anxiety? How much was it related to specific contexts, and how much is it applicable more broadly?

Readiness (12:35–59)

Listening to Luke

13:35 "Do up your belt and be ready with your lamps lit, **36** like people waiting for their master to come back home from the wedding celebration, so that when he comes and knocks at the door, they'll be ready to open up. **37** Happy times for those slaves whom the master comes and finds ready and watching out for him! I'm telling you, he'll do up his belt and sit them down and come and serve them. **38** So if he turns up at the second or third watch of the night and finds them like that, it'll be great for them. **39** And be aware of this, that if a householder knew what time a thief would be coming, he wouldn't have let his house be burgled. **40** So make sure you're ready, because the Son of Man is going to come at a time you won't be expecting him."

41 Peter then asked him, "Lord, were you directing this parable to us or to everyone?"

42 The Lord replied, "Who's going to be the reliable and sensible manager that the master will put in charge of his household to make sure they get meals in a timely way? **43** Good on that slave when the master returns and finds him doing just that. **44** I'm telling you for sure, he'll put him in charge of his possessions. **45** But if that slave starts thinking, the master is not coming just yet, and starts to abuse his male and female slaves, and to eat and drink and get drunk, **46** then when that slave's master returns on a day he wasn't expecting him or at a time he wasn't thinking about it, then he'll slice him in two and put him with the unbelievers. **47** That slave who knew very well his master's wishes but neither got ready for him nor did his bidding will be subject to quite a beating. **48** And the slave who didn't know but still did what deserved a beating will get beaten a bit less. All given a lot to do will have a lot expected of them, and all those entrusted with a great deal, all the more will be expected of them.

⁴⁹ "I came to bring fire to the earth and I wish it was already flaring up. ⁵⁰ I've got a baptism that I'm to undergo, and I can't wait for it to happen. ⁵¹ Do you imagine I came to bring peace to the world? No, I'm telling you, but rather division. ⁵² From now on five people in one household are going to be divided, three against two and two against three. ⁵³ A father will be in conflict with his son and son with his father, a mother with her daughter and a daughter with her mother, a mother-in-law with her daughter-in-law and a daughter-in-law with her mother-in-law."

⁵⁴ And he started also to say to the crowds, "When you see a cloud coming up from the west, straightaway you say there's going to be a shower and that turns out to be so. ⁵⁵ And when a southerly blows, you say, it's going to get warm and so it does. ⁵⁶ Hypocrites, you know how to read what's going on from the earth and sky, but how come you don't read the signs of what's going on in the present time?

⁵⁷ "Why don't you make your own assessment of what is just? ⁵⁸ When you head off with your opponent to the magistrate, make an effort to sort it out with him on the way, so he doesn't drag you up before the judge and the magistrate hand you over to the officer and the officer throw you into jail. ⁵⁹ I'm telling you, you won't get out of there until you've paid the very last cent."

Thinking About Luke

In a relaxed state you would not put a belt round your flowing tunic, but if you are about to do things and become active, you would normally put on your belt or sash or do it up to keep your loose garment from getting in the road. The reference to lamps implies nighttime. So we have a scene painted that will reflect what might have been imagined back in those days. Rich people had slaves and houses that they could secure with a locked gate. Jesus often used imagery reflecting scenes from everyday life. It is important not to overinterpret them as though every master is an image of God or Jesus, because quite often he is referring to a corrupt or manipulating master. This master has been to a wedding celebration somewhere that has gone on into the night, as they often did, and then he comes home. That could be any time. Slaves need to be ready to open up for him.

The main point here is to be ready, but there are playful allusions that suggest a little more. Was this master half-drunk that he comes home and starts serving his slaves? Perhaps so, but it might also hint at Jesus' acts of kindness such as when John's Gospel reports his washing his disciples' feet. Weddings were also often used as symbols of hope and salvation. We can imagine that as this saying was repeated in the early days of the church, people would apply it especially to the expectation of Jesus' return, hence the reference here to being ready for the return of the Son of Man (Luke 12:40). The previous verse reinforces the message with its image of the burglar. Here, too, we are not to imagine Jesus is a burglar!

The call to disciples to be ready comes to us already in Mark 13:33–37, which uses the imagery of slaves needing to be ready because their master could return at any time. Mark's Gethsemane scene also emphasizes the need to stay alert. Matthew expands Mark's theme with the image of the ten young women needing to keep their lamps alight for when their master would return home with his bride (Matt 25:1–12). When Luke has Peter ask about the parable, he may well want those hearing his account to think of Peter's leadership and of leadership in early Christian communities and their responsibilities.

At one level, such warnings might be reduced to an appeal to fear: watch out that you're not caught napping! Matthew, in particular, appears to be dealing with members of his community who are quite happy to call Jesus Lord but who have lost connection with what Jesus was about. It is like people reducing faith to having been "saved," securing access to heaven, and then not really caring about being good news. Matthew has Jesus call such people goats in his parable of the last judgment (Matt 25:31–46) and at the end of the Sermon on the Mount had already confronted such empty discipleship of those who called Jesus Lord (Matt 7:21–23). It is like someone thinking they have a fine marriage because they once had a fine wedding.

Watching and being ready is, at best, not about fear as a motivation, but about making sure you're staying connected with the vision and agenda of Jesus. Like working at a marriage, it is about keeping your relationship of love with God, with others, and, indeed, even with yourself alive and growing. Then the timing does not really matter because it's the relationship that counts. That's a healthier motivation than having the fear of missing out driving you to be good, just in case.

As Luke moves on in 12:41–48, we are back in the world of slavery. It is a world of abuse and oppression, abuse by some slaves of others, and, effectively, also abuse by the master. It is not difficult to imagine that some would have taken the master to be an image of God or Jesus and used such imagery as a channel for their hate towards those who refuse the gospel. Hate has no place in our justice system, much as journalism sometimes courts victims to express it after trials because it gives them the reporting that many will love. At most, these are images that emphasize accountability and reinforce the need to remain alert to living in love and resisting abuse.

In 12:49–53 Luke brings words of Jesus that are deliberately shocking. Peace was a favorite idea of the time and Rome hailed its achievements in bringing peace by suppressing danger and also dissent. To live by a vision of good news for the poor was, on the other hand, to expose oneself to confrontation and death. Like fire, water, too, could be an image of disaster and suffering and also of judgment. John the Baptist's baptism was in that sense an undergoing of judgment in advance. People feared floods and drowning and so Jesus could speak of the ordeal he was to face as a baptism, being immersed in rejection and suffering.

To embrace the vision of good news for the poor was not to sweep things under the carpet or to be nice. It was to bring radical love to need and tread on the toes of those whose vested interests included keeping some people down while they themselves prospered. Jesus was not a chaplain to the status quo, but a subversive who put love at the center, and that would and still does challenge prevailing values.

The words about division in families will doubtless have had direct relevance for many in Luke's community, especially fellow Jews, and those memories will have been painful. Family loyalty and family power loomed very large in those times and has its equivalents today. Love calls out such power and seeks to dethrone such gods, including family gods. Love can therefore generate conflict and division, but, unlike in many movements, it does not then turn to hate, let alone violence against those who dissent. It calls people like Zacchaeus down from the tree.

The local weather forecast, if they had one, would indeed see rain mostly coming from the west and the southerlies bringing warm air up from Africa. Luke's Jesus leaves it wide open what signs people are meant to be seeing. Probably it is less about impressive cosmic signs and more about signs of what was wrong in the society of the time, why for many there was no good news and why things needed to change.

Our passage ends with some simple advice about pursuing reconciliation rather than being contentious. In that sense, take justice into your own hands, make your own assessment of what is just. A commitment to the vision of the kingdom should give you the insight to see what really matters and deal with injustice. That applies also to this advice about dealing with conflict. Matthew chooses to bring it when he has Jesus speak about managing anger in the Sermon on the Mount (Matt 5:25–26). It sounds like practical advice to avoid imprisonment, but it is also about seeking connection and working at relationships even where there is conflict.

Reflection: Jesus' images from everyday life reflect the world of slavery and abuse. This means they have limitations, but what is their point and how might it be interpreted and misinterpreted?

Warnings and Allusions to What Was to Come (Luke 13:1–35)

Listening to Luke

13:1 At that time some people came with the news about the Galileans whose blood Pilate had mixed with their sacrifices. **2** In response Jesus told them, "Do you think these Galileans were any worse than all other Galileans that they suffered such a fate? **3** Not at all, I'm telling you, but unless you all turn to God you'll all similarly perish. **4** Or what about the eighteen people the tower fell on and killed in Siloam? Do you reckon they were more deserving of such a fate than all the rest of Jerusalem's inhabitants? **5** Not at all, I'm telling you, but unless you turn to God you'll all similarly perish."

6 And he told them this parable: "There was this guy who had a fig tree and planted it in his vineyard, and he came looking for fruit on it and found none. **7** So he said to his vineyard worker, 'Look, for three years I've come looking for fruit on this fig tree and haven't found a thing. Chop it down. Why have it waste the space?' **8** But in response the worker said, 'Master, let it be for this coming year, until I've dug around it and given it some manure, **9** and if it produces fruit, all's good; but then if it doesn't, you can cut it down.'"

10 He was teaching in one of their synagogues on the Sabbath **11** and a woman turned up who had had a disability demon for eighteen years, and she was bent over and hadn't ever been able to straighten herself up. **12** When Jesus saw her, he called her to come near and said to her, "Woman, you're free of your disability," **13** and he laid hands on her and immediately she was able to straighten up and started praising God. **14** The chief leader of the synagogue in response was annoyed that Jesus healed her on the Sabbath, and told the crowd, "There are six days for doing work and that's when you can come and get healed, but not on the Sabbath." **15** The Lord responded to him by saying, "You're hypocrites, you'd all untie your cow on the Sabbath or lead your donkey to its eating trough and then away to get a drink, wouldn't you? ¹⁶ And as for this daughter of Abraham whom Satan has tied up for some eighteen years, should she not have been freed from this bondage on the Sabbath?"

¹⁷ After he said this, everyone who was opposing him was ashamed, and the whole crowd came to be really happy at the wonderful things that had come about through him.

¹⁸ So he said, "What is the kingdom of God like and what can you compare it with? ¹⁹ It's like a mustard seed that someone takes and plants in his garden and it grows and turns into a tree, and the birds fly down from the sky and nest in its branches."

²⁰ And again he said, "What can you compare the kingdom of God with? ²¹ It's like yeast, which a woman takes and mixes in with three measures of flour until the whole lot rises."

²² And he went on going through their towns and villages teaching as he made his way toward Jerusalem.

²³ Someone asked him, "Master, are only a few going to be saved?" He responded, ²⁴ "Focus on entering through the narrow gate because there are many, I tell you, who will want to go in through it and won't be able to. ²⁵ From the time the householder gets up and locks the gate you'll start being left outside knocking on the gate and saying, 'Master, open up for us,' and in response he'll say, 'I don't know you or where you're from.' ²⁶ Then you'll start saying, 'We ate and drank with you and you taught on our streets.' ²⁷ And he will tell you, 'I don't know you or where you're from. Get away from me all of you, you evil doers!' ²⁸ And there will be weeping and grinding of teeth, when you'll see Abraham and Isaac and Jacob and all the prophets in the kingdom of God, but yourselves excluded. ²⁹ And people will come from east and west and north and south and will recline together sharing a meal in the kingdom of God. ³⁰ Because, look, many who are first will be last and last who'll be first."

³¹ At that time some Pharisees approached him and told him, "Get away and leave this area, because Herod's wanting to kill you." ³² He said to them, "Go and tell that fox, 'Look, I'm expelling demons and performing healings today and tomorrow and I'll be done by the third day. ³³ Just today and tomorrow, and then I need on the following

day to head off, because it isn't on for a prophet to perish outside of Jerusalem.' ³⁴ Jerusalem, Jerusalem, killing the prophets and stoning those sent to you, how often did I want to gather your children together as a hen gathers its chickens under its wings, and you refused. ³⁵ Look, your house is abandoned. I'm telling you, you're not going to see me until the day comes when you'll say, 'Blessed is the one who comes in the name of the Lord.'"

Thinking About Luke

Luke has Jesus challenge the notion that disasters are a way that God punishes people. It is a crude notion, but we can still meet it where people who face suffering or illness might blame themselves and even see their plight as brought upon them by God. Or see others' plight in such terms. Luke has Jesus reject such ideas. Events happen. We are not to think of God generating or manipulating them. There would have been cruelties perpetuated by Pilate, and this probably refers to the time of year when lay people could themselves offer sacrifices and for some reason brought slaughter upon themselves at the hands of Pilate's soldiers. We are not told why. Were they also seen as subversive, as Jesus would be?

Falling towers and such phenomena as earthquakes, storms, and fire, let alone disease and pandemics, are not God's initiatives; they are part of reality. Rejecting such crude notions makes sense. This, then, stands against the kind of comfort people might find in the belief systems that declare such events part of a divine plan, or people's karma, enabling them to accept such events as "meant to be." Often the claims that positive events are engineered by God, for instance, as answers to prayer, help reinforce such notions. It is all being controlled by God. Luke's Jesus distances himself from such notions.

The warning that follows each reflection, however, namely that people might face a similar fate if they do not turn to God, repent, puts the focus elsewhere. It is another way of talking about judgment day when all people will be held to account, a central message of John the Baptist and one that Jesus will have also shared. Luke has been using such warnings in this part of his gospel and more will follow. Such warnings can easily go off the rails and become the main way preachers appeal to people to change. We are then in a religion of fear, not love, and the appeal is to pure self interest, not to partnership with God and a life motivated by love.

The focus on warning about the day of judgment returns in the parable about the fig tree and its failure to bear fruit. This is a widely used image in biblical tradition and among the sayings of Jesus. No fruit? Cut the tree down! John the Baptist had spoken of the axe ready to cut such unfruitful trees down. Good on the slave for giving the tree a chance with a bit of care!

The incident in the synagogue, which is found only in Luke, recalls other such stories. Religious leaders object not to Jesus' healings but to his performing them on the Sabbath day. Mark tells the story of Jesus healing a man's hand on the Sabbath (Mark 3:1–6). Come back and do it tomorrow, Jesus! Then it would be okay. Luke's hearers would sympathize with the common sense of responding to human need there and then. Such stories preserve evidence not of Jesus' disregard for Sabbath law but of his seeing response to human need as a law that overrides Sabbath law.

Luke then brings the parables of the mustard seed and of yeast. These will be from the source he shares with Matthew (Matt 13:31–32). Mark also has the parable of the mustard seed (Mark 4:30–32). As often when he has two sources, Matthew combines them, such as he does with the sending out of the twelve disciples. Luke instead passes over Mark's story when he uses Mark 4 and instead brings here the version of the parable that he found in his other main source. It is the kind of parable that will have been told many times and been allowed to grow bigger than the image allows. For, at most, the mustard seed grows up to be a big bush, not a tree, and as Mark's version indicates, the birds would not nest in its branches but under its shade.

Birds were often an image of non-Jews, gentiles, so there may be a hint here of gentiles finally also joining the movement. Just a few verses later Luke has Jesus speak of people from all directions of the compass coming to feast in the kingdom of God (Luke 13:29), also a reference to gentile inclusion.

The sayings about entering through the narrow gate and about a householder shutting his gate on people also serves to underscore warnings about judgment day. The householder's words refusing entry are in fact a quotation from Ps 6:8. On the positive side is the reference to gentiles coming from all directions. It uses the image of hope as being present at a shared meal, a common image among Jesus' sayings to depict the future. The next chapter will return to the image, portraying the invitation to all to accept the invitation to be included. Again, it is two-sided. Its negative side is the warning about missing out.

Only Luke has the advice from Pharisees to leave Herod Antipas's territory and Jesus' response, calling him a fox and insisting that he would soon go, and that Jerusalem would be his destiny, portraying himself as likely to suffer the fate of prophets before him. It is also only in Luke that we hear of Jesus ultimately having to face not only Pilate but also Herod Antipas (Luke 23:6–12).

Luke returns to the source he shares with Matthew in having Jesus speak of having wanted to gather Jerusalem's inhabitants together like a hen its chickens. Elsewhere he attributes such statements to God's Wisdom who had sought to do this down through the ages, so that is probably implied here too. In other words, Jesus is speaking not of his recent experience of ministry—he had not, according to Luke, been in Jerusalem since he commenced his yearlong ministry; he is speaking, rather, on behalf of Wisdom.

Foxes and chickens . . . not a good combination! I remember once, while looking after a farm, getting up one morning to find the chicken run completely empty. Only feathers remained, signs of the struggle. I had seen a fox the days before checking out the scene, but was confident the enclosure was well secured. I was wrong. The fox had dug its way in, killed, and taken all five hens. Herod the fox had already done for John the Baptist. Soon he and Rome's foxery would do the same to Jesus. Rome's army would then do the same to Jerusalem in 70 CE, leaving the temple a pile of ruins.

Luke appears to be depicting Jesus and his significance from a later perspective, which his hearers would appreciate. Jerusalem's house, the temple, would indeed be laid waste by the time of Luke's audience, having been destroyed by the Romans in 70 CE in response to the Jewish revolt of 66–70 CE. Luke represents hope as Jesus' return to Jerusalem at his second coming to commence his messianic rule from there, and this would be how the final statement would be read, "Blessed is the one who comes in the name of the Lord." Words normally addressed to pilgrims coming to the temple to worship would be addressed to Jesus when he returned.

Reflection: Luke portrays Jesus' warnings with subtle allusions to what was to come, both positively and negatively. To what might people of Luke's day see him alluding?

4

Conflicting Priorities

Challenging the Norms (Luke 14:1–35)

Listening to Luke

^{14:1} Once he went to the house of one of the leading Pharisees for a meal on the Sabbath, and they were keeping a close eye on him. ² And, lo and behold, a man suffering from fluid retention was there in front of him; ³ and so Jesus said to the Law specialists and Pharisees, "Is it lawful to heal on the Sabbath or not?" ⁴ They kept quiet. So, taking hold of the man, he healed him and set him free. ⁵ And he said to them, "Suppose your son or your cow were to fall into a ditch, wouldn't you immediately pull them out on the Sabbath day?" ⁶ They couldn't answer that.

⁷ He then told a parable to those who had been invited, when he saw how they chose the best places. ⁸ He said to them, "When you're invited to a wedding feast by someone, don't choose the best place at the table; otherwise, someone more distinguished might have been invited by him ⁹ and then he'll come and tell you, 'Give up your place for this man,' and then you'll start to feel ashamed and take the least significant place. ¹⁰ But when you're invited, go and take the least significant place, so that your host will end up telling you, 'My friend, move up higher.' That will then earn you admiration among everyone reclining

there with you. ¹¹ Because, you see, everyone who exalts himself will be brought low and everyone who humbles himself will be lifted up."

¹² And he said to the person who had invited him, "When you prepare a dinner or banquet, don't invite your friends or siblings or relatives or rich neighbors, because then they will invite you in return and in that way repay you. ¹³ Instead, when you put on a banquet, invite the poor, people with disability, the lame, the blind, ¹⁴ and that way you'll be blessed, because they don't have the wherewithal to repay you, so you'll be repaid at the resurrection of the righteous."

¹⁵ One of those seated with him when he heard this said, "Blessed is the one who will eat bread in the kingdom of God." ¹⁶ Jesus responded to him by saying, "A certain fellow once put on a great feast and invited lots of people. ¹⁷ And when the feast was ready, he sent his slave to tell those invited that it was all set to go. ¹⁸ But one by one they all started to excuse themselves. The first said, 'I just bought a field, and I need to go and look at it. Can I ask you to have me excused?' ¹⁹ And another said, 'I just bought five pairs of oxen and I'm going to check them out. Can I ask you to have me excused?' ²⁰ And another said, 'I just got married to my wife and so I can't come.'

²¹ "So the slave returned and told his master all of this. Then the householder got mad and told his slave, 'Go quickly out into the streets and laneways of the town and bring the poor, the disabled, the blind and lame here.' ²² Then the slave said, 'Master, I did what you told me, and there's still room.' ²³ The master told the slave, 'Then go out to the highways and hedges and make people come, so my place will be full. ²⁴ I'm telling you, none of those men whom I invited are going to get a taste of my banquet.'"

²⁵ Crowds of people were joining him as he went along, so he turned round and said to them, ²⁶ "If anyone comes to me and doesn't hate his father and mother and wife and children and brothers and sisters and even his own life, he can't be my disciple. ²⁷ Whoever doesn't carry his cross and follow me can't be my disciple.

²⁸ "If any of you wanted to build a tower, wouldn't you first sit down and work out the cost, whether it was feasible, ²⁹ so that you wouldn't end up having laid the foundation and then not being able to finish the build and have everyone looking on then start to make fun of you, ³⁰ saying, 'This guy started to build but couldn't get it done'?

³¹ "And if you were a king going out to do battle with another king, wouldn't you first sit down and get advice about whether with ten thousand men you could bring it off against a man heading for you with twenty thousand men? ³² Otherwise, you'd send a delegation to sue for peace while he was still at a distance. ³³ Similarly, any of you who is unwilling to renounce all your possessions can't be my disciple.

³⁴ "Salt is good but if salt loses its taste, what can you do to make it salty again? ³⁵ It's no good, not even for the soil or for manure, but people throw it out. If you've got ears, listen!"

Thinking About Luke

This is the second time that Luke reports that Jesus was invited to a Pharisee's place to eat. The first is when the woman appeared and Jesus talked about forgiveness (Luke 7:36–50). This time the assumption is that this was not a private occasion. There were others there, including Pharisees and Law specialists.

There are many references to meals in Luke 14, and they need to be understood within the world of their time. Houses often had an area near the front where people could come and share a meal, usually around a low table, lying down on their side around the table rather than sitting on chairs. People who owned houses usually had the wherewithal to have numbers of people around for meals.

While in our contexts meals are routine and we mainly eat well, in the first century eating well was reserved for the well to do, such as the tax collectors and others who made money. Meals were places of celebration but also of meeting. As noted earlier, people who imagined a positive future often did so by imagining a banquet. For some, that would be a banquet just for them. Jesus envisaged a banquet to which all would be invited. In a local village someone putting on a banquet would send out invitations and then when the banquet was ready would send his slaves to tell people it was ready.

In Luke's first story in Luke 14 the meal is the context for what appears to have been a regular cause of conflict between Jesus and other teachers. That they invite him for a meal reflects the fact they would have at least felt that they had something in common. He was a teacher as were they. Often the people with whom conflict becomes most intense are those closest to us, and this is likely to have been the case with Jesus and the Pharisees.

Luke paints a scene in which those teachers, while happy to dine with Jesus, nevertheless viewed him with suspicion. What might he be up to now? Into the scene, the front area of the Pharisee's house, open to the street, comes a man suffering from some kind of fluid retention, which we might call now as edema or dropsy. Our interest might be in the man but the storytellers who passed on this anecdote are not interested enough to give us detail. Instead, their focus is the controversial action of Jesus' healing on the Sabbath, reckoned by Jesus' critics to be a breach of the Sabbath command not to work. Luke told a similar story in the previous chapter.

Jesus' response to the eloquent silence of his critics, which he knew how to read, was to appeal to common sense, as he did in the similar episode back in Luke 13:10–17. If you'd lift your child or an animal out of a ditch on the Sabbath, then surely healing a person is equivalent. They could have responded: "Yes, that is an emergency, but this man will have the same ailment tomorrow. Come back and heal him then!" Luke is having Jesus imply that such reasoning is extreme and unreasonable. No need to come back tomorrow. It is okay to heal on the Sabbath. Mark has Jesus declare: "The Sabbath was made for people, not people for the Sabbath" (Mark 2:28). Effectively, people matter most to God. God is not going to be upset when you help people, as though for God the rules matter most.

The next section in Luke 14 requires a sense of humor and is probably at one level a provocation rather than advice. Taken literally, Jesus is depicted as offering a clue about how to get people to admire you and win kudos. While some will want to read it that way, it is more likely a confrontation, which actually challenges those wanting to be top dogs, something, Luke says, that provoked the parable. The social background is that it was often the custom that hierarchy played a role in where people reclined around a meal table. The more important you were, the closer you would be located to the host. Give up that game, argues Jesus. The closing statement (Luke 14:11) declares that the people whom God will praise are those who don't push for recognition but, knowing God loves them, love themselves and have no need to compete for top positions above others.

The confronting humor continues in Jesus' advice about whom to invite to dinner. It seems absurd and laughably self-serving. Transfer your needy selfish obsession to putting others, needy people who can't repay you, in your debt, and then get the reward finally from God, your greed fulfilled. Caring for needy people not because you care but because it makes you feel good and superior is a form of abuse. Jesus is playing with social customs of his day, where there was an unwritten rule of trying never to be in anyone's debt. If you do a favor, you expect a favor in return.

The advice to invite those who cannot repay you prepares for the parable of the great feast that follows. Taken out of the context of playing the greed game, Luke does portray Jesus as challenging traditional agendas and highlighting the need for compassion for the poor. Good news for the poor and embracing it as one's agenda is something very different from the self-indulgence of those who play the game of greed, including those who do so spiritually by taking Jesus' advice literally.

Jesus' parable of the great feast is one of his best known. In Matthew's Gospel, we see it developed into a wedding feast for a king's son. The king not only finds the invited guests making excuses for not coming. He responds by sending his army to destroy their city, an allusion to the destruction of the temple and the sacking of Jerusalem in 70 CE (Matt 22:1–14). Matthew takes it even further by having a guest who did come expelled from the wedding feast for wearing the wrong clothes, an allusion to church members who acclaim Jesus Lord but no longer clothe themselves in the love that Jesus represents.

The parable story reflects a world where rich households had slaves and could afford to put on feasts. It is a playful story employing a storyteller's art of exaggeration. All those invited refuse to come when told the feast was ready. The story confronts those who really should have been recognizing Jesus' message from God and embracing it but instead refuse to join. The feast is an image that Jesus regularly uses of the hope of the kingdom of God. In Matthew's version there is then only one initiative to get others in. In Luke there are two, to match what he knows would eventuate, as he will go on to depict in his second volume, the Acts of the Apostles. The two reflecting first those Jews who did in fact respond and then the gentiles to whom the gospel would also go.

In the sayings about discipleship that follow the parable, we are back with the serious provocative playfulness whose meaning is missed when we take it too literally. Nothing elsewhere suggests that Jesus advocated hating one's family. Like Jesus' statements about cutting off one's hand or plucking out one's eyes, when we have used them to do wrong, the hate statements are meant to make people sit up and take notice. Matthew softens them by having Jesus speak of loving one's family less (Matt 10:37–38).

Why such dramatic and extreme statements? Families exercised enormous power and many still do. Frequently people have to make decisions between what family values demand and what they know to be right and just. This can be where family wealth and inheritance matter most. It can also be where people have carried the put downs and deprivations they experienced in formative stages of their life, which plague them well into adulthood, until they find some love that sets them free. Embracing love and compassion, for oneself and for others, is what partnership with God and being a follower of Jesus means. The radical love that Jesus represents can set people free from all the obsessions, often rooted in family values, that make people unloving and greedy.

The final statement about salt also makes no sense if read literally. Salt remains salt and so salty. That's its chemistry. Jesus' saying reflects the fact that they had salt in a mix with other things and too much of other things means too little salt effect. The challenge is the same, as is the warning. Never lose the flavor of love. We would say: beware of watering down, removing the taste by contamination with what produces the flavor of greed, even when it comes because of influences from those close to you. You will be better for them by remaining pure.

Reflection: What norms do you see being challenged in Luke 14, and how do you recognize their existence and power today?

Defending Love (Luke 15:1–32)

Listening to Luke

15:1 Now tax collectors and sinners were all coming to listen to him. **2** And the Pharisees and the scribes started grumbling about it, saying, "This guy welcomes bad people and shares meals with them."

3 Then Jesus told them this parable: **4** "Who among you with a hundred sheep and having lost one of them wouldn't leave the ninety-nine in an isolated area and go looking for the lost sheep until he'd found it? **5** And then, having found it, would be really happy and carry it on his shoulders **6** and come home and call his friends and neighbors together to tell them, 'Celebrate with me, because I found my lost sheep'? **7** I'm telling you, there'll also be such joy in heaven over one sinner who repents and turns to God, more than over ninety-nine who have no need of repentance.

8 "And which woman with ten drachmas and losing a drachma wouldn't light a lamp and sweep her house and have a thoroughly good look for it until she found it? **9** And when she'd found it, she'd call together her friends and neighbors and say to them, 'Celebrate with me, because I've found the drachma I lost.' **10** Just so, I tell you, there's joy before God's angels over one sinner who repents and turns to God."

11 And he said, "There was once a man who had two sons. **12** And the younger of them said to his father, 'Dad, give me my portion of your estate which will be coming to me.' So he divided his wealth between them. **13** Not many days later the younger son got it all together and set off for a land far away and wasted his inheritance through a profligate lifestyle. **14** When he'd spent all his inheritance, a severe famine hit that land, and he found himself in trouble. **15** So he went and hired himself out to one of the citizens of that area, and he sent him out onto his farm to look after his pigs. **16** And he would have liked to have eaten from the carob pods from which the pigs had to eat, but no one gave him anything. [17] Then he came to his senses and said, 'How many of my dad's slaves have more than enough food, and here am I dying of hunger. [18] I'll get up and go to my father and say to him, "Dad, I did the wrong thing by heaven and by you, [19] and I don't deserve to be called your son any more; treat me like one of your slaves."' [20] So he got up and went to his father.

"While he was some way off, his father saw him and was thrilled and ran down and put his arms around him and kissed him. [21] His son said to him, 'Dad, I've done the wrong thing by heaven and by you; I don't deserve to be called your son anymore.' [22] But his father said to his slaves, 'Hurry and bring the best robe and put it on him and put a ring on his finger and sandals on his feet, [23] and bring the calf we've been fattening up and butcher it, so we can eat and celebrate, [24] because this my son was dead and has come back to life; he was lost and has been found'; and they started to celebrate.

[25] "Now the elder son was out on the farm and when he came back and was getting close to the house, he heard music and dancing, [26] and, calling one of the slaves, he asked him what all this was about. [27] He told him, 'Your brother has come, and your dad killed the fattened up calf because he's got him back safe and sound.' [28] But he was angry and didn't want to go in. His dad, however, went outside to call him in. [29] In response, he said to his father, 'Look, all these years I've served you and I never once deviated from what you told me to do, but you never gave me even a goat to help me celebrate with my friends; [30] and now this son of yours who spent the inheritance you gave him on prostitutes has come and you've gone and killed the fattened up calf for him.'

[31] "His father replied, 'Look, my lad, you've always been with me and everything I've got is yours, [32] but I had to celebrate and be happy, because this your brother was dead and now has come back to life and was lost and has now been found.'"

Thinking About Luke

If the previous two chapters in Luke include anecdotes about Jesus facing criticism because of his willingness to heal people on the Sabbath, this chapter focuses on another criticism. Why was he having to do with people considered anything but good and holy? Why wasn't he ensuring he kept company with those who pursued a life of obedience to God's Law? While not all tax collectors will have been corrupt, many doubtless were exploitative, taking a larger cut than they should have, and in any case, they were not, it was fair to assume, sticklers for observing issues of purity, especially with regard to food. As for those called "sinners," who they might have been is left to our imagination: women entertainers who turned up at their parties? Others engaging in corrupt behaviors of various kinds? Certainly, bad people, as we assume most would have seen them, and nothing suggests that Jesus swept sin under the carpet.

The critics had both moral and ritual concerns, which amounted to whether you were committed to obey God's commands. If your starting point is that God's priority is that people keep the commandments, a reasonable assumption, then you should be doing everything to please God. We do not have any evidence that Jesus advocated disobeying God's commands, but there is clear evidence that he understood God's priorities as first and foremost caring about people.

That might lead to a situation where priorities compete. Do I keep the Sabbath or do I heal, doing some work to help someone? Do you need to do so on the Sabbath? Can't it wait? Sometimes that is not realistic. And similarly, if I'm going to reach out to people who have messed up their lives and messed up others' lives, do I protect myself from being exposed to their evil influences or do I prioritize helping them? Jesus did the latter. Mark tells an anecdote about Jesus going to Levi's place and eating with such people. When criticized, he declared: "The sick need a doctor, not the well" (Mark 2:17).

One of the problems with brief anecdotes such as those showing Jesus in conflict with Pharisees is that they have been passed on without the broader context. In that broader context, we know that not all Pharisees were like those with whom Jesus on occasion was in conflict. The Pharisaic tradition, which became the rabbinic tradition of Judaism, is much richer and diverse and is done an injustice if we generalize from such anecdotes to conclude that they were representative of all Pharisees, let alone all of Judaism. That is to feed the evil of anti-Semitism. There were some, however, like that, and, indeed, there have been Christians with similar prejudices.

The anecdotes serve not to stereotype groups but to raise issues about priorities in the way we interpret our religious traditions.

Jesus does so and does theology by appealing to common human experience. When he first told the parable about the lost sheep there were probably some sheep farmers present. The image had already been used in moral teaching, as far back as in ancient Egypt, where there is wisdom teaching that advises that kings should care for their subjects as a shepherd does for his sheep. We are more familiar with the image of David the shepherd king and Ps 23, which declares that God is our shepherd. The Latin for shepherd, *pastor*, comes into our language in describing ministry and pastoral care. In the ancient world it was mostly used of rulers, more about political leaders than pastors.

Jesus' appeal to common sense among sheep farmers, that they would surely go and look for a missing sheep, is partly self-defense against his critics, but really it is about God and asserting and defending God's priorities. Jesus is just acting out God's priorities. Every sheep matters, surely! Everyone matters, surely, is the argument, and that concern, that commandment, overrides all other concerns and commandments. Jesus engages with these disreputable people because they matter to God. They are not to be written off but invited back into a relationship with God.

Luke may well have added the statement here and also after the parable about the woman, that heaven will rejoice when sinners repent. In some ways it does not capture the issue, because those Pharisees, for sure, would also have been glad if sinners repented. The criticism was rather about Jesus' willingness to show acceptance and friendship to these people, seek them out, even before they repent. His critics' view was that they would be happy to associate with such people and show them acceptance but only after they repented. That is a significant difference. Love comes first and then the possibility of repentance follows. Love does not set repentance as the necessary prerequisite before love is shown.

The next parable about the woman who's lost a drachma is making the same point. A drachma, like a denarius, was roughly the equivalent of a day's wage. Here the focus is not on who is in need, as in the lost sheep, but rather on what matters to the woman. Of course, she wants the drachma for herself, and of course God wants these unwanted, unloved, and deemed-unworthy people. This is God's interest. The argument is that it is in God's own interests, as the creator, we might say. This comes through most strikingly in the parable that follows.

The so-called parable of the prodigal son is also a reading from thinkable everyday life. It may rarely have happened like that, but it was imaginable and made enough sense to its hearers to bring home its point. One son asks for his share of what will be coming to him and the outcome is that each of the two sons gets his share. The one son heads off to a land far away and wastes all his money. How, we are not told, but later his brother will allege that he spent a lot on prostitutes. When a famine comes, he is down and out and ends up being employed on a pig farm, which for a Jew would be a matter of deep shame, since pigs and pork were deemed unclean.

The lad comes to his senses, heads back home. That would all make sense to people listening to the parable. What happens next is the key to the parable. One possibility would have been that the father, who might well have resented his son's setting off in the first place, might have had second thoughts about welcoming him back. My son will have to make up for it, might have been in his thoughts. Instead, he did what many dads would have done. He ran down the road and was overjoyed to see him. That's the natural human thing to do. Social norms about whether doing so might be a bit undignified for a respectable father are all left by the wayside. Love matters most and the father initiates celebration, even killing the calf they'd been fattening up for a good feast some day.

Those with a sensitivity to biblical imagery might have smiled at the image of the feast, commonly used to depict salvation and hope. Into this celebratory event comes the elder brother, who resents what is going on because it is not fair. The connection to Jesus' critics would have been clear for all to see. They objected to Jesus' treating those bad people with the same love they assumed fitting only for themselves, and giving them the same status.

The second son's objections were reasonable enough. It is important to see that he is not portrayed as someone evil. He's making a fair claim that would have made sense to people listening to the story. Jesus' claim is that there is a wider frame of reference, which is not about what people deserve but about what they need. And when you've made love your highest priority and your joy, then you're going to find your hopes fulfilled, and God's hopes fulfilled, when you see such restoration. You won't be doing sums about merit.

In all three parables Jesus is defending himself and defending love, but he is also doing more than that. He is doing theology; that is, he is confronting people with a way of thinking about God that challenges common

CONFLICTING PRIORITIES

assumptions. God is not, as many by implication assume, obsessed with having people keep rules and having himself obeyed, like a ruler and alas like some who claim leadership in our world. And God is not like fathers who similarly focus on their own power and control. God is more like the compassionate parent, the mother or father who cares and engages in an open and affirming relationship. Nor is God like leaders or parents who absolve themselves of responsibility in order to remain popular and so never confront what needs to be confronted to prevent harm and abuse. Sin is real and so therefore are forgiveness, healing, and change.

Reflection: What was the main point of contention between Jesus and his critics?

Money Matters (Luke 16:1–31)

Listening to Luke

16:1 And he told his disciples, "There was once a rich man who had a household slave, and he was charged with wasting his assets. **2** So summoning him he said to him, 'What's this I'm hearing about you? Give an account of your household management, because you can't any longer be in charge of household finances.' **3** The household slave said to himself, 'What'll I do, because my master is taking away from me the job of managing the household accounts? I can't dig and I'm ashamed to be a beggar. **4** I know what I'll do, so when I'm removed from managing the accounts, people will welcome me into their homes.'

5 "So he summoned each person who owed his master something and said to the first, 'How much do you owe my master?' **6** He said, 'A hundred measures of olive oil.' He told him, 'Get your bill and sit down quickly and write fifty.' **7** Then he said to another, 'And you, how much do you owe?' And he said, 'A hundred measures of wheat.' He tells him, 'Get your bill and write eighty.' **8** And the master commended the dishonest slave because he acted shrewdly. For the people of this age are cleverer in dealing with the current generation than the sons of light.

9 "I'm telling you, make friends for yourselves of those who handle corrupt finance, so that when your money runs out, they'll welcome you into eternal dwellings. **10** The person reliable in dealing with minor matters can be counted on to be reliable in dealing with major ones and the person who is corrupt in dealing with minor matters will be corrupt in dealing with major ones. **11** If you turn out to be corrupt in dealing with finances, who's going to trust you with what is genuine? **12** And if you turn out to be unreliable in relation to someone else's things, who's going to give you something to manage for yourself? **13** No slave can serve two masters; for either he'll hate one of them and like the other or be devoted to one and despise the other. You can't serve God and money."

¹⁴ The Pharisees who were into money were listening to all of this and started ridiculing him. ¹⁵ So he said to them, "You justify yourselves in front of people, but God knows your hearts, because what may be hailed as good in people's eyes might be an abomination in God's. ¹⁶ The Law and the Prophets have been in force up until John and since then the kingdom of God has been proclaimed and everyone is resisting it. ¹⁷ Yet it is easier for heaven and earth to pass away than for one stroke of the Law to fall. ¹⁸ Anyone who divorces his wife and marries another commits adultery, and whoever marries a woman divorced by her husband commits adultery.

¹⁹ "There was once a rich man who decked himself out with purple and fine linen and engaged every day in sumptuous meals. ²⁰ And there was a poor man named Lazarus who'd been left covered in sores at his gate, ²¹ looking to get something to eat from what fell from the rich man's table, but exposed to dogs who would come and lick his sores. ²² Now it happened that the poor man died and was carried off by angels to be placed in the arms of Abraham. The rich man also died and was buried. ²³ And in Hades being in torment he lifts his gaze and sees Abraham far away and Lazarus in his arms. ²⁴ So he called out, 'Father Abraham, pity me and send Lazarus to dip the tip of his finger in water and cool my tongue because I'm in agony in these flames.' ²⁵ But Abraham said, 'My child, remember that you did so well in life and Lazarus did so poorly. Now, here, he is being comforted and you're experiencing agony. ²⁶ And as well as all this, there's a great chasm set up between us and you, so that anyone wanting to cross over from here to you can't, nor from there to us.' ²⁷ He said, 'I beg you, father, then send him to my father's house, ²⁸ because I have five brothers, to let them know so that they won't end up in this place of agony.' ²⁹ Then Abraham tells him, 'They've got Moses and the Prophets, let them listen to them.' ³⁰ But he said, 'No, father Abraham, but if someone were to go to them from the dead, then they would turn their lives around.' ³¹ He told him, 'If they don't listen to Moses and the Prophets, then they won't obey even if someone rises from the dead.'"

Thinking About Luke

In the previous chapter Luke presents Jesus as responding to critics for reaching out to disreputable people. He recounts three parables. There is every reason to suggest that the first parable in Luke 16 also belongs originally to Jesus' defense of his actions. It is typically tongue in cheek. They were criticizing Jesus for offering God's forgiveness to such people and arguing that he had no right to do so.

In response Jesus told a parable about a cunning household slave who knew he was about to lose his job and went out and got people to write down their debts, the very thing Jesus was doing when he went out to offer God's forgiveness, when according to his critics he had no right to do so. Tongue in cheek, Jesus was talking about himself and of course the master praised him, as God would affirm Jesus by resurrection. Yes, I'm a rogue, you think, but I'm not really.

There have been problems from early times trying to interpret the parable. It may well have been something that Jesus knew had happened, which might have added to the confusion because it was not a neat fit. Some suggest that Jesus' only point is that it is a good idea to take initiatives in critical situations, to act decisively, but that is too little. Others tried to apply it more literally. We see this in the comment added in 16:9 at the end, which suggests that it is a good idea to have friends who have money who might help you out, even if they are not saints.

Clearly, others attached more sayings to the story, including about trustworthiness (Luke 16:10–12) and then also the saying about serving God or money (Luke 16:13), which Matthew also knew and incorporated into the Sermon on the Mount (Matt 6:24). Luke then uses it to have Jesus attack his critics as being greedy (Luke 16:14–15).

The attack on those who resist the gospel continues in the statement in Luke 16:16. There Luke effectively has Jesus say that what is going on continues a trend of rejecting God's will seen in the past, first during the time when Moses and the prophets set forth God's will and then since John the Baptist, when, in addition, the message of God's kingdom was being proclaimed, which the Pharisees resist. Like Matthew's version of the saying, Luke has Jesus speak of an effective assault on the kingdom (Matt 11:12), fighting against God's will, God's reign.

Against such resistance Jesus then emphasizes in 16:17 that in no way is the Law to be set aside, as the Pharisees are effectively doing by their greed and their rejection of God's will. Not even a stroke of the Law is to be set aside! Matthew incorporates this into his introduction to Jesus' exposition of the Law in the Sermon on the Mount, preceded by his declaration that he had in no way come to abolish the Law and the Prophets and followed by the declaration that setting any of it aside would effectively ban one from the kingdom (Matt 5:17–19).

We then have what might seem like a change of subject when Jesus declares divorce and remarriage as contrary to God's will and as effectively to commit adultery. The connection with the context is very likely to be divorce and remarriage for financial gain, getting a bigger dowry. A dowry was normally a financial contribution that the wife's family made to the marriage. That made marrying and remarrying profitable. The assumption behind the charge is that marriage is permanent and cannot be dissolved, so that any attempt to act as though it can be dissolved had to be a breach of the original marriage, thus adultery.

Mark has a similar prohibition (Mark 10:9–12), as do Paul (1 Cor 7:10–11) and Matthew, the latter acknowledging an exception, namely that where adultery has taken place that marriage has ended and, according to both Jewish and Roman law, must end (Matt 5:32; 19:9). Over time, the church had to grapple with whether to treat this prohibition as absolute law and so forbid divorce altogether or whether to acknowledge that in some circumstances it could be appropriate as the more loving thing to do, a stance that many would espouse today. Staying faithful to the gospel and to love is the highest priority. Already Paul intimated that there could be exceptions where one partner wanted to follow Christ and the other found it intolerable (1 Cor 7:12–15). Domestic violence and serious breakdown of relationships make it the caring way forward.

The focus on money and wealth continues in the parable with which Luke 16 concludes. It is a story told elsewhere in Jewish tradition and in its present form looks very much like a Jewish story reworked to reflect what fellow Jews were now claiming about Christ. It is unmistakably another challenge to greed and inequality, a key theme in Luke, and probably one that also addressed issues of his own day. If you are not good news for the poor, you clearly have not understood the gospel.

Like Jesus' statement in 16:16, the parable asserts that the rich man was among those who did not heed Moses and the Prophets. The dramatic conversation of the rich man now crying out in agony goes on to refer to Jesus' resurrection. Still, they do not hear! Luke will be confronting people of his own day.

The imagery of what might go on in Hades, the place of the dead, reflects an assumption that many shared, namely that effectively a person's fate is decided at death. Luke appears to share this view when he has Jesus say to the man crucified beside him that they would soon be together in paradise (Luke 23:43). The more common view was that at death people would enter a waiting space and be only semiconscious and then at the last day be raised from the dead to full consciousness with a body and be held to account at the last judgment. Imagining the future inevitably produced diverse images and theories, which are sometimes contradictory.

Ultimately the belief is that we face God in the end and face up to ourselves. The rationale behind such belief is that it is simply so unfair that there is so much inequality and injustice in this world that one day surely it must be put right. That also generates fantasies that sometimes look rather more hateful and vengeful than a commitment to love with justice would tolerate and would have no place in any human system of justice today. Holding back from such fantasies is preferable and being satisfied in the faith that in the end we can have confidence in one detail, which may indeed be enough: in the end, God. God who confronts and God who cares and loves is our hope. All else is in God's hands and we can leave it there and set the fantasies of hate and revenge aside.

Reflection: What do you see as Luke's main theme in this chapter and how does it relate to the message of Jesus?

Advice and Warnings (Luke 17:1–37)

Listening to Luke

17:1 He told his disciples, "It's inevitable that scandals will arise, but woe to those who bring them about. **2** It would be better for them to have a millstone hung round their neck and be thrown into the sea than that one of these little ones be abused. **3** So be on guard! If your fellow believer does wrong, confront them about it, and if they face up to it, forgive them. **4** And if someone wrongs you seven times and then turns to you seven times saying, 'I'm sorry', forgive them."

5 The apostles then said to the Lord, "Increase our faith." **6** The Lord responded, "If you have faith the size of a mustard seed, you could say to this mulberry tree, 'Be uprooted and planted in the sea' and it would obey you.

7 "Would any of you with a slave out ploughing or looking after sheep, when he returns from out on the farm, say to him, 'Come right now and take your place for a meal?' **8** Wouldn't you rather say to him, 'Prepare a meal for me and put your kit on and serve me till I've had something to eat and drink, and then after that you can have something to eat and drink'? **9** You wouldn't surely thank the slave for doing what he's told, would you? **10** So just like that, when you have done all you've been told to do, say, 'We're just unworthy slaves, who've just done what we ought to have done.'"

11 And while he was on his way to Jerusalem, he traveled through Samaria and Galilee. **12** And when he came to one of the villages, ten men with leprosy met him, while keeping their distance. **13** And they called out to him, "Jesus, master, have pity on us!"

14 When he saw them, he said to them, "Go and show yourselves to the priests." And as they went off, they were healed. **15** One of them, realizing that he was healed, returned giving thanks out loud to God,

[16] and fell at his feet expressing his gratitude. Now he was a Samaritan. [17] In response Jesus said, "Weren't there ten of you who got healed? Where's the other nine? [18] Are none of them found returning to give thanks to God except this foreigner?" [19] So he said to him, "Get up and go! Your faith has made you whole."

[20] When he was asked by the Pharisees when the kingdom of God was to come, he replied, "The kingdom of God won't come in a way to be observed, [21] nor will they say, 'Look, here it is' or 'There!' For, you see, the kingdom of God is among you." [22] He told his disciples, "The days are coming when you'll be wanting to see one of the days of the Son of Man and you won't see it. [23] And they'll say to you, 'Look, there!' or 'Look, here!' Don't go and follow after them. [24] For as lightning flashes across the sky from one end to the other, that's how the Son of Man will be when his day comes. [25] But first he'll have to endure a lot of suffering and be rejected by this generation.

[26] "And as it was in the days of Noah, that's how it will be in the days of the Son of Man. [27] They were eating and drinking and marrying and getting married right up until the time when Noah entered the ark, and the flood came and annihilated them all. [28] It'll be just like in the days of Lot. They were eating and drinking, buying and selling, planting and building; [29] then the day came when Lot left Sodom and fire and sulfur came down from heaven and annihilated them all. [30] It'll be the same on the day when the Son of Man is revealed.

[31] "On that day whoever is on his roof shouldn't go down to retrieve his possessions and similarly nor should anyone out on his farm turn back. [32] Remember Lot's wife. [33] Whoever tries to save his life will lose it and whoever loses it will keep it. [34] I tell you, there'll be two people that night in one bed and one will be taken and the other left; [35] and two women will be working at the grinder together and one will be taken and the other left." [37] In response they said to him, "Lord, where?" He said to them, "Where the corpse is, that's where the vultures will be gathered."

Thinking About Luke

Luke 17 is a loose collection of sayings of Jesus that will have been passed on, adapted, and supplemented to serve the church. The warning about abuse is found also in Mark 9:42, probably Luke's source at this point. It is a typically dramatic saying, not meant to be taken literally, but intended to make a serious point. Abuse of little ones: referring to any believer or meaning children? Originally it probably did refer to children and most likely addressed pederasty, a common crime of the time and one that, alas, has survived well. The language used, *skandalon*, which comes through into English as "scandal," was sometimes used to refer to sexual wrongdoing and probably refers to that here. In Mark, warnings follow about cutting off limbs and plucking out eyes (Mark 9:43–48). Matthew uses them when he has Jesus address sexual wrongdoing in the Sermon on the Mount (Matt 5:29–30).

Luke moves straight on to the saying about the need to forgive (Luke 17:4). Matthew has a more elaborate form of the saying and associates it with handling issues of discipline in the church (Matt 18:15–22). What might seem obvious is far from that when we reflect on all the other various ways in which people handle hurt and conflict, from gossiping to third parties to holding grudges. The instruction is: go and sort it out with the person! Don't sweep it under the carpet in an endeavor to keep the peace or be "nice"! Be prepared to be open and to reconcile!

We then skip to another playful exaggeration about faith (Luke 17:5–6). Whether replanting mulberry trees or moving mountains, confidence is encouraged, which also needs to remain grounded and avoid fantasies of greed.

The next section assumes the world of slavery (Luke 17:7–10). It would have made sense to people for whom slavery was an acceptable part of life. For us it is not. So, the argument is not persuasive. On the other hand, the challenge to the claim for rewards can make some sense for us. If for me, caring about others is part of who I am, I don't expect any special reward for it. It is a reward in itself. We've done what we want to do, which is also what we ought to do. We don't need special kudos. We have learned to love and value ourselves without having to carry on making a case for it. Worthless slaves? Not really. Anything but! Certainly not slaves to the need to seek approval and reward.

The story about the lepers (Luke 17:11–19) has a sting in its tail, at least for those proud of being the special people of God and harboring prejudice. The hero is someone they might look down on: a Samaritan! Like in the parable of the good Samaritan, the outsider becomes the insider.

Prejudices are overturned. That does not mean they are reversed, as sadly happened in history and helped generate anti-Semitism. The story has echoes of Mark's story of the leper whom Jesus healed and sent off to the priests, who exercised the role of the health authorities to declare the person free of the leprosy (Mark 1:40–44). Apparently biblical "leprosy" was a contagious skin disease, but it is not to be confused with Hansen's disease, the leprosy we know today.

Luke moves from there to bring some of Jesus' teaching about the kingdom of God (Luke 17:20–21). Some have translated the words as "the kingdom of God is within you" instead of "among you," but the latter is almost certainly more correct. It is not about inward spirituality but about what was happening among people. Then the question is whether it is claiming that the kingdom of God is coming into reality among them already through Jesus' actions or whether it would one day suddenly be among them when the Son of Man comes, as the following verses suggest. Then, however, one would expect not "is among" but "will be among you," but that is less likely given that the coming of the Son of Man will be there for all to see. Either way, Luke is probably having Jesus ward off speculation, and doing so either by having him claim that it's happening now or having him claim that it will happen all of a sudden when you don't expect it, or perhaps both.

Luke shifts then from talking of the kingdom of God, which for him is both present and future, to talk about the coming of the Son of Man, very much a concern of the early church as they looked for Jesus' return (Luke 17:22–37). Matthew, too, has this material but incorporates it into the last of the five main speeches he attributes to Jesus, in Matt 24, as he expands upon Mark 13.

Luke has Jesus foretell his impending suffering and then use imagery typical of future expectation of the day. Noah's flood and Sodom's destruction serve as models of what is imagined on judgment day. People will be carrying on as normal and then suddenly Jesus will arrive and that will be the end. We see from Paul's speculations that they seem to have imagined that Jesus would appear from above, usually accompanied by angels, and would whisk away the righteous to join him in the air (1 Thess 4:15–18). This is represented dramatically by talking of the sudden elevation of individuals. We are in the realm of imagination seeking to clothe hope.

The closing question about where this might happen may seem strange to us, but for Luke and his hearers, the event is to be expected at Jerusalem. That is where Jesus' corpse will be, at least for a time. This matches a widespread view that saw history coming to a climax by God's action to restore Jerusalem and raise those on the nearby Mount of Olives from their graves. They might have seen an allusion to Jesus' death with reference to the corpse and understood the vultures as representing the people's representatives from Israel and Rome who would bring Jesus to his death. Luke will later address the inhabitants of Jerusalem and speak of the day when he would be returning to them (Luke 21:28).

Our passage is an assortment of advice and hope. Underlying its diverse sayings is the message of God who loves and who wants people to share that love. That had very concrete implications whose relevance remains, not least in relation to abuse of minors, but also in how to handle hurt and conflict, and how to abandon the merry-go-round of being occupied with making up for one's sense of lack of worth. Celebrating being made whole in thanksgiving, in contrast to prejudices of others and ourselves, is part of experiencing the kingdom of God in the present. Love can then fantasize and dream, knowing that hope has its basis not in speculation but that same love.

Reflection: How might Luke's depiction of Jesus' advice have had significance for people of Luke's day and how might it speak in our day?

Colliding Values (Luke 18:1–43)

Listening to Luke

18:1 And he told them a parable about the need to be always persistent in prayer and not to become discouraged. **2** "There was once a judge in a town who had no regard for God nor respect for people. **3** Now there was a widow in that town, and she used to approach him asking, 'Get me a fair go in relation to my opponent.' **4** And for some time he wasn't prepared to do so. Then later he said to himself, 'Even though I have no regard for God nor respect for people, **5** yet, because this widow is so persistent in bothering me, I'll deal with her case, so that she'll finally stop coming and wearing me out.'" **6** The Lord said, "Hear what the unjust judge is saying. **7** Isn't God going to make sure his chosen ones who keep crying out to him day and night get a fair go, and be patient with them? **8** I'm telling you, he'll quickly attend to their rights. But when the Son of Man comes, will he find faith on earth?"

9 And to some who were confident in themselves that they were righteous and despised everyone else he directed this parable. **10** "Two men went up to the temple to pray. One was a Pharisee; the other was a tax collector. **11** The Pharisee stood by himself and prayed, 'God, I thank you that I'm not like the rest of humankind, extortioners, unjust, adulterers, or like this tax collector. **12** I fast twice a week, I pay a tithe on everything I get.' **13** Now the tax collector, standing a long way off, didn't want to lift his eyes to heaven but beat his chest saying, 'God, pardon me, a sinner.' **14** I tell you, he, rather than the other guy, went off home set right with God, because those who exalt themselves will be humbled and those who humble themselves will be exalted."

15 People also started bringing toddlers to him that he might touch them, but his disciples told them off for doing so. **16** Jesus, however, called them over and said to them, "Let the little children come to me and don't stop them, because the kingdom of God is made up of such little ones as these. ¹⁷ I'm telling you, whoever does not accept the kingdom of God like a little child won't get into it."

¹⁸ Now there was a man from the ruling class who asked him, "Good teacher, what do I need to do to inherit eternal life?" ¹⁹ Jesus said to him, "Why are you calling me good? No one is good but God alone. ²⁰ You know the commandments: don't commit adultery, don't murder, don't steal, don't lie, honor your father and mother." ²¹ He responded, "I've kept all these since my youth." ²² When Jesus heard this, he said to him, "There's just one thing you're missing. Sell what you have and distribute the funds to the poor and you'll have treasure in heaven and then come and follow me." ²³ When he heard this, he become sad, because he was very rich.

²⁴ Noticing this, Jesus said, "How hard it is for those with possessions to enter the kingdom of God. ²⁵ It's easier for a camel to pass through the eye of a needle than for a rich person to enter the kingdom of God." ²⁶ When people heard him say that, they said, "Who then can be saved?" ²⁷ He told them, "What's impossible for human beings is possible with God." ²⁸ Peter said, "Look, we've left everything we had and have taken up following you." ²⁹ He said to them, "Truly I tell you, there's no one who has left his household or wife or brothers or parents or children for the sake of the kingdom of God ³⁰ who will not receive much more in this age and eternal life in the age to come."

³¹ And taking the twelve aside, he told them, "Look, we're going up to Jerusalem and everything written in the Prophets about the Son of Man is going to come to fulfillment; ³² for he'll be handed over to the gentiles and will be ridiculed and abused and spat on, ³³ and they'll beat him up and put him to death, and on the third day will rise from the dead."

³⁴ But they didn't understand any of this and its meaning was hidden from them, so they had no idea what he was talking about.

³⁵ As they approached Jericho there was a blind man sitting begging on the side of the road. ³⁶ Hearing that a crowd was passing through, he inquired what was going on. ³⁷ They explained to him that Jesus of Nazareth was on his way through. ³⁸ So he shouted out, "Jesus, Son of David, have pity on me!" ³⁹ Those who were up at the front of the crowd told him off, to be quiet, but he cried out all the more, "Son

of David, have pity on me!" ⁴⁰ Jesus stopped and instructed that he be brought to him. When he came, he asked him, ⁴¹ "What do you want me to do?" He said, "Lord, to help me get my sight back." ⁴² Jesus said to him, "Receive your sight! Your faith has healed you." ⁴³ And immediately he got his sight back and started following him, praising God, and all the folk who saw this gave thanks to God.

Thinking About Luke

Luke brings two last parables from his special sources before returning halfway through this chapter in 17:15 to Mark. Luke introduces the first parable as urging people not to give up praying. Looking at the parable on its own, we see that it is typical of parables of Jesus, which teach about God along the lines: if you can imagine a human being responding in this way, can't you think about God like that, too? So, in the famous parable of the prodigal son, part of the message is: you would have compassion as a dad, wouldn't you? Can't you think of God as having compassion, too?

A judge with no regard for God or respect for human beings ends up addressing the widow's need. Can't you then see that God will surely hear the cries of his people? The focus is hope and the background is people crying out for change, for liberation. The Jewish people longed for change. John the Baptist and Jesus belonged to movements looking for change. Have faith. It will happen. Don't give up hoping and praying for it. Translated into the wider world of the Jesus movement and the church, it is a message of hope. For them, that now also included Jesus' return as Son of Man, God's agent for leadership when that time would come. Will he find people holding onto their faith and hope? That is the challenge that Luke has Jesus bring.

The second episode is less a parable and more a story designed to challenge attitudes. (As long as we do not generalize the reference to Pharisees and end up doing what this Pharisee does, but in the form, "I am proud that I am not like this Pharisee.") The message is clear and confronts self-righteousness. Whenever our sense of value is at the expense of respect for others, we can know we have missed the point. Loving ourselves as we love our neighbors is embracing, not excluding.

This is not about a phony humility or a false one, such as sometimes happens when people compose prayers of confession that ask people to confess what they may not be guilty of. It is rather a matter of openness and honesty. Humility is not an act, let alone a manipulation in the interests of being exalted. It is about being down to earth, down on the *humus*, on ground level with the awareness that we don't need to play games but can simply be ourselves. That means being honest about our weaknesses and failings and about our strengths. That way we get right with God and with ourselves, and we are likely to have better relationships with others because we show them the same love we have for ourselves.

At this point in the chapter Luke goes back to Mark's text. Luke left off following Mark back in Luke 9:49–50, where he was using Mark 9:38–41. Now he returns to Mark, but leaves out Mark's account of Jesus' warnings against abuse (Mark 9:42–50) and his response to questions of divorce (Mark 10:2–12). He had, after all, included a saying about abuse in Luke 17:1–2, and about divorce in Luke 16:18. Instead, now in Luke 18:15–17, after more than eight chapters where he has used other sources, he picks up Mark again where Mark mentions people bringing infants to Jesus (Mark 10:13–16).

The story follows well after the contrast between the Pharisee and the tax collector because one way of talking about nonmanipulative lowliness is to speak of recovering the trustfulness of a little child, not yet into competing with others for approval. Luke has used Mark's story of Jesus' response to his disciples' ambitions for greatness by putting a little child before them (Luke 9:46–48), but that now lies many chapters back. The same message is, however, repeated here in Luke 18:17. To embrace the kingdom of God is to embrace God's way of being, that is, to embrace love and openness. Not to do so is by definition not to want such oneness with God.

By picking up Mark's story of Jesus' welcoming children, Luke preserves the positive attitude towards children, not just as illustrations of how adults might be, but as persons in their own right. Love and care for children might come naturally for some but then and now this is not always the case, and it took centuries before there was an understanding of how formative the years of childhood are. It is not too hard to imagine the rationale for the disciples telling people off for bringing their children. Jesus is busy and won't want to be bothered with children. They're not real persons yet.

Luke's retelling of Mark's story removes one of the possible readings of the incident in Mark. In Mark, parents bring their children. For "children"

Mark uses a word that can mean a child of any age. He had used it of a twelve-year-old girl in Mark 5:42. Luke changes it to a word meaning infants. This change may have been incidental, but possibly Luke was aware of how Mark's story could be heard or misheard. For some might have been familiar with teachers who engaged in pedophilia and people who offered them the favor of using/abusing their children. They would then hear the word translated "touch" as implying sexual fondling, as it sometimes did. Matthew, who keeps Mark's word for children, nevertheless removes the reference to touching, replacing it with a reference to Jesus' laying on hands and praying for them.

Pederastic relations with children were not uncommon. No wonder then, for those who read it this way, that the disciples told the parents off. Luke also omits the detail that Jesus then took the children into his arms and blessed them, possibly cautious about misunderstandings. While some might indeed have had such thoughts when they heard Mark's story, nothing suggests it was Mark's intended meaning, and the changes in Matthew and Luke may be no more than stylistic variations.

Luke then continues with Mark in bringing the account of the rich man wanting eternal life. Luke puts him not unreasonably in the ruling class, literally "ruler," but probably not meaning an actual ruler, but someone from the ruling class. Apart from that, he repeats Mark's story with just a few omissions. He has Jesus leave out "Don't defraud," as does Matthew, because it is not one of the Ten Commandments, and also, like Matthew, omits the detail about Jesus' positive emotional response to the man for his efforts thus far, following a tendency both have to delete references to such emotions.

Unlike Matthew, he has no problem with Jesus declaring that only God is good. Like Mark, he saw no problem in Jesus' not claiming to be good: "Why are you calling me good? No one is good but God alone" (Luke 18:19). Jesus' response is simply good Judaism and there is no reason to suggest that his response was anything other than a genuine answer. That includes his going on to point to the commandments. You have eternal life now and in the future by embracing life with God and so keeping the commandments. This is not about keeping them to reap eternal life as a reward but keeping them as part of a continuing relationship of oneness with God, the God of love.

This is also more than not breaking the commandments, ticking the boxes, never doing what is wrong. Such obedience appears to be the claim of the rich man, which Jesus does not dispute. Not doing what is wrong is one thing; doing what is right is another. Jesus tests this by challenging him to sell up and distribute the proceeds to the poor. The agenda of being and staying rich outweighed such perspectives and the man was left sad and disappointed that he couldn't make it.

This is a story being passed on to make a point. Originally it fits with Jesus' pattern of challenging some people to leave their possessions and households and join him on the road with his itinerant group. He didn't tell all to do so. Some he told to stay home, but to all he gave the challenge to embrace God's agenda, the vision of the kingdom of God, which meant good news for the poor. No amount of refraining from breaching the commandments or claiming faith or conversion counted, if there was not a commitment to share God's life, eternal life, and that meant sharing God's eternal love.

Luke follows Mark in bringing the sequel in which Jesus spells out the challenge to rich people and engages with the disciples and their concerns. Making your wealth your priority is not compatible with wanting to share God's life and priorities. That was and is hard to hear. Jesus then consoles the disciples' anxiety about having left all to follow him by pointing to the compensation of a being part of a new family. They had been asked to be part of what was effectively a protest movement against the economic system of the day, which through its hierarchical structures and tight family controls kept some people poor and kept others rich. Greed is very inventive and finds ever new forms of achieving its goal. Whether making the break in protest or sticking within it, to have eternal life is to embrace love and justice, a radical change of one's life agenda.

Like Mark, Luke follows this story with Jesus' announcement about his impending fate, but instead of bringing Mark's account of James and John wanting to have key leadership posts in the coming kingdom, Luke skips over this material in Mark 10:35–45, and moves on to the account of the healing of the blind man, named Bartimaeus in Mark. Luke does not omit the material in Mark 10:35–45 altogether. Rather, he obviously saw it as appropriate to adapt and bring as part of Jesus' final advice to his disciples on the night he was betrayed (Luke 22:24–30).

Luke knows another story about Jericho from a special source, namely the encounter with Zacchaeus, which he brings in Luke 19:1–10. To fit both into his account, he rearranges the order of events, so that the healing of the blind man no longer takes place on the way out of Jericho, as in Mark, but on the way in, and has the Zacchaeus episode now take place as Jesus was leaving.

In Mark, the healing of Bartimaeus like the healing of the blind man at Bethsaida functions also symbolically to contrast with the disciples' blindness in failing to see greatness not as might and power but as lowliness and love, qualities central to Jesus and to God. Luke appears no longer to use it symbolically. He has been selective in his use of Mark's material, does not include the healing of the blind man at Bethsaida, and has fitted so much more into his account. Mark has Jesus three times speak of his impending fate as Son of Man (Mark 8:31; 9:31; 10:33–34) and on each occasion has the disciples show they are blind to the values Jesus represents: Peter rebukes Jesus (Mark 8:32); the disciples argue about who among them will be the greatest (Mark 9:3–34); and James and John ask for the top positions in the kingdom (Mark 10:35–36). Luke, instead, has Jesus deal with the issue in his farewell words.

Reflection: What values are in collision in this chapter?

Making Money Work (Luke 19:1–27)

Listening to Luke

^{19:1} Having entered Jericho, when he was on his way through, ² a man named Zacchaeus, who was a chief tax collector and wealthy, ³ wanted to see who Jesus was and couldn't do so because of the crowd, for he was rather short. ⁴ So he ran on ahead of the crowd and climbed up a sycamore tree so he could see, because Jesus was about to come through that way. ⁵ Now when Jesus came to the place, he looked up and saw him and said, "Zacchaeus, quick, come down because I'm coming to stay at your house today." ⁶ So he hurried down and was glad to welcome him in.

⁷ All those who saw this started criticizing the fact that he was going in to be guest of a man who was a sinner. ⁸ But Zacchaeus stood up and said to the Lord, "Look, master, half my possessions I'll give to the poor, and, if I've defrauded anyone of anything, I'll pay them back fourfold." ⁹ Jesus said to him, "Today salvation has come about in this house, because he, too, is a son of Abraham; ¹⁰ for the Son of Man came to look for and save the lost."

¹¹ While they were listening to this, he went on to tell a parable because he was getting near Jerusalem and people were thinking that all of a sudden the kingdom of God was going to appear. ¹² So he said, "A certain nobleman went off to a faraway country to have himself appointed to a kingdom and then return. ¹³ Calling ten of his slaves together, he gave them ten minas [roughly a thousand days' wages] and told them, 'Do business with it till I return.'

¹⁴ "The citizens hated him and sent a delegation off after him with the message, 'We don't want this fellow ruling over us.'

¹⁵ "So when he returned, having been entrusted with his kingdom, he gave instructions for these slaves to whom he had given money to

be summoned, so he could find out what profit they had made. **¹⁶** The first came and said, 'Master, your mina has produced ten more minas.' **¹⁷** And he said to him, 'Well done, my good slave, you were reliable in a small task, now you can be in charge of ten towns.' **¹⁸** The second came and said, 'Your mina, master, has made five more minas.' **¹⁹** He told this man, 'You're to be in charge of five towns.'

²⁰ "Then another came and reported, 'Master, look, here's your mina, which I received and wrapped up in cloth. **²¹** I was scared because you're a hard man, and you take what you didn't deposit and you reap what you didn't sow.' **²²** He said to him, 'Based on words from your own mouth I condemn you, you wicked slave. Did you know I'm a hard man, taking what I didn't deposit and reaping where I hadn't sowed? **²³** Then why didn't you put my money in the bank? I could have then come and collected interest on it.' **²⁴** And he said to those present, 'Take the mina from him and give it to the guy who's got the ten minas'—**²⁵** they said to him, 'Master, he's already got ten minas'—**²⁶** 'I tell you, those who've got something will be given more and those who don't, even what they have will be taken away from them. **²⁷** But, as for these enemies of mine who don't want me to rule over them, bring them here and kill them in front of me.'"

Thinking About Luke

Luke now brings a story from an independent source and for this reason has relocated the healing of the blind man to when Jesus enters Jericho rather than to when he leaves, as originally in Mark. The story of Zacchaeus raises the issues again for which Jesus was criticized. What was he doing entering the house of someone apparently known to be corrupt, who then even confesses up to the fact? Luke had Jesus address that issue back in Luke 15 with the parables of the lost sheep, lost coin, and lost son. Normally an observant Jew would at least be hesitant to enter someone's house known to be a sinner. As Ps 26 puts it, "I do not sit with the worthless, nor do I consort with hypocrites; I hate the company of evildoers, and will not sit with the wicked" (Ps 26:4–5).

There is another connection with what precedes. Indeed, just a few verses earlier Luke had told the story of another rich man, a man of the ruling class, who asked Jesus how he might inherit eternal life and was then told that it entailed more than not breaking commandments. It entailed embracing the spirit behind the commandments such as being willing to care about the poor. He was not prepared to go that far (Luke 18:18–23). By contrast, Zacchaeus, who was even a leading tax collector, was prepared to make that change. He is the countermodel to that rich ruler. Salvation happened for him, and the evidence for it was his change of attitude towards wealth.

When Luke writes, literally, that salvation came about in Zacchaeus' house, he does not mean Jesus is salvation and so salvation came to his house when Jesus arrived. The salvation was about what happened to Zacchaeus. It is possible to read the story as though Zacchaeus was saying, I already give half my possessions to the poor, and pay back anyone I defraud, but that is very unlikely. Rather, Zacchaeus is portrayed as anything but generous and Luke's hearers would assume that he was a leader in exploitation.

The story assumes he must have known something of Jesus' message and there must have been conversation. We simply hear of the transformation. Salvation happened for Zacchaeus, and it did not happen for the rich man in the previous chapter. Then Luke has Jesus add: "because he, too, is a son of Abraham." This reflects the fact that Jesus saw his ministry as directed towards his fellow Jews, fellow descendants of Abraham. Matthew has Jesus express it more directly: "I was sent only to the lost sheep of the house of Israel" (Matt 15:24) and before Easter commissioned his disciples to confine their outreach similarly (Matt 10:5–6). As Luke has Jesus put it, "for the Son of Man came to look for and save the lost" (Luke 19:10). Reaching beyond the lost of Israel would come later. The message is: Zacchaeus belongs, too. He's not to be written off. No one is to be written off, not even someone like Zacchaeus.

Luke then reports Jesus' approach to Jerusalem and brings a parable that appears to play with some real history about Jerusalem which will have been familiar to some of Luke's (perhaps fellow) Jewish hearers. Josephus, the Jewish historian, writing about the same time as Luke, tells us what happened when King Herod the Great died in 4 BCE. His son Archelaus succeeded him and set off to Rome to be installed as king in his father's stead, while at the same time a delegation of citizens also went pleading that he not be made king, pointing to his known cruelty and corruption. Matthew also reflects this assessment of Archelaus when he writes of Joseph in his infancy story: "when he heard that Archelaus was ruling over Judea in place of his father Herod, he was afraid to go there" (Matt 2:22).

In fact, Archelaus was not appointed king but to the lesser status of ethnarch and even then not of all of his father's realm, but only Judea, Idumea, and Samaria, while other parts of his father's territory were allocated to his half-brothers, as tetrarchs. Antipas received Galilee and Perea; and Philip received the Golan Heights and northern Transjordan. After ten years, in 6 CE, the Romans deposed Archelaus on grounds of his cruelty and appointed their own prefects to run the territory, the best known in later years being Pilate.

It seems that the parable plays with details of what happened and was perhaps inspired by it, but it is making a rather different point. The motif of kingship will come again when Jesus is hailed as king at his entry to Jerusalem, but in the parable its significance is minor. To try to match up Jesus as king to the nobleman does not work, not least because the nobleman is cruel and exploitative. Nor is there a match up between the citizens rejecting him and people rejecting Jesus.

The focus is simply on slaves being given a huge amount of money. A mina was a hundred drachmas, so a hundred times an average day's wage. The task given them was: make money for me! Some did and some didn't. The message seems to be: followers of Jesus ought to get on with the mission of love and when he returns he will reward them. This may indicate the parable was generated not by Jesus himself but by preachers in the early church. In any case, it is a warning about being faithful and active followers and against doing nothing.

The parable is better known in the version that Matthew brings, which, on the one hand, lacks the echoes of history and, on the other, has the amounts given the slaves put in terms of talents. A talent in currency of the time was worth sixty minas. The message there, too, is a warning about making money, in other words, being active. In both parables the money appears to symbolize not an individual's talents and skills, but more like the gift of the Spirit, the richness of the gospel. What is a misreading of Matthew has led to "talents" being seen as one's natural gifts and abilities, also supporting a valid wisdom about putting them to good use, but not really what the parable appears to mean.

The cruel world of slavery is assumed as normal and serves as an image of discipleship. The massacre of dissenters was not unbelievable in their world and sadly a spirit not laid to rest in ours. Learning from love, we have to untangle the threads of wisdom from the parable and leave its violence behind. But perhaps, for Luke, that violence also points forward in the narrative at another level to the violence about to be inflicted on Jesus.

Reflection: Have you got talents or perhaps minas? What does that mean as Luke and Matthew portray it? What has it got to do with Zacchaeus's salvation?

5

Jesus and Jerusalem

Challenging the Jerusalem Authorities (Luke 19:28–48)

Listening to Luke

19:28 He said this and then made his way up to Jerusalem. **29** When he got close to Bethphage and Bethany, near the hill called the Mount of Olives, he sent off two of the disciples, **30** telling them, "Go into the village opposite, and, as you're entering it, you'll find a young donkey tethered there that no one has yet mounted. Untie it and bring it. **31** And if anyone asks you, 'Why are you untying it,' reply along the following lines: 'The master needs it.'" **32** So off they went on their commission and found it just like he'd told them. **33** As they were untying the young donkey, its owners said to them, "Why are you untying the donkey?" **34** And they said, "The master needs it."

35 So they brought it to Jesus and put their outer garments on it and mounted Jesus on it. **36** As he rode along, people spread their garments out on the road. **37** When he was already approaching the descent down the Mount of Olives, the whole mob of disciples started joyfully shouting praise to God for the wonders they had seen, **38** saying, "Blessed is the king who comes in the name of the Lord; peace in heaven and glory in the highest." **39** And some of the Pharisees in the crowd said to him, "Teacher, tell your disciples to stop."

⁴⁰ In response he said to them, "If they were to keep silent, the stones would shout out."

⁴¹ And when he came near and looked at the city, he wept over it, ⁴² saying, "If only you knew on this day what can lead to peace. But now it is hidden from your eyes. ⁴³ For the days are coming for you when your enemies will set up siege works around you and surround you and hem you in from all sides, ⁴⁴ and dash you and your children within you to the ground, and no stone will be left standing in you, because you did not recognize the time of your visitation."

⁴⁵ And entering the temple he started to expel those who were selling things ⁴⁶ and said to them, "It is written, 'My house shall be a house of prayer' but you have made it a brigands' den."

⁴⁷ And he was teaching daily in the temple, but the chief priests and scribes and leading citizens were wanting to do him in, ⁴⁸ but didn't find an opportunity to do so, because all the people were hanging on his words.

Thinking About Luke

Luke now returns to Mark, retelling the story of fetching the young donkey. Matthew recognizes what probably inspired the story, namely, the words of Zechariah the prophet,

> Rejoice greatly, O daughter Zion!
> Shout aloud, O daughter Jerusalem!
> Lo, your king comes to you;
> triumphant and victorious is he,
> humble and riding on a donkey,
> on a colt, the foal of a donkey. (Zech 9:9)

In the early retellings of Jesus' last days elements from Zechariah feature, including: "blood of my covenant" (Zech 9:11); striking the shepherd and scattering the sheep (Zech 13:7); and references to Judas's throwing his thirty pieces of silver into the treasury (Zech 11:7). Matthew follows his citation of Zech 9:9 by taking it very literally and reporting that Jesus sat on "them," the donkey and its foal!

Did Jesus enter Jerusalem seated on a young donkey or was that a story generated by what was read as prophecy? Zechariah's royal figure is a triumphant warrior, very different from Jesus, but quite possibly the saying inspired the picture.

Finding the young donkey might have been through some unreported prior arrangement. More likely Luke (and Mark) is implying miraculous foreknowledge. A major parade with Jerusalem's population lining the streets, a television spectacular, was highly unlikely. The Romans would have pounced. If there were some celebrations by Jesus' followers, hailing him as Messiah, as king, then it would likely have been a smaller event, not enough to warrant too much attention. The welcome matched what welcomed any pilgrim, using the words of Ps 118. "Blessed is the one who comes in the name of the Lord" (Ps 118:26), preceded by the cry "Save us," "Hosanna!" (Ps 118:25), which Mark brings but Luke omits. John's Gospel also recounts the scene, but suggests that these were responses from the crowd that the disciples understood only later and only then saw a connection with Zechariah (John 12:16).

The scene inspired retellings that celebrated faith and imagination as subsequent generations through to the present day have imagined themselves there joining in the celebration and waving palm branches, a detail Luke omits. Luke does, however, add his own touches and one of these is to have the crowd's acclamation, "Peace in heaven and glory in the highest," echo the song of the angels at Jesus' birth: "Glory to God in the highest and peace on earth to people who please him" (Luke 2:14). The return of the would-be king, Archelaus, reflected in the parable of the minas, brought slaughter, for which he was deposed in 6 CE. By contrast, Jesus is a king who brings peace, a contrast also to Rome's rule, whose propaganda claimed it as the bringer of peace.

Another added touch is the reference to Pharisees asking Jesus to shut his disciples up, to which Jesus replies that then the stones would start crying out (Luke 19:40). Luke then introduces material that reflects deep love for Jerusalem (Luke 19:41–44). He will do this again when he adds the scene of wailing women whom Jesus addresses on his way to his crucifixion with the words, "Daughters of Jerusalem, don't weep for me; but weep for yourselves and your children" (Luke 23:28).

Luke is retelling the story in the light of events that followed, in particular the sacking of Jerusalem and the destruction of the temple in 70 CE. Luke shows elsewhere that he envisages future hope as centered in Jerusalem, to which Jesus would return as the Messiah. He has Jesus foretell the disaster of 70 CE when the Romans laid siege to Jerusalem and finally turned the temple to ruin, massacring many Jews in the process. His comment that they had not recognized their visitation implies that, had they heeded God's call to peace and hope in Jesus, the disaster might never have occurred. Luke reflects on the disaster with great empathy while, like Matthew, still seeing Jerusalem's demise as God's judgment (Luke 21:22).

The reflection on those events continues when Luke returns to Mark and tells of Jesus' action in the temple. He has omitted much of Mark's story, including the symbolic cursing and withering of the fig tree and the suggestion that now a new community of faith would be a spiritual temple. He even trims the temple scene to Jesus expelling those who were selling things, not even mentioning what they were selling and omitting Jesus' overturning of the tables of the currency exchange people.

Mark has Jesus cite Isa 56:7, "My house shall be a house of prayer for all peoples," where Isaiah looks to the day when all nations would gather to worship God in the temple. Jesus' citing this passage is especially fitting given that he is speaking in the huge outer court of the temple where gentiles were welcome, the Court of the Gentiles. Mark will have in mind the expansion of the gospel to reach out to the gentiles, as he had prefigured it in the feeding of four thousand gentiles. Luke, however, had omitted that feeding with its symbolic significance in Mark and also trims back the quotation to leave out "for all peoples," probably because he knew he would be introducing that theme in his next book, Acts.

He retains, however, the second half of Jesus' statement, namely, "but you have made it a brigands' den." It is possible to translate the last two words as a "robbers' den." Some then think Mark and so Luke are having Jesus object to sellers overcharging, but that seems most unlikely. The word at stake was also used to describe bandits and revolutionaries and is used of those crucified for subversion either side of Jesus. Luke has been focusing on the Jewish revolt, which in its final stages had revolutionaries holed up in the temple. That was the tragedy that Luke has Jesus foresee and confront.

John's Gospel brings the temple confrontation in the first year of what it depicts as a three-year long ministry of Jesus. The others, who describe Jesus' ministry as lasting just one year, more plausibly place it in Jesus' last days. With it we again face the issue of what might have happened. It took place in the outer court of the temple some six football playing fields in size. It is highly unlikely that Jesus embarked on the massive task of clearing the whole area of merchants, not least because soldiers were stationed in the tower which overlooked it and would have pounced on such an act.

More likely is an action on the part of Jesus in one area of the court from which he could then disappear into the crowds, who quite possibly numbered thousands at the festival when Jerusalem was filled with Passover pilgrims. Some action, interpreted as an attack on the temple, is likely to have happened and helps explain why it featured in Jesus' demise. For any attack on the temple would also have been understood as an attack not only on the temple authorities but also on the imperial authorities, who saw the security of the temple as part of their responsibility.

Luke then follows Mark in mentioning that the temple authorities looked for an opportunity to do away with Jesus but found themselves constrained by the fact that he was so popular. He goes straight on from there in the following chapter to bring Mark's account of Jesus' disputes while teaching in the temple, omitting Mark's reflections on faith and community (Mark 11:20–25).

Reflection: Luke's account refers both to what happened and to what would happen in the following decades before Luke writes. What impact might Luke's way of telling the story have had on those who had known of or perhaps experienced such events?

Defending Jesus' Profile (Luke 20:1–44)

Listening to Luke

20:1 One day he was teaching the people in the temple and sharing with them the good news of the gospel when the chief priests and the scribes along with the elders confronted him **2** and said, "Tell us by what authority you are doing these things or who gave you this authority?" **3** In response he said to them, "Let me ask you a question, too. Tell me, **4** John's baptism, was it sanctioned by heaven or just a human initiative?"

5 They discussed it among themselves along the lines, "If we say by 'heaven,' he'll say: 'Then why didn't you believe him?' **6** But if we say it was a 'just a human initiative,' all the people will stone us, because they have come to believe that John was a prophet."

7 So they replied, "We don't know where he got it from." **8** Then Jesus said to them, "So nor will I tell you by what authority I'm doing these things."

9 And he began to tell the people this parable. "There was a man who planted a vineyard and leased it out to tenant farmers and went abroad for some time. **10** At the appropriate time he sent a slave to the tenants, so they'd give him what the vineyard had produced, but the tenants beat him up and sent him away with nothing. **11** Then he tried again sending a slave, but they beat him up, too, and sent him off humiliated and empty handed. **12** So he tried a third time, and they did the slave an injury and sent him cracking. **13** Then the master of the vineyard said, 'What am I going to do? I'll send my beloved son; perhaps they'll treat him fairly.'

14 "When the tenants saw him, they discussed among themselves as follows: 'He's the heir. Let's kill him so we can take his inheritance.' **15** And they took him outside the vineyard and killed him. What do you think the owner of the vineyard will do? [16] He'll go and kill these tenants and hand the vineyard over to others." Those listening to him said, "No way!"

[17] Looking at them, he said, "What's this scripture saying: 'The stone that the builders rejected, it's become the chief cornerstone'? [18] Everyone who stumbles over that stone will be smashed, and whomever it falls onto will be crushed."

[19] The scribes and the chief priests wanted to lay hands on him at that moment, but were scared how the crowds might react, because they recognized that he was telling the parable about them. [20] So they got people to spy on him and give the impression they were genuine, so that they could catch him out in what he was saying and so be able to hand him over to the power and authority of the governor. [21] They therefore put a question to him, "Teacher, we know that you are speaking and teaching with integrity and you're not beholden to trying to impress but are truthfully expounding the way of God. [22] Is it lawful for us to pay tax to the emperor or not?"

[23] Recognizing their strategy, he said to them, [24] "Show me a denarius. Whose image and inscription does it have?" They responded, "The emperor's." [25] Then he said, "Give to the emperor what is the emperor's and to God what is God's." [26] And they couldn't catch him out in what he said in front of the people and, marveling at his response, they said nothing.

[27] Then some Sadducees, who deny resurrection, approached him [28] and put to him the question: "Teacher, Moses wrote the rule for us, that if someone's brother dies who has a wife, but was childless, his brother should take the wife and raise up offspring for his brother. [29] Now there were seven brothers and the first took a wife but died childless; [30] so also the second [31] and then the third took her, and so also the rest of the seven, and died, not leaving any children. [32] Then later the woman also died. [33] Whose wife will she be at the resurrection? For all seven had had her as their wife."

[34] Jesus said to them, "People of this era marry and are given in marriage, [35] but those deemed worthy to reach that era and the resurrection from the dead neither marry nor are given in marriage, [36] because they can no longer die, but are like angels and are children of God, being children of the resurrection. [37] And the fact that the

dead are raised was something Moses indicated in the passage about the burning bush, when he says, 'Lord God of Abraham and God of Isaac and God of Jacob.' [38] God is God not of the dead but of the living, for all come to life through his agency." [39] Some of the scribes said in response, "Teacher, that was a good answer." [40] And they no longer dared to ask him anything.

[41] Then he said to them, "How come they say that the Messiah is David's son? [42] Because David himself says in the book of Psalms, 'The Lord said to my master, "Sit at my right hand [43] till I turn your enemies into a footstool for your feet."' [44] David calls him 'master'; so how can he be his son?"

Thinking About Luke

Luke now brings the episodes he found in Mark where Jesus found himself confronted with questions while teaching in the temple (Mark 11:27—12:37). The first is when his critics challenge him about his right to do what he did in the temple, reduced in Luke to expelling those who were selling things. Jesus' response of asking them in turn about John the Baptist's right to do what he did silences the critics. The story reminds us of the close links between Jesus and John the Baptist. There was nothing illegal about John's offering people God's forgiveness as they symbolically allowed him to immerse them in the Jordan, but it was unusual. Normally priests were the ones who were authorized to manage procedures such as sacrifices in order to gain forgiveness. Hence their unease, but at the same time their difficulty in challenging what John was doing.

The parable that follows uses vineyard imagery already employed by the prophet Isaiah to challenge Israel for its engagement in unjust behavior (Isa 5:1–7). There, the vineyard itself is a symbol of Israel. Here the focus is on the tenants. Unlike in Isaiah's image, the outcome is not the destruction of the vineyard for producing wild grapes, but the expulsion and execution of the tenants for being unwilling to give its owner some of its produce. Their behavior symbolizes past history in rejecting the prophets and their message, and most recently in rejecting John's message. Their killing the owner's son therefore reads as a reference to their response to Jesus.

If details are matched up and treated more like an allegory, not the usual way parables function, then the parable represents God's expectation that at least Israel's leaders should heed the call to uphold what is right. It then shows their failure coming to a climax in their rejection of Jesus as Son of God. Certainly, very early in the movement in the church's early decades, we find evidence that people saw Jesus as God's Son whom he sent into the world, such we see, for instance, already in Paul, who can write of God sending his Son (Gal 4:4). Luke, like Mark, has Jesus declared to be God's beloved Son at his baptism. The parable may well therefore have come into being in its current form in these early years of the church, although it could potentially have had its origins with Jesus at the level of a typically confronting parable rather than an allegory. Read as an allegory, the ending, which indicates handing over the vineyard to new tenants, would amount to a claim to leadership of Israel now by the church and its leaders.

In Mark, the appended quotation from Ps 118:22 about the rejected stone becoming the cornerstone of a new building hints at the replacement of the temple by the new faith community of disciples, a key theme in this and following chapters in Mark. The Hebrew word for stone, *eben*, is so close to the word for son, *ben*, that behind its use here is a deliberate play on words. Jesus the son/stone is the foundation of a new building not made with hands, a new temple.

Luke, who does not take up the imagery of the church as a new temple, instead uses the image to speak about judgment, indicating that this rock would bring a shattering and a crushing of the critics, hinting at the belief that Jesus would come as judge and Son of Man to execute judgment.

Luke then adds to Mark's observation that his critics knew the parable was directed at them, by suggesting that they therefore decided to get people to spy on Jesus to try to get evidence that would have him arrested. This is a fair interpretation of what ensues, because the attempt is made to trap Jesus into saying something that could be reported to the authorities. Again, however, he meets the challenge. His response could be read as separating obedience to the Roman authorities from obedience to God, as if to divide life into civil and spiritual realms. It can then be used as a basis for arguing that faith has nothing to do with politics, the political sphere having its own separate values. Jesus' response, however, is more subtle, because in reality all belongs to God.

The Sadducees then approach with a question designed to ridicule belief in resurrection. Jesus' response is instructive and corrects what many still assume to be belief in resurrection, namely that it means the physical body coming back to life again in the same way as before. This was not how they saw it. When Paul, for instance, speaks of resurrection in 1 Cor 15, he does not mean such resuscitation, as though people simply reappear with the same kind of body that they now have. Instead, he speaks of people's corpses being transformed into a spiritual body. This is assumed also in the stories of Jesus' resurrection, where he has a spiritual body that has the ability to appear and disappear.

Because they believed it will not be the same kind of body that people have now, some of the features that characterize human bodies in the present will no longer apply. That includes having sex, so they will not marry. They will be, as Mark, and so Luke, explains, like angels. This answers the Sadducees ridiculing question, which also assumes bodies will be as they are now.

Luke adds to Mark the comment that they will, like angels, not die and so adds that as a reason why sex is not needed. This reflects a limited understanding of sexual relations, as primarily for reproductive purposes, a widespread view among many, including Greco-Roman philosophers of the time, who frowned on sex for pleasure or sex as an expression of intimacy and closeness, as Gen 2 assumes and affirms. The whole notion of the age to come as one where sex will have no role could easily lead people to denigrate sexuality, and some went on to argue that all should already behave in the way they will in the age to come and so abstain from sexual relations altogether. Paul found himself in 1 Cor 7 having to push back against such views and explain that this might be an option for some, but for others marriage and sexual relations belonged to God's good creation and were not to be denigrated (1 Cor 7:7; a view also countered in Matt 19:10–12).

There would have been many arguments with Sadducees about resurrection over the years and not all of them would be convincing. That would apply to the reference to God as the God of Abraham, Isaac, and Jacob, which originally is not a reference to their being alive, but for the sake of argument was read as indicating that they were, at least in a waiting state before resurrection.

Belief in resurrection of the dead arose in part from the conviction that where life has been unfair and unjust it must some day be put right, if not in this age, then in the age to come. While there is evidence that Jews, like many cultures in their world, had some belief in a survival after death, usually in the form of a half-conscious life, if justice was to be done, people would have to front up in person before God for reward or condemnation. For that they would need to have the equipment that embodiment brings. So, they would need to be raised up from the dead and have a body.

This belief sometimes envisaged a resurrection of the good to join the living and enjoy the reign of the coming Messiah and only thereafter join everyone else for the day of judgment. There were in fact diverse notions about how the future would look. Generally, however, there was the belief that people would have to be really present in the end to face God, and to be really present had to mean to be present with eyes to see, ears to hear, and feelings to experience what was about to happen to them. Their resurrection body would make all this possible, while at the same time not having other physical aspects, including sexuality. Hope often led to imagination of what might be and could produce an array of images and ideas. Behind them all, the wonderful and the weird, is a firmer ground, namely that in the end there is God and God cares and in God we can trust both for this life and the life beyond.

The following episode in Mark has a teacher of the Law ask Jesus about the greatest commandment (Mark 12:28–34). Luke leaves this out because he had already used it to introduce the parable of the good Samaritan, which he has Jesus use to expound what the second greatest commandment (loving one's neighbor) and being a loving neighbor means (Luke 10:25–28). Luke even changes the question with which the teacher approaches Jesus in Mark, "What is the first commandment of all?" (Mark 12:25). He replaces it by the question that the rich man of the ruling class had brought to Jesus: "Good teacher, what do I need to do to inherit eternal life?" (Luke 18:18). Thus, the introduction that leads to the parable of the good Samaritan reads: "Teacher, what do I have to do to inherit eternal life?" (Luke 10:25).

The final episode, as in Mark, has Jesus challenge the notion that the Messiah was to be seen as Son of David (Luke 20:41–44; Mark 35–37). It does so on the basis of the view of that time that David wrote the Psalms, and so points to the fact that in Ps 110:1 the author, which the superscription to the psalm claims to be David, reports what God said to David's master or lord. Psalm 110:1 was one of the most widely used passages to explain the significance of Jesus' resurrection as God enthroning him as the Messiah: "The Lord said to my master, 'Sit at my right hand till I turn your enemies into a footstool for your feet.'"

We now recognize that, while some psalms might possibly go back to David, most do not but come from later times, including Ps 110. We can nevertheless seek to appreciate why the argument against the adequacy of the title Son of David came to be made. We appear to be dealing here with a reflection, arising from within the early church, that Son of David did not adequately capture Jesus' true identity. That Jesus was Son of David, meaning the Messiah (anointed one) of David's line, was widely assumed and is reflected in the Gospel traditions. The church, however, would come to see that Jesus had to be seen as more than the Jewish Messiah. His importance as bearer of God's word and wisdom would not be able to be communicated to a wider non-Jewish world if such categories remained dominant. Indeed, Messiah—Greek *Christos*, which comes through into English as Christ—soon lost its Jewish royal messianic meaning, and became more like a surname, as people moved from speaking of Jesus the Christ to speaking of him simply as Jesus Christ.

Reflection: What significance might the issues Luke portrays Jesus as facing have had for his audience? What significance might they have for our day?

Reflecting on Demise and Imagining Hope (Luke 20:45—21:38)

Listening to Luke

20:45 While all the people were listening, he said to his disciples, **46** "Beware of the scribes who like to walk around in robes and want to be greeted in the marketplaces and have the best seats in the synagogues and the best places at feasts, **47** who also devour widows' households and for show pray long prayers. They'll face even greater condemnation than others."

21:1 Then he looked up and saw rich people putting their gifts into the receptacles for offerings. **2** He saw also a poor widow there putting in two little coins, **3** and said, "Truly I'm telling you, this poor widow just put in more than all the rest. **4** For they were all contributing from what was spare cash for their offering, but she out of her poverty contributed her whole livelihood."

5 When some were talking about the temple, how it was adorned with magnificent stones and dedicated gifts, he said, **6** "The days are coming when all you're looking at will be left with no stone now resting on another that won't be not toppled down." **7** They asked him, "Teacher, when will this happen and what will be the indication that it's about to occur?" **8** He said, "Watch out you're not led astray, because many will come in my name saying, 'I'm the one' and 'The moment has come.' Don't go after them. **9** When you hear of wars and uprisings, don't panic; this all needs to take place first, but it doesn't mean the end will suddenly be then."

10 Then he said to them, "Nation will rise up against nation and kingdom against kingdom, **11** and there will be big earthquakes and famines and pandemics in various places, terrifying things and great portents coming out of the sky. **12** And before all this, they'll lay their hands on you and persecute you, hauling you up before their synagogues and into prisons, dragging you before kings and governors because of my name, [13] and it will be an opportunity for you to testify. [14] Get it into your heads not to rehearse what you will offer in your defense, [15] because I'll give you something to say and wisdom that all your opponents won't be able to resist or refute. [16] You'll be handed over by your parents and siblings and relatives and friends, and some of you they'll kill, [17] and you'll be hated by everyone because of my name. [18] But not one hair of your head will perish. [19] By perseverance you'll manage to keep hold of your lives.

[20] "When you see Jerusalem encircled by armies, then know that its devastation is close. [21] Then those in Judea should escape to the hill country and those inside the city should get out and those out on the land shouldn't enter it, [22] because these are days when she will be facing divine vengeance in fulfillment of all that is written. [23] Pity those who are pregnant and those breastfeeding babies in those days, because enormous distress will come to the land and divine anger expressed towards this people, [24] and they'll fall by the sword and be taken captive into all the gentile lands and Jerusalem will be trampled down by the nations until the times set for gentile domination are over. [25] There will be portents in the sun and the moon and the stars, and on earth the nations will face distress at not knowing what it is about, and the sea and the waves will roar, [26] with people fainting from fear and anxiety about what is coming over the world, for the powers of the heavens will be shaken. [27] Then they will see 'the Son of Man coming in a cloud' with power and great glory, [28] and when these things start happening, stand up and lift up your heads because your liberation is at hand."

[29] And he told them a parable. "Look at the fig tree and all trees. [30] When they are sprouting and you notice it, you know that summer is coming. [31] So, also when you see these things happening, know that the kingdom of God is near. [32] Truly I tell you, this generation will not pass away before all this happens. [33] Heaven and earth will pass away, but my words will never pass away.

[34] "Watch you never let your minds be swamped with hangovers or drunkenness or day-to-day worries and then have that day suddenly spring on you [35] like a trap, because it's coming upon all who dwell on the face of the earth. [36] So stay awake and always pray that you'll have

the strength to escape from all that's going to happen and be able to take your stand before the Son of Man."

³⁷ During the day he was teaching in the temple and overnight he would go out and stay on the hill called the Mount of Olives. ³⁸ And in the morning all the people would get up early to come and listen to him in the temple.

Thinking About Luke

Jesus' warnings about the hypocrisy of some scribes belongs closely to what follows. In contrast to their hypocrisy and grandstanding and their exploitation of the poor, including widows living in poverty, Jesus highlights such a widow's authentic devotion. The contrast is stark and feeds then into what follows, where Luke has Jesus go on to predict the disasters that would befall Jerusalem and its people.

Predictions about the future as they would have been seen by a famous figure of the past were a standard feature of ancient biography. Sometimes such advice for future generations was written up as separate works in themselves, often called testaments. The Testaments of the Twelve Patriarchs, for instance, which took its final form in the second century CE but had its origin in the previous century, presents the parting advice of each of the twelve sons of Jacob. Among the Gospels we see various attempts to represent what the authors believed would have been Jesus' parting advice. In Mark it is chapter 13. Matthew expands what he found in Mark 13 with an additional chapter (Matt 24–25). Luke revises and expands Mark 13 here in Luke 21, but also has Jesus give parting advice during his last meal with the disciples (Luke 22:24–38). In John's Gospel we have the most extensive attempt, which runs from John 13 to John 17.

Luke, writing probably in the 80s CE, reworks what Mark wrote around 70 CE in the light of what he and his hearers will have experienced or heard about, especially in the intervening years, not least the destruction of the temple and capture of Jerusalem in 70 CE and its aftermath. One of the key changes that Luke has made is that instead of having Jesus' words addressed just to Peter and Andrew and James and John on their own outside the temple (Mark 13:1–3), Luke has Jesus utter them in the temple for all the Jerusalem crowd to hear (Luke 21:5–6).

Luke follows Mark in the first section, which predicts the destruction of the temple. Mark has Jesus warn of people who would come claiming to be himself or the Messiah (Mark 13:6). Luke repeats this, but adds that they would also be saying that, effectively, with the destruction of the temple, the end was at hand (Luke 21:8). Mark appears to have Jesus ward off those claiming to be the Messiah during the revolt (Mark 13:6). Luke follows Mark in this and in having Jesus say that the destruction of the temple did not herald the end, but he adds that Jesus also warned people off from believing that the end of the world would follow closely after the destruction of the temple, as Mark appeared to imply, because Luke knew that this had not been the case.

In the interim, before the end of the world and Jesus' return, his followers would be subject to trial, persecution, and sometimes death. Luke had previously reported Jesus' words assuring the disciples that when they faced trials, they need not be anxious about how to respond because the Spirit would guide them about what to say (Luke 12:11–12). For that he drew on the source he shared with Matthew (Matt 10:19–20). He now brings Mark's version of the same advice in which Jesus promises that he himself would help them (Mark 13:11). It was not uncommon to merge these two ways of speaking, namely of the risen Jesus and of the Spirit, because ultimately it was about God's help.

Mark has Jesus refer to the presence of a sacrilegious image in the temple (Mark 13:14), imagery based on Dan 9:27. Daniel uses the image to speak of the erection on the altar in the Jerusalem temple of a sacrilegious image by Antiochus IV Epiphanes of the Seleucid dynasty of Syria which controlled Judea. It provoked the revolt of 167–64 BCE. Its equivalent in the first century CE would have been a similar action carried out or intended by the Roman authorities. We know of the Emperor Caligula's failed attempt in the 40s CE to have an image of himself as Zeus erected in the temple. Even placing military standards with their emblems often reflecting images of gods in the temple would have been an outrage. Mark may well have had in mind similar provocation, perhaps at the moment when Jerusalem fell.

Luke omits the reference altogether and instead has Jesus refer to the siege of Jerusalem and its impending devastation and urges people to escape for their lives. Luke's additions at this point are instructive. He adds in Luke 21:22 that what was to happen would be an expression of God's judgment on the inhabitants of Jerusalem, who in Luke are those who are listening. He then adds additional material in Luke 21:23–24, which mentions slaughter but also people being taken away as prisoners. Perhaps he was aware that some were taken to be slaves and worked on the construction of the Colosseum in Rome.

He also adds in Luke 21:24 an explanation that portrays these events as somehow divinely planned. There was a time allotted for gentiles to trample down Jerusalem, but this allocated period would come to an end. A little later, he indicates that this will occur when Jesus returns to Jerusalem as Son of Man and liberates it, good news for Jerusalem's inhabitants who survive.

Luke then leaves out the section in Mark about the coming afflictions being the worst ever experienced and God's shortening the time to enable people to survive (Mark 13:19–20) and also omits the warnings about false prophets performing signs and wonders and predictions cited from Isa 13:10 and 34:4 (Mark 13:24–25), except for reference to the powers of the heavens being shaken (Isa 34:4b). Instead, he moves straight to Mark's reference to the Son of Man coming in a cloud (Luke 21:27), an allusion to the book of Daniel and its depiction of one like a human (like a son of man) to whom God would give authority to rule after a succession of empires led by emperors depicted as animals (Dan 7:13). This image of the one like a human being then became the inspiration for the expectation that one day this son of man, entitled the Son of Man and sometimes identified with the hope for the Messiah, would come as God's agent to rule. This, therefore, came also to be a way of speaking of Jesus and his return to act as God's agent.

Luke omits the detail in Mark about the Son of Man sending angels out to gather the elects from all corners of the earth (Mark 13:27), possibly because he sees the Son of Man's action first as returning on earth to Jerusalem as he will explain. Instead, he addresses his Jerusalem hearers with the promise: "When these things start happening stand up and lift up your heads because your liberation is at hand" (Luke 21:28). Luke envisages Jesus' return to liberate Jerusalem and rule there as God's Messiah. This had been the hope of the faithful Jews who, according to Luke, surrounded Jesus' birth and hailed him as their Messiah (Luke 1:69; 2:25, 38). It is reflected as a hope also in Luke's account of the disciples on the road to Emmaus, who expressed their hope that Jesus would liberate Israel (Luke 24:21) and at the beginning of Acts where the disciples ask him, "Lord, is this the time when you will restore the kingdom to Israel?" to which he replies that they are not to know the timing, reflecting the assumption that it would certainly happen (Acts 1:6–7).

Luke then returns to Mark in 21:29, using the image of trees beginning to shoot as indicating summer is approaching to say that the events mentioned should be read as indicating that the end is near, which only Luke describes as the nearness of the kingdom of God (Luke 21:31). He then takes up Mark's prediction that this would happen within a generation.

Luke then concludes his account of Jesus' predictions for the future with the exhortation that people make sure they are ready for it, because it might come all of a sudden. They should make sure they won't be caught napping or, worse still, preoccupied with self-indulgence. Rather they should be praying that they may survive, to be able to stand with confidence before the Son of Man. Luke envisages that some of those listening to Jesus daily in the temple would be able to do so, underlining the fact that for Luke these predictions and promises are directed not to a small in-group of disciples, as in Mark, but to the inhabitants of Jerusalem, the city that, on his understanding, would take central place in the coming reign of Jesus the Son of Man on his return.

It is very likely that Jesus issued warnings about what might befall Jerusalem and its temple, but whatever he might have said, it was then developed, as was the custom of biographers of famous people, into a full-blown final speech directed to future generations. Belief that God cared inspired the imagination about what might come. There is evidence that they lived in an era and among circles that did not see history lasting long. Luke can still have Jesus predict, like Mark, that what they were imagining would all take place within their lifetime. Paul too thought Jesus would return in his lifetime (1 Thess 4:15; 1 Cor 15:51). These projections of hope have proved to be mistaken, as one might expect when people imagined the future within the limits of the knowledge and faith of their time.

As we no longer see the world as flat and its universe as but a few thousand years old, so we are not able to share their projections about the future. What we can share is the one firm detail in which we can trust, namely that in the end there is God and God cares. And while we will not likely share Luke's particular view that Jesus would liberate Jerusalem and make it his capital, we can embrace the vision of the kingdom that will mean good news for the poor and engage ourselves in that hope as our agenda. We do so, too, in the light of opposing trends, not least, as we face new forms of violence done to people and pollution done to our planet.

Reflection: How did Luke envisage the events of his era and how it would end? How can we relate to such a vision in ways that acknowledge its limitations?

Jesus' Last Meal (Luke 22:1–21)

Listening to Luke

22:1 The Festival of Unleavened Bread called the Passover was approaching. **2** And the chief priests and the scribes were looking for a suitable way to kill him, because they were afraid of the people. **3** Then Satan entered Judas, called Iscariot, who was numbered among the twelve; **4** and he went off and spoke with the chief priests and officers about how he might hand him over to them. **5** And they were glad and agreed to pay him for it. **6** So he went along with the arrangement and looked for an opportune time to betray him to them without the crowd knowing.

7 The first day of the Festival of Unleavened Bread arrived when the Passover lambs were to be sacrificed. **8** So Jesus sent off Peter and John, instructing them, "Go and prepare for us to eat the Passover meal." **9** They said to him, "Where do you want us to get it ready?" **10** He told them, "Look, as you enter the city, a fellow will meet you carrying a pitcher of water. Follow him into the house he goes into, **11** and you'll say to the head of the house, 'The teacher is asking you, "Where's the room where I'm going to eat the Passover meal with my disciples?"' **12** And he will show you a big furnished room upstairs. Make the preparations there." **13** So they set off and found things just as he had told them and prepared the Passover meal.

14 When the time came, he took his place at the meal along with the apostles **15** and said to them, "I've been very much looking forward to sharing this Passover meal with you before I suffer, **16** because, I tell you, I'll not eat it again until it is fulfilled in the kingdom of God. **17** And taking a cup and giving thanks, he said, "Take this and share it among yourselves, **18** because I'm telling you, from now on I'll not be drinking from the fruit of the vine until the kingdom of God comes."

¹⁹ Then, taking a loaf of bread and giving thanks, he broke it up and gave it to them saying, "This is my body given for you. Do this in my memory," **²⁰** and similarly the cup after the meal, saying, "This cup is the new covenant in my blood poured out for you. **²¹** But look, the hand of the one who is betraying me is with me at the table."

Thinking About Luke

Luke identifies the Festival of Unleavened Bread with Passover. Strictly speaking, the festival lasts seven days and begins with Passover Day (Lev 23:4–6). Passover celebrates Israel's rescue from Egypt, when according to the ancient story God brought death on Egyptian families but passed over the homes of Israelites (Exod 12:12–13). It takes place on the 14th day of the Jewish month of Nisan, roughly equivalent to March or April in our calendar year.

In the way they reckoned days, a day ran from sunset to sunset, so Passover Day began after sundown and its first event was the Passover meal, which remains a central Jewish festival. The meal itself comprises roast lamb accompanied by additional items such as bitter herbs, and four glasses of wine drunk at various stages of the ritual.

Following Mark, Luke has Jesus celebrate Passover with his disciples (on Thursday evening by our reckoning) before facing his arrest, trial, and execution also on Passover Day (for us Friday, the next day). While agreeing that Jesus died on the Friday, John's Gospel differs in saying that this took place on the day before Passover, which began that Friday evening and continued the next day and so was a Sabbath Day. Then the final meal in John was not a Passover meal, but rather Jesus was killed at the time when the Passover lambs would have been slaughtered, on the day before Passover Day, the so-called Day of Preparation. Uncertainty remains about who was right historically. Did John's tradition want to portray Jesus as the Passover lamb? Or did Mark's tradition want to associate Jesus' last meal and so its celebration as the Eucharist with the Passover?

The exact year, traditionally 33 CE, continues to be subject to debate, not least because Jesus' birth was before Herod the Great's death in 4 BCE, so that many now date Jesus' death as occurring in 29 CE, or it could be earlier, if Jesus was thirty when he commenced his ministry (Luke 3:23) and it lasted just one year, as the first three Gospels suggest, rather than the three years that John suggests.

Basically, Luke follows Mark in the events that follow, but also makes some minor adjustments. He begins like Mark with another reference to the intent on the part of the temple authorities to have Jesus killed and their concern at the same time not to do so publicly for fear of the crowd's response. Luke then omits Mark's story about the woman who anointed Jesus (Mark 12:3-9), because he had brought a version of that story much earlier in Luke 7:36-50. Instead, he goes straight on to the report about Judas's initiative to help the authorities, which follows well after the statement about the authorities' concerns.

Nothing is said about Judas's motive for doing so. Luke adds that Satan, understood as the chief of demonic powers, entered and inspired him, but that still does not tell us why. Was Judas resenting Jesus for some reason? Was he wanting to provoke him (or God) to respond with divine intervention? Nothing suggests so. Was it for personal reward? Again, nothing suggests so. Like the other Gospel writers, Luke simply presents Judas as wicked.

Luke's modification of the story of arrangements for the Passover is that he names Peter and John as those whom Jesus sent. Like the story of finding the young donkey in Luke 19:29-34, this does not read like good prior arrangement but as an exercise of inspired foreknowledge. Jesus and the disciples then come and take their place at the meal table for Passover, literally: they recline, as was the custom, around a low table.

There follows Luke's version of what became the basis for the celebration of Holy Communion, the story of Jesus' last meal with his disciples. For his retelling, Luke clearly has access not only to Mark but also to a tradition close to what Paul recalls in 1 Cor 11:23-26. We might have expected some reference to elements in the Passover Seder, the ritual followed in celebrating Passover, but at most the fact that Luke refers not to one but to two cups may echo that ritual. Otherwise, nothing suggests the meal was a Passover meal and perhaps originally it was not.

Luke' reference to two cups, one before the offering of the bread and one after, led to some revision in the manuscript tradition, probably in response to the doubling of the cups, which some must have seen as a mistake. Accordingly, some ancient manuscripts end the report after Jesus offers the bread, omitting the second cup and the words accompanying it. That did not really fix the problem because it then meant that Luke got the events in the wrong order: the cup before the bread! More probably, the longer version is what Luke wrote and the reference to the first cup belongs to the addition he brings where he portrays Jesus' attitude to this as his final Passover meal.

Right from the outset Luke sets this meal in relation to the hope of the kingdom of God (Luke 22:16). There were also other Jewish groups who held meals—including with bread and wine—that foreshadowed the hope they held for the future, when they and their group would feast together in the kingdom of God. Jesus and his group were no different except that the future hope was not exclusive, but a feast of hope to which all were invited. It is one of Jesus' favorite ways of speaking about future hope, whether in sayings or in parables.

In Mark, the reference to the future comes at the end of the account where it is attached to Jesus' words about the cup: "Truly I tell you, I won't be drinking of the fruit of the vine anymore until that day when I drink it anew in the kingdom of God" (Mark 14:25). Luke has it there as well as in Jesus' initial statement about eating the Passover in 22:16. Luke thus underlines that the basic meaning of the meal is its foreshadowing of the vision of the kingdom of hope, bringing about change, peace, and justice. To participate in it is to embrace that hope and make it our agenda, for which it also nourishes us.

The novel component in this meal of hope is the personal way in which Jesus tweaks it. At his last meal with his disciples, he not only looks forward, he also presents himself to them as he had done during his ministry. He indicates that he was giving his life for it and for them, identifying himself with the gifts of bread and wine, and inviting them to participate in what he was doing.

In portraying this, Luke's account has Jesus first offer a cup (probably understood as one of the four cups of the Passover meal ritual) and invites them to share it and repeats the reference to the future hope but now not referring to eating the Passover in future but to drinking the wine in future. Only then does Jesus take a loaf of bread, give thanks, and break it up, as one might normally have done at the beginning of a meal, saying grace, as we might put it. We are almost certainly dealing with unleavened bread, flat bread, like a pizza base. Over time one way of referring to the meal was "breaking bread" (e.g., Luke 24:35; Acts 2:42).

While one might see in the breaking a symbol of Jesus going to be broken, none of the accounts put the focus on the breaking itself or just on it. Rather, the focus is the sharing and what is being shared. Mark has Jesus declare: "This is my body" (Mark 14:22). Paul has a longer form: "This is my body for you" (1 Cor 11:24), and Luke has a fuller form: "This is my body given for you," and like Paul, he has Jesus add: "Do this in my memory" (Luke 22:19).

Like Paul, Luke thus has the meal also be a way of remembering Jesus, looking back to the past. This adds to the focus on the future, already implicit in the meal. The words with which Jesus identifies himself with the bread and the wine indicate also a reference to the present, giving rise to our designating the meal as a Communion. It has, therefore, future, past, and present dimensions.

What exactly Jesus meant by his words linked to the bread and the cup has been a source of controversy down through the ages. Some of this has been the result of taking the statements literally, as if bread ceases to be bread and becomes Jesus' actual body and the wine, his blood, a miraculous event that implies Jesus is present in physical form. This is almost certainly not what is meant, but we should respect that people's sense of Jesus' presence among them in this celebration would quite easily have generated such an explanation. It is best to read it as Jesus saying: "This is me. I am giving my life for you, as I also have done in my ministry. Feed on who I am and this vision for which I now lay down my life."

As people came to see Jesus' death as unleashing change and explained it as doing what people believed sacrifices did, namely changing things, so people could see this meal as a sacrificial meal. This was all the more so because it was common as part of an act of sacrifice that those sacrificing also engaged in a meal in which they fed on the body of the animal which had been sacrificed and now provided food. Luke's expansions of Jesus' body "given for you," and especially of his blood "poured out for you," reflect sacrificial language.

The reference to covenant may well also have evoked the imagery of covenant sacrifices, which accompanied agreements or covenants and included shared meals as an aspect of celebrating coming to an agreement. We read of such sacrifices at the celebration of God's covenant with Israel (Exod 24:5–8), which may well lie behind the account in Mark. In Luke and Paul, however, it seems that Jeremiah's prophecy of a new covenant that would bring change (Jer 31:31–33) lies behind their depiction of Jesus' words, when he refers to "the new covenant" in his blood. The promise of the coming kingdom of God was indeed something new and included the promise of forgiveness and renewal.

This second sharing of a cup in Luke, in which Jesus speaks of the new covenant, comes "after the meal," as does the sharing of the cup in Paul's account (1 Cor 11:25). Both assume that between the breaking of the bread and this sharing of the cup there was a meal. The two acts did not occur together in close succession. The breaking of the bread was at the start of the meal. Only at the end of the meal was the cup of wine then shared.

Our Holy Communion, Mass, or Eucharist has both actions occur together, and it seems that already in Paul's day they had been brought together as a single ritual at the end of a meal, such as is assumed in Paul's comments in 1 Cor 11. Over time, the two acts came to be separated from a meal altogether, such as has then become the norm through to our own day. That indirectly contributed to putting the focus on the substance of what was eaten rather than the action of sharing, and led also, for instance, in Matthew, to changes in the wording. Thus, Matthew has Jesus' words have a matching form: "Take, eat. This is . . ." and "Drink . . . . This is . . . ."

In his own way, Luke allows us to see that what has become a ritual celebration remains a commitment to future hope and change, so central to his depiction of Jesus, a celebration of belonging and being nourished in the present, and a way of remembering that did much more than remember.

In Mark, Jesus announces that one of the disciples would betray him before going on to share himself with them in bread and wine. Luke has reversed the order, which adds to the drama. For immediately after Luke has Jesus share himself in bread and wine with his disciples, he speaks about one of them sharing that meal who was going to betray him. It was a dramatic turn of events. It will introduce the next section, to which we now turn.

Reflection: What is the focus of Jesus' last meal in Luke? How might this inform the way we celebrate and understand the celebration of Holy Communion to which it gave rise?

Falsely Charged with Subversion (Luke 22:22–71)

Listening to Luke

22:22 "The Son of Man is going as was foreordained, but woe betide that man through whom he is betrayed." **23** And they started questioning each other about who from among them it would be who was going do this.

24 And a dispute broke out among them as to who among them was to be counted the greatest. **25** He said to them, "The kings of the gentiles love to exercise power over them and those in authority over them love to be called benefactors. **26** But it's not to be like that with you. Rather the greatest among you, let him be like the more junior and the leader like a slave. **27** Who is the greater, the one with a place at the table or the one serving him? Isn't it the one with a place at the table, but I am among you as one who serves.

28 "You've stuck with me in the tough times I've faced; **29** so I'm entrusting you, the way my Father entrusted me, namely, with responsibility to rule a kingdom, **30** so that you may eat and drink at my table in my kingdom, and you shall sit on thrones to exercise judgment over the twelve tribes of Israel.

31 "But Simon, Simon, look out, because Satan is wanting to sift you guys like wheat, **32** but I have prayed for you, yourself, that your faith not fail and that one day you'll return to strengthen your brothers." **33** He said to him, "Lord, I'm ready even to go to jail with you and to face death." **34** Jesus said, "I'm telling you, Peter, the rooster won't have crowed today before you will have denied you know me three times."

35 And he told them, "When I sent you off without a bag and backpack and sandals, were you missing anything?" They answered, "Nothing." **36** He then said to them, "But now, whoever's got a bag, let him take it, likewise a backpack, and anyone without a sword, let him sell his cloak and buy one. ³⁷ I'm telling you, what's been written about me has to happen, namely the bit about being 'counted among the lawless,' because things written about me are coming to their fulfillment." ³⁸ They said to him, "Lord, look, we've got two swords."

He said to them, "That'll do."

³⁹ Then he left and went, as he usually did, to the Mount of Olives, and his disciples followed him. ⁴⁰ Reaching his spot, he told them, "Pray that you won't face testing times."

⁴¹ And he himself went off from them on his own about a stone's throw away and, kneeling down, he started praying, ⁴² "Father, if you're willing, take this cup from me; but let not my will but yours be done." [⁴³ And an angel from heaven appeared, strengthening him. ⁴⁴ And becoming distressed, he was praying very intensely and his sweat fell to the ground like drops of blood.] ⁴⁵ Then he got up from praying and came to the disciples and found them sleeping because of grief, ⁴⁶ and said to them, "Why are you sleeping? Get up and pray that you won't face testing times."

⁴⁷ Then, while he was still speaking, a crowd turned up and the man called Judas, one of the twelve, was leading them and approached Jesus to kiss him. ⁴⁸ Jesus said to him, "Judas, are you betraying the Son of Man with a kiss?" ⁴⁹ When those around him saw what was going to happen, they said, "Lord, shall we give them a whack with our sword?" ⁵⁰ And one of them struck the high priest's slave and cut off his right ear, ⁵¹ in response to which Jesus then said, "Enough of that!" and, touching his ear, healed him. ⁵² Then Jesus said to the chief priests and temple officers and elders who had all come along, "Have you come out with swords and clubs as if against a bandit? ⁵³ I was there with you day after day teaching in the temple and you didn't lay a hand on me, but this is your moment and the power of darkness."

⁵⁴ Arresting him, they took him off and brought him to the high priest's house. Now Peter was following them at a distance. ⁵⁵ And people had lit a fire in the middle of the forecourt and had sat around it and Peter sat down with them. ⁵⁶ One of the female slaves, seeing him in the light of the fire and having a good look at him, said, "This guy was also with him." ⁵⁷ Peter denied it, saying, "Ma'am, I don't know the

fellow." ⁵⁸ And quite soon after another who saw him said, "You're also one of them." Peter replied, "Look mate, I'm not."

⁵⁹ And about an hour later another person insisted, "This fellow really was with him; after all, he's a Galilean." ⁶⁰ Peter said, "Mate, I don't know what you're talking about." Then immediately, while he was saying that, the rooster crowed. ⁶¹ And the Lord turned round and looked at Peter and Peter remembered the Lord's prediction, how he told him, "The rooster won't have crowed today before you'll have denied me three times." ⁶² And Peter went outside and cried his eyes out.

⁶³ The men who had charge of Jesus were ridiculing him and beating him, ⁶⁴ and blindfolding him, they asked him, "Prophesy: who hit you?" ⁶⁵ And they hurled abused at him in lots of other ways.

⁶⁶ And when day came, the people's council of elders assembled, including the chief priests and scribes, and they brought him before the council, ⁶⁷ and said to him, "If you're the Messiah, tell us." He answered, "If I tell you, you won't believe me; ⁶⁸ and if I question you, you won't respond. ⁶⁹ But from now on the Son of Man will be seated at the right hand of the power of God." ⁷⁰ All of them then said, "Then are you the Son of God?" He replied, "You're saying I am." ⁷¹ They said, "Why do we need any more evidence? We've heard it ourselves from his own mouth."

Thinking About Luke

As we noted at the end of the previous section, having shared himself with them in bread and wine, Jesus immediately speaks of his betrayal: "But look, the hand of the one who is betraying me is with me at the table" (Luke 22:21). This is Luke's rearrangement, and it makes for a dramatic contrast. One might imagine that for Luke's hearers this may have had direct relevance at times, especially when members of their own community turned against them and reported them to the authorities. Did such experiences generate the figure of Judas or was his story part of what actually happened? In any case, it underlined the vulnerability both of Jesus and of his followers.

Luke neatly makes this story the point of transition to his depiction of Jesus' parting advice to his disciples. Depicting the parting words of heroes was a standard element in telling their story, to ensure their impact would be felt by future generations. To compose his version of Jesus' parting words Luke uses material that he found earlier in Mark. He had brought the detail about the disciples arguing over who was to be the greatest (Luke 9:46; Mark 9:33–34) and repeats it here (Luke 22:24). He had omitted the ambitious request of James and John wanting to have the top jobs in Jesus' kingdom (Mark 10:35–40) and also what followed (Mark 10:41–45). He now takes up that second part (Mark 10:41–45) and brings it here in an edited form as Jesus' response to the dispute about greatness (Luke 22:25–27). It fitted so well in Luke after Jesus had confronted them with the fact one of them would betray him.

Thus, in Luke 22:24–27, Luke combined both Mark 9:34 and Mark 10:41–45 as the beginning of Jesus' parting words to his disciples, and by implication to all who would become his disciples. Advice about leadership was very pertinent for the early church, as it still is. Greatness is not about having power over people. It is about being a caring, serving person, not so much in obedience to Jesus as a master, as in imitation of his own stance, for he came to serve, as Mark had put it, not to be served. Mark had highlighted that love as also reflecting God's priorities (Mark 8:33).

This had been a very difficult thing to grasp and take seriously when, all around them then and around us now, greatness is seen as making oneself great at the expense of others. Images of God based on royal courts where the kings of this world make themselves the center of adulation so easily corrupt our thinking and fill the space in worship, leaving little room for the alternative model that Jesus represented.

Jesus did not avoid royal language nor language of God as father, often similarly laden with notions of power and control, but subverted the latter with his image of the father in the prodigal son parable and used royal language to talk less about power than about hope. The kingdom of God would mean hope for the poor and hungry and the removal of injustice and oppression.

It fits well then, that Luke follows his comments about true greatness in Luke 22:24–27 with a saying that Matthew also cites (Matt 19:28; Luke 22:28–30). It depicts the disciples as sharing in leadership of the coming kingdom of God. It fits the imagery of royal houses that the ruler would have his lieutenants dine with him. Describing their role as judging is less about forensic decisions and more about determining what is right. This picture of hope imagines rule over Israel, represented by its twelve tribes, and reflects a time when the focus was primarily on Israel, as it had been in Jesus' ministry. Such was how they imagined hope.

Luke then moves on to mention Jesus' declaration to Simon Peter that he would deny him. Mark had brought this after reporting their departure to the Mount of Olives and had Jesus tell them that they would be scattered, but that he would appear to them in Galilee (Mark 14:27–28). Luke omits this as he will omit references to Jesus appearing to his disciples in Galilee. Instead, he relocates the prediction of Peter's denial to be within Jesus' parting words, and rewrites it in the light of subsequent history, thus adding that Peter would be rehabilitated and assume leadership in the early church: "one day you'll return to strengthen your brothers" (Luke 22:32).

The focus of Jesus' parting words on the future church is evident also in the advice about how to equip themselves for mission, which would have to be different from what they needed when they were active in the limited confines of Galilee. In this sense, Luke has Jesus offer advice for when they would scatter into the empire. Then they would need a backpack and a bag, but also a sword to ward off wild animals out on the highways. That is the likely meaning, rather than that they needed swords to ward off bandits, let alone engage in acts of rebellion against the state. When Luke has them inform Jesus they had two swords and Jesus say that this would be enough, he may well be ensuring that Jesus' command is not misconstrued as in any way dangerous for the state, because for that they'd need a good deal more than just two swords.

Only after Jesus has completed his parting words does Luke pick up the detail from Mark about their going back outside the city to the Mount of Olives, but then Luke trims Mark's story. He omits reference to the place as Gethsemane and to his taking Peter, James, and John aside. He also omits Mark's detail that Jesus left to pray three times and each time on his return he found them not alert, but sleeping. As a storyteller Mark appears to have had the common fondness for sets of three, reflected in these three prayers, Peter's denial three times, three references to the temple's destruction, and much more.

Luke, perhaps aware of Mark's artistry, reduced the story to a single act of prayer about seeking escape but affirming submission to God's will. The bracketed verses appear to have been added to Luke at some stage to give more emotional content, which Luke would characteristically not include (choosing to omit such when Mark has it). The disciples are to look out for trouble, which was about to come. They are to pray what Luke had already presented as the final request in his version of the Lord's Prayer, not to be led into testing times (Luke 11:4).

Trouble, a testing time, did then come in the form of Judas leading a band of chief priests, temple officers, and elders. Luke fills out the reference in Mark to one of those present, presumably a disciple, cutting off the ear of the high priest's slave (Mark 14:47). For he adds that the disciples raised the possibility of taking action with the sword and then started doing so, in response to which Jesus tells them to stop. This is another message reassuring anyone listening to Luke's Gospel that Jesus and his movement were not into violence. Matthew and John also sense that Mark's account did not say enough to counter misunderstanding, so also have Jesus tell them off. It is a slight enhancement when Luke mentions that it was the right ear, since people tended to see the right side as superior, so it was all the more serious! Our forensics would point out that the person doing so would have to have been left-handed or have done so from behind, but that is not Luke's concern. Unlike John, Luke does not mention the servant's name, Malchus (John 19:10).

Luke had omitted Jesus' citation in Mark of Zech 13:7 to predict that all would flee for their lives and so also omits its fulfillment (Mark 14:27, 49–50). Instead, this Gospel takes us straight to the account of Peter's denial, which Luke brings in full, whereas Mark had recounted it partly before and partly after his account of Jesus' trial before the Sanhedrin (Mark 14:54, 66–72). One of the reasons for that change is that Luke relocates the account of the Jewish trial to the next morning. Luke must have been aware that it would have been extremely unlikely that the temple authorities would run such a trial at night on Passover Day. Instead, he has Jesus taken to the high priest's house and mentions only what Mark reports as happening after the trial (Mark 14:65), namely the mockery by those who had charge of Jesus (Luke 22:63–65).

In relocating the interrogation by the high priest before the Sanhedrin to a morning meeting (Luke 22:66–71; Mark 15:1), Luke has also reworked the substance of Mark's account (Mark 14:55–64). It appears that there was some degree of historical memory in what happened in Jesus' final days, but much of how it played out was left to the imagination. This helps explain some of the differences in the Gospel accounts as well as the common features. Mark or his tradition may well have imagined what happened after Jesus' arrest as a trial before the Sanhedrin and, accordingly, had reported an interrogation with witnesses, a charge of blasphemy, and a guilty verdict.

This may well have reflected what some in the early church had had to face when brought before their local synagogue communities. Luke reports it as happening in the morning, and not as a trial but just as an interrogation (Luke 22:66–71). This is closer to what John's Gospel reports, according to which there was no trial, but just a hearing before the high priest and some officials, but, unlike in Luke, that it took place in the night of the arrest (John 18:12–14, 19–24).

Claiming to be the Messiah and so God's adopted Son was not, in fact, blasphemy. Psalm 2 illustrates the use of "Son of God" as a royal title, where the king reports, "I will tell of the decree of the LORD: He said to me, 'You are my son; today I have begotten you'" (Ps 2:7). As Messiah, king of the Jews, Jesus could also be called "Son of God." However, as believers began to fill out the notion of messiahship into something much greater, the charge of blasphemy would have seemed more fitting and so it would have been seen as fitting by Mark's time. They meant much more in claiming that Jesus was the Son of God than that he was the Jewish Messiah.

For his account, Luke not only transfers the occasion of Jesus before the council to the next morning, when Mark reported they met again (Mark 15:1), but, as noted above, he appears no longer to portray it as a trial but rather just as an interrogation. There are no witnesses mentioned, true or false, as in Mark, and there was no verdict. Luke has also omitted the accusation that Jesus had claimed he would destroy the temple and build another in three days, one not made with hands, the first half of which was false but the second half true.

In Mark, this is the first of three occasions when the temple's destruction would feature (Mark 14:57–58), reflecting Mark's propensity for sets of three. The next is when those mocking him on the cross return to the accusation (Mark 15:29). The third is when the temple curtain is ripped from top to bottom when Jesus dies, a symbolic act of judgment on the temple authorities (Mark 15:38). Luke omits all but the last of these and instead has Stephen in Acts falsely charged before his martyrdom with claiming Jesus would destroy the temple (Acts 6:14) and responding by confronting the temple establishment (Acts 7).

Thus, Luke removes any reference to charges against Jesus related to the temple in his depiction of the hearing. He also takes the high priest's question, "Are you the Messiah, the Son of the Blessed?" (Mark 14:61) and separates it into two questions, one about messiahship and the other whether he was the Son of God. This may well reflect the fact that he was aware that "Son of God" had come to mean much more than being the royal Messiah, although in Luke there is no reference to a charge of blasphemy.

In response to the question about messiahship, Luke has Jesus not say directly, "I am," as in Mark, but "If I tell you, you won't believe me; and if I question you, you won't respond" (Luke 22:67–68), perhaps recalling their earlier not answering his question about John the Baptist's authority (Luke 20:7). The answer, however, is clearly yes, as implied when Luke has Jesus refer to his impending status as the Son of Man. Here, too, Luke has made a subtle change. Instead of having Jesus say that they will see the Son of Man coming with the clouds, as in Mark 14:62, he omits the seeing and the coming and instead has Jesus speak of his impending exalted status, which for Luke was Jesus' present status (Luke 22:69).

The purpose of the interrogation, according to Luke, appears to have been to confirm their suspicions that Jesus was claiming to be the Messiah and so to be able to report this to Pilate. This is what we, in fact, see, as Luke continues where he has them present Jesus as subversive, refusing to pay tax, and as a would-be Messiah king (Luke 23:1–2). The depiction of events in Luke 22 serves not only to help people fill out the scarce information about what happened, but also to present what happened to Jesus as what might also happen to them when they were hauled up before the authorities on false charges. Yes, he was the Messiah, but he was not the kind of subversive that this normally implied. That would have relevance not only for correcting history but also for refuting charges that they too faced. However, Jesus was subversive in a much broader sense, in inspiring people to believe in a coming kingdom or empire of God.

Reflection: How might the people of Luke's day have found their own story reflected in Luke's story of Jesus in this passage?

A Travesty of Justice and a Model of Faithfulness in Adversity (Luke 23:1–47)

Listening to Luke

²³:¹ They all then got up *en masse* and took Jesus to Pilate. ² And they started by laying charges against him, saying, "We found this fellow leading the people astray and blocking them from paying taxes to the emperor and claiming to be the Messiah, a king." ³ So Pilate asked him, "Are you the king of the Jews?" He answered, "If you say so." ⁴ Pilate said to the chief priests and the people, "I don't find this fellow guilty." ⁵ They insisted, "He's stirring up the people through his teaching all through Judea and having started off in Galilee before getting here."

⁶ When Pilate heard that, he asked if he was a Galilean ⁷ and, having found out that he was under the jurisdiction of Herod, he sent him off to Herod, who happened to be in Jerusalem during those days. ⁸ Herod was very pleased to see Jesus, because for some time he had wanted to see him because he'd heard about him and was hoping he might see a miracle performed by him. ⁹ He asked him lots of questions, but he gave no reply. ¹⁰ The chief priests and scribes stood by launching accusations against him. ¹¹ Herod, too, treated him with contempt, along with his soldiers, and made fun of him by putting him in a fine robe and sent him back to Pilate. ¹² Herod and Pilate became friends with one another on that same day, for previously they had been at loggerheads.

¹³ Pilate then summoned the chief priests and the leaders and the people ¹⁴ and said to them, "You brought me this fellow as someone leading the people astray, but look, having assessed him in your presence, I don't find this fellow guilty of the things you're charging him with, ¹⁵ and nor does Herod, because he sent him back to us. And look,

nothing he's done warrants the death penalty; ¹⁶ so I'll punish him and let him go."

¹⁸ They shouted out together, "Take him and release Barabbas to us!" ¹⁹ Now Barabbas had been put in prison because of a riot that took place in the city and because of murder. ²⁰ Again Pilate addressed them wanting to release Jesus. ²¹ But they called out, "Crucify, crucify him!"

²² A third time Pilate spoke to them, saying, "What crime has he committed? I don't find he's done anything warranting capital punishment. So, I'll just punish him and let him go." ²³ They pressured him, shouting out loud their demand that he be crucified; and their voices prevailed. ²⁴ So Pilate decided to grant their request. ²⁵ He set free the fellow they'd been asking for who had been put in prison because of rioting and murder, and handed Jesus over to their wishes. ²⁶ Then they took him off and, grabbing Simon of Cyrene, who was coming back in from the countryside, they forced him to carry the cross behind Jesus.

²⁷ A big crowd of people followed him, including women who were mourning and weeping for him. ²⁸ Turning to them, Jesus said, "Daughters of Jerusalem, don't weep for me. Weep rather for yourselves and your children, ²⁹ because the days are approaching when they'll say, 'Blessed are those who can't bear children and the wombs that have not produced offspring and the breasts that have not breastfed babies.' ³⁰ Then they'll start saying to the mountains, 'Fall on us!' and to the hills, 'Cover us!' ³¹ because, if they're doing this while the wood is green, what'll happen when it's dry!"

³² And they brought also two other criminals to be executed along with him. ³³ And when they reached the place called "The Skull," they crucified him there along with the criminals, one on his right and one on his left. ³⁴ [Jesus said, "Father, forgive them, because they don't know what they're doing."] Dividing up his clothes, they tossed up for them. ³⁵ The people stood there watching. The leaders mocked him, saying, "He saved others; let him save himself, if he's God's chosen Messiah!" ³⁶ The soldiers also ridiculed him by coming up to him offering him sour wine ³⁷ and saying, "If you're king of the Jews, save yourself!" ³⁸ For above him was the charge against him: "This is the king of the Jews."

³⁹ One of the criminals hung up alongside him slandered him, "Aren't you the Messiah? Save yourself and us!" ⁴⁰ The other responded

to him by telling him off and said, "Have you no respect before God, because you're under the same verdict? ⁴¹ And for us, that's just, we're getting what our deeds deserve, but he's done nothing wrong." ⁴² And he said, "Jesus, remember me when you come into your kingdom." ⁴³ He replied, "Truly I tell you, today you'll be with me in paradise."

⁴⁴ And it was around the sixth hour and then darkness descended over the whole land until the ninth hour ⁴⁵ because the sun didn't shine. And the curtain of the temple was torn down the middle. ⁴⁶ Then Jesus cried out in a loud voice, "Father, into your hands I commit my spirit." And having said that, he took his last breath. ⁴⁷ When the centurion saw this happen, he gave thanks to God and said, "Truly this fellow was innocent."

Thinking About Luke

Luke has been rewriting the story of Jesus' last days that he found in Mark. He has just relocated the interrogation of Jesus by the high priest in front of the council to the morning. He then follows Mark in having the council members all take Jesus to Pilate. Whereas Mark simply reports that they accused Jesus of "many things" before Pilate, Luke helps his hearers fill out the detail by listing three charges.

The first is about misleading the people through his teaching, leading them astray. It could simply refer to disagreements over interpreting the Law, but most likely it also includes a suggestion of subversion. That would fit the other two charges. Luke will doubtless want his hearers to remember what Jesus said when asked about taxes (Luke 20:22–26) and so recognize the second charge as false. With regard to the third charge, that Jesus claimed to be the royal Messiah, we may assume that Luke implies that this was, in fact, true, but not in the way that this would normally have been understood, namely as claiming to be a leader to oust the Romans.

As in Mark, Pilate picks up this accusation about claiming to be the Messiah, the king of the Jews. There, in Mark, Jesus gives no answer. In Luke he replies, but in a way that would have implied yes. The charges are sufficiently ambiguous that Luke's reporting that Pilate saw no problem makes sense. The assumption is that he did not hear the claim to messiahship as a claim of a subversive kind and that he did not hear the charge about misleading teaching as subversive.

Luke portrays Pilate as assessing that Jesus was not guilty of the charges. Matthew goes even further by adding a scene where Pilate's wife is told in a dream that Jesus is innocent and where he then washes his hands to say the same (Matt 27:19, 24). In all four Gospels we are dealing with their authors' reconstruction of history to make sense of it for their hearers. That included drawing on tradition, as Luke and Matthew do in using Mark, but also attempting to fill out the story so its significance comes through. They would also have viewed it in the light of contemporary situations of their day. These included increasing tension with the Jewish community, some of whom had become informants to the authorities, and also a concern to present this newfound form of Jewish faith as posing no threat to civil order or the state.

Going behind their reports to reconstruct what actually happened is not easy. Clearly it was a Roman execution. John's Gospel may well draw on authentic tradition when it reports that soldiers were also involved in the arrest (John 18:3). It is highly likely that Pilate would have been concerned about populist movements causing unrest. It is very unlikely that the council's bringing Jesus to Pilate was the first he knew about him. Pilate apparently made no attempt to round up Jesus' followers, so that reflects that he did not assume that Jesus was the leader of a military group. At the bare minimum, it is likely that Pilate would want to have Jesus taken out, to avoid unrest when so many were in Jerusalem for the Passover, and because Passover weekends were often occasions of unrest. Had he heard anything about Jesus' teaching, especially talk of change and the coming empire or kingdom of God, one can understand that he would have wanted to pounce.

It is also highly unlikely that only Pilate was involved. Again, John's Gospel may preserve some authentic tradition behind its story, which has the high priest concerned about Jesus (John 11:49–50). The concern was that Pilate might overreact in response to Jesus and his group and impose oppressive limitations on everyone. That fear would certainly make sense, given the other probabilities, and might well explain their involvement in having Jesus removed, and in that sense sacrificed for the protection of everyone else against a vicious Roman response.

In the context of the 80s and 90s CE, when Luke was writing, the enemy at one level was not so much Rome but the resurgent Judaism that now had official recognition by the state and whose leaders opposed what they saw as a deviation from their faith in the form of these communities promoting faith in Jesus. This situation, which we can trace especially behind the three later Gospels, may well have led to a retelling that placed the primary blame for Jesus' death on the Jewish leadership rather than the Romans. At worst, this later generated the claim that the Jews killed Jesus and the anti-Jewish hate that ensued.

Luke, alone, has a hearing before Herod Antipas, Herod the Great's son who was put in charge of the northern area of his kingdom after his death and given the status of a tetrarch (not a king as Mark loosely calls him). Was there such a hearing before Herod or did Luke imagine it must have been so? The same goes for whether this created a friendship between Antipas and Pilate and for Antipas dressing Jesus in a fine robe. Luke gives no substance to the accusations before Antipas, so that we can assume he means us to see them as the same as those presented to Pilate. Mark's account has Jesus subjected to mockery and abuse by Pilate's soldiers, including being clad in a purple robe and being crowned with a crown of thorns. Luke omits all this and may well have been using it when he describes what Antipas's soldiers did. Is Luke protecting Roman soldiers?

Having Pilate repeat declarations that Jesus was not guilty will have been important for Luke's hearers and carry with it the implication that their faith communities were not a threat to the state. The state, through its prefect, Pilate, had declared such charges false. Having both Pilate and Antipas see Jesus as not guilty may also reflect the Jewish legal principle of requiring two agreeing testimonies before issuing a verdict. Here, two agreed: he clearly is innocent.

The depravity but also the unacceptable behavior of the accusers, according to Roman values, becomes even worse when they want to have an insurgent against Rome set free rather than Jesus, the very kind of thing Christians were being accused of! Mark's account reports that the Romans followed a custom of freeing a prisoner at the festival. Luke suppresses this detail, perhaps because it might be deemed unacceptable, and instead has the accusers take the initiative. If there was, in fact, a custom of releasing a prisoner and Barabbas, an insurrectionist, came up as an option, then in either a storyteller's mind or in actual history, it would reflect the fact that Jesus was seen broadly as belonging in the same category of someone who caused unrest.

Violence towards people who were arrested was to be expected and, alas, is still present in autocratic regimes. Punishing Jesus, that is, beating him up, and releasing him was Pilate's suggestion, not exactly portraying him in a good light, but shamefully the accusers want him executed. It would have been seen as a gross failure of his duty as a Roman official that Pilate failed to uphold the law and instead gave in to pressure. Depicting it like this preserves the integrity of Rome's assessment, which Luke and his hearers will want authorities to note in their day, namely that Jesus was innocent of all charges! No official at any time should give in to such pressure, including when Jesus' followers are similarly, falsely accused, as was happening in Luke's world.

As noted above, Luke passes over Mark's account of the soldiers' acts of abuse against Jesus (Mark 15:16–20) and moves straight on to the account of Jesus' being taken to the execution site, briefly mentioning that Simon of Cyrene carried the cross for him. At this point Luke adds a scene that depicts local women wailing at what they see, reminiscent of women's choruses in Greek drama, which give voice to the grief and pain of tragic events being depicted (Luke 23:27–30). Luke has Jesus point them to the tragedy that would befall Jerusalem in 70 CE, which would have been felt keenly by many members of Luke's community.

At this point, rather than a little later, as in Mark, Luke mentions the two crucified on either side of Jesus (Luke 23:32–33). He describes them as criminals, instead of Mark's term, which identifies them as *lestai*, sometimes translated thieves, but more likely the term for insurgents, another trace of the general category into which Pilate would have put Jesus (Mark 15:27). Some later manuscripts add here a reference to Jesus' praying that God forgive them, meaning those crucifying him (Luke 23:34).

Luke abbreviates Mark's account of the crucifixion, leaving out the location's name, Golgotha, just giving its translation, "The Skull," and has him offered a drink by soldiers only as mockery. Mark then brings the first of three allusions to Ps 22, which we suspect had been employed already by others before him, in telling the story of Jesus' death. Mark often used sets of three. The first allusion is about tossing up for his garments (Mark 15:25): "They divide my clothes among themselves, and for my clothing they cast lots" (Ps 22:18). The second is the report of the three mockeries (Mark 15:27–32): "All who see me mock at me; they make mouths at me, they shake their heads; 'Commit your cause to the LORD; let him deliver— let him rescue the one in whom he delights!'" (Ps 22:7–8). The third is the cry, "My God, my God, why have you forsaken me?" (Mark 15:34; Ps 22:1). Luke has only the first. He also omits Mark's note that Jesus was crucified at the third hour, 9 a.m. (Mark 9:25), the first of three references to time, three hours apart, again reflecting Mark's fondness of threes.

Luke revises Mark's set of three mockeries, from passersby, from the chief priests, and from those crucified with him. Instead, he has mockeries from Jewish leaders, then soldiers who mockingly offered him sour wine, and then one of his co-crucified (Luke 23:35–39). Thus, he leaves out the reference to the accusation that Jesus allegedly said he would destroy the temple and rebuild it in three days (Mark 15:29), because he had omitted it from his account of Jesus' interrogation before the Jewish council.

Before introducing the scene where one of his co-crucified mocks him, Luke mentions the charge attached to the cross. Crucifixion was cruel and functioned as a deterrent. Luke brings the title in the form "This is the king of the Jews" (Luke 23:38). In Luke it fits well among the mockeries because all refer to the charge that as such he was claiming to be the Messiah.

Luke then develops a scene in relation to the third mockery by having the other criminal dissent; and, in response to his positive response, he has Jesus promise that on that very day he would join him in paradise (Luke 23:39–43). This reflects what appears to be Luke's understanding of life after death, reflected also in his parable of the rich man and Lazarus, which is not that souls wait in a half sleep till the day of resurrection, but enter a conscious state, for the righteous, like a return to a heavenly garden of Eden, paradise (Luke 16:19–31). John's Gospel assumes a similar state of consciousness after death when it has Jesus promise that those following him into death would join him in the afterlife (John 12:26; 17:24).

Luke then picks up Mark's second reference to time, namely the sixth hour, midday, and Mark's depiction of the scene as then enveloped in darkness for the next three hours (Mark 15:33; Luke 23:44). This is creative imagery on Mark's part rather than the reporting of an impossibly long solar eclipse as some have wondered, because length is determined by movement, size, and distance, and the longest eclipse ever recorded was just under eight minutes. Darkness it was indeed, in a metaphorical sense. Luke goes on to mention the splitting of the temple curtain before Jesus' death, rather than after it, as in Mark.

Luke also changes Jesus' final cry from one that voiced the pain of abandonment, "My God, my God, why have you forsaken me?" (Mark 15:34; Ps 22:1), a potential source of confusion (was Jesus really abandoned?), replacing it with the more confident word of the psalmist, "Father, into your hands I commit my spirit" (Luke 23:46; Ps 31:5). This coheres with Luke's trend to present a calmer, less emotional Jesus, better matching the ideals of his world about how brave men should be. It meant also that Luke omitted Mark's report that someone heard the Aramaic or Hebrew of "my God," "Eli," and thought he was calling for Elijah, a prophet widely expected to appear at the climax of history.

It is striking that Luke then revises Mark's account of the centurion's response: "Truly this was a son of God" or more likely, "Truly this was the Son of God" (Mark 15:39). In Mark it is the third of three acclamations, the first two being made by God's voice from heaven at his baptism and transfiguration. Instead, Luke renders it: "Truly this fellow was innocent" (Luke 23:47). Perhaps Luke read Mark's wording in the former sense, "Truly this was a son of God," understanding it as an acclamation of innocence. That is certainly how he portrays it, reinforcing the emphasis throughout his account that Jesus was innocent of the charges brought against him.

The tone of Luke's account matches the summaries reflected in his account of preaching in the early days of the church in Acts. Jesus went about doing good but was executed as a result of collusion between the Jewish and Roman authorities (Acts 2:22–24; 10:37–39). He was innocent and so are his followers in Luke's day. His death was a miscarriage of justice and a failure on the part of Rome's appointed official.

For Luke and Luke's hearers, his story was their story. As in the summaries in Acts, the focus is not, as we might expect after reading Paul's account of the gospel, on Christ's death as an atoning sacrifice. It is rather on his death as the mark of faithfulness to the end.

We might also see it as the story of so many who have raised their voice for hope and justice. In doing so, it is important not to flip from advocating love to embracing hate, or recreating a "them and us" perspective that damns them. Then we would find ourselves not onside with Jesus but as bearers of the spirit he sought always to expel and from which he sought to liberate people so that they could instead embrace open-eyed and informed generosity and love.

Reflection: Luke was making sense of Jesus' death in ways that his hearers could appreciate and that might inspire them. How did he do so and what does it say to us today?

Affirming Hope (Luke 23:48—24:53)

Listening to Luke

23:48 All the crowds of people who had come to watch the spectacle, seeing what happened, went off home upset. **49** And all his acquaintances stood at a distance watching all this, including the women who had been following him from Galilee.

50 Now there was a man named Joseph, a leading councilor, a just and fair person, **51** who was not in agreement with the council's decision and what it had done. He was from Arimathea, one of the Jewish cities, and he was looking forward to the coming of the kingdom of God. **52** He approached Pilate and asked if he could have Jesus' body **53** and, retrieving it, he wrapped it in linen cloth and put it in a stone tomb where no one as yet had been laid. **54** It was the Day of Preparation and the Sabbath was about to begin.

55 Now the women who had traveled together from Galilee followed him and saw the tomb and how the body was placed there. **56** They then went off and prepared spices and ointments, but, in keeping with the commandment, held off from doing anything on the Sabbath. **24:1** Then at dawn early on the first day of the week they came to the tomb with the spices they had prepared. **2** But they found the rock rolled away from the entrance to the tomb, **3** and going inside they didn't find the body of the Lord Jesus. **4** Then, while they were puzzled by this, two men stood before them in dazzling clothes. **5** Overcome with fear, they fell face down to the ground, but they addressed them, saying, "Why are you looking for the living among the dead? **6** He's not here but has risen. Remember how he told you while he was still in Galilee **7** that the Son of Man was to be handed over into the custody of wicked men and to be crucified and on the third day to rise again." **8** Then they remembered what he had said.

⁹ So returning from the tomb they reported all this to the eleven and all the others. ¹⁰ The women were Mary Magdalene and Joanna and Mary, James's mother, and the other women who were with them. They were telling the apostles about this, ¹¹ but their report seemed to them like a fairy tale, and they didn't believe them. ¹² Peter then got up and ran to the tomb and stooping down saw only Jesus' clothes and so went off home amazed at what had happened.

¹³ Now the same day two of them were on their way from Jerusalem to a village about sixty stadia away, called Emmaus, ¹⁴ and they were having a conversation about all these things that had happened. ¹⁵ While they were deep in conversation discussing the matters, Jesus himself joined them and walked along with them, ¹⁶ but their eyes were kept from recognizing him. ¹⁷ He said to them, "What's all this you're talking about along the way?"

And they just stood there very sad. ¹⁸ Then one of them, called Cleopas, said to him, "Are you the only stranger in Jerusalem unaware of what's gone on just recently in this city?"

¹⁹ He responded: "What?"

They said to him, "The business with Jesus of Nazareth, a man who was a mighty prophet in word and deed before God and all the people, ²⁰ and how the chief priests and our leaders handed him over to be condemned to death and crucified him. ²¹ And we were hoping that he would be the one coming to liberate Israel, but, along with all this, it's now three days since these things happened. ²² What's more, some of our womenfolk astonished us, after they'd been to the tomb ²³ and didn't find his body; they came to us saying they'd also seen a vision of angels, who were saying he was alive. ²⁴ Then some who were with us went to the tomb and found it just as the women had said, and also didn't see him there."

²⁵ Then he said in response, "You really are ignorant and slow to believe all that the prophets foretold. ²⁶ Wasn't it necessary that the Messiah suffer and then enter his glory?" ²⁷ And starting with Moses and all the prophets he explained to them from all the Scriptures what applied to him.

²⁸ When they approached the village to which they were traveling, he acted as though he was going on farther, ²⁹ but they urged him, "Stay with us, because it's evening and the day is already coming to an

end." So he joined them and stayed with them. ³⁰ And when he took his place at table with them, he took a loaf of bread, blessed it, and broke it up and distributed the pieces among them, ³¹ and their eyes were opened and they recognized him. And then he vanished into thin air in front of them. ³² They said to one another, "Didn't it warm our hearts when he was talking to us along the way and how he opened up the meaning of the Scriptures for us?"

³³ That moment they got up and returned to Jerusalem and found the eleven and those with them all together, ³⁴ who told them, "The Lord really has risen from the dead and has appeared to Simon." ³⁵ They then reported their experience on their journey and how he had made himself known to them through breaking up the loaf of bread. ³⁶ While they were reporting these things, Jesus himself came to stand among them and addressed them. "Peace be with you!" ³⁷ They were startled and scared, thinking they were looking at a ghost.

³⁸ Then he said to them, "Why are you so troubled and why do you let doubts arise in your minds? ³⁹ Look at my hands and my feet; it's me. Touch me and see, because a ghost doesn't have flesh and bones as you can see that I have." ⁴⁰ And having said this, he showed them his hands and feet. ⁴¹ When they still couldn't believe their eyes for joy and were amazed, he said to them, "Have you got anything to eat here?" ⁴² They gave him a piece of broiled fish, ⁴³ which he took and ate in front of them.

⁴⁴ Then he said to them, "These are my words which I spoke to you while I was still with you, namely that everything written in the Law of Moses and the Prophets and the Psalms about me has to be fulfilled." ⁴⁵ Then he opened their minds so they could understand the Scriptures. ⁴⁶ And he told them, "Thus it is written that the Messiah was to suffer and rise from the dead on the third day, ⁴⁷ and that the challenge to turn to God for forgiveness of sins is to be proclaimed to all peoples, beginning from Jerusalem, ⁴⁸ and you are witnesses to these events. ⁴⁹ And I am going to send upon you the gift promised by my Father; but you are to remain in the city until you are clothed with power from above."

⁵⁰ He then brought them out to Bethany and, lifting up his hands, he blessed them. ⁵¹ And while he was blessing them, he parted from them and went up into heaven. ⁵² They fell down and worshiped him and then returned to Jerusalem full of joy ⁵³ and spent their days praising God in the temple.

Thinking About Luke

Luke brings his account of Jesus to a climax with stories of Jesus' resurrection. All four Gospels acclaim that God had raised Jesus from the dead. Pilate and the authorities had said no, but God had said yes to who Jesus was and what he did. The stories told by the authors of the Gospels vary considerably, but all affirm Jesus' resurrection. In some ways the situation they faced in giving more detail was similar to what they faced in writing about Jesus' origins. Like good historians they needed to fill in the gaps from their imagination, just as Luke, for instance, needed, like a good historian, to create speeches for the leading figures in the early church in Acts based on any traditions he had, plus creative historical imagination.

Thus, the element of creative historical imagination is at play in these stories, which seek to fill out the meaning of Jesus' resurrection, and this accounts for the variations and discrepancies among them. Mark, for instance, has the women encounter a young man in the empty tomb, presumably an angel (Mark 16:5); Luke has them encounter two men, later identified as angels, and call it a vision (Luke 24:4, 23); Matthew has an angel descend from heaven and roll the rock away and then sit on top of it and also introduces an earthquake into the story (Matt 28:2).

Similarly, Mark has the women told by the young man to instruct Peter and the disciples to head for Galilee where Jesus would appear to them, but they said nothing (Mark 16:7–8). Luke, on the contrary, has them go and tell the eleven disciples what they had seen and heard (Luke 24:9). Matthew has them even meet the risen Jesus on their way to give the disciples the instructions, as commanded in Mark (Matt 28:9–10). John has just one woman, Mary Magdalene, come to the tomb, see no angelic figure, but return to tell the disciples, as a result of which Peter and the beloved disciple race to the tomb and John's favorite disciple believes, but it is Mary who has the first encounter with Jesus, after first thinking he was the gardener (John 20:1–16). He restrains her from holding onto him because, as he explains, he has to ascend to God (John 20:17). Then that evening he appeared to the eleven and gave them their commission and breathed the Spirit on them (John 20:18–23). In John, resurrection, ascension, and Pentecost all happen on the same day.

To try to harmonize these accounts as though they are purely historical reports is not to understand the creative nature of such accounts, where one should expect differences and discrepancies as authors sought to give their hearers stories to bolster the central claim. Our earliest account comes roughly twenty years before the first Gospel, Mark, was written. Paul, who brings it, does so as something that had been passed on to him, so probably a much older account. It affirms Jesus' resurrection on the third and then adds that he appeared to Cephas (Peter), then to the twelve, then to over five hundred people, then to James and the apostles, and finally to Paul himself (1 Cor 15:3–9). The Gospel stories attempt to fill in the details.

Paul's tradition makes no reference to the women (reflecting typical male priorities?) and the accounts that the Gospels have tell us only of appearances to the twelve (strictly speaking, the eleven, without Judas). Acts mentions the appearance to Paul (Acts 9) and perhaps the events of the Day of Pentecost in Acts 2 may be related to Jesus' appearance to over five hundred, though it does not depict it as such.

If we are to understand these stories and their significance, we need to enter their world and its assumptions. They include belief in resurrection. This was expected to occur at the climax of history. As Paul explains:

> We will not all die, but we will all be changed, in a moment, in the twinkling of an eye, at the last trumpet. For the trumpet will sound, and the dead will be raised imperishable, and we will be changed. For this perishable body must put on imperishability, and this mortal body must put on immortality. (1 Cor 15:51–53)

Paul expected this to occur in his lifetime but notes that some had died. He describes them as asleep. This reflects the view that in the interim state after death and before the day of resurrection people did not cease to exist altogether but lived in a half-conscious state. Some streams of thought, however, depicted this as a very conscious state, as in Luke's parable of the rich man and Lazarus (Luke 16:19–31) and his depiction of Jesus' promise to his co-crucified that the man would join him in paradise (Luke 23:43). Over time, this view prevailed, namely that people would be fully conscious after death, the common assumption in our day. Usually in Jesus' and Paul's time the interim state was seen as only a half life of limited consciousness, hence as close to sleep.

The underlying assumption is that to be conscious you needed ears and eyes; you needed a body. You needed to be raised from the dead. That, however, was not understood as a resuscitation but as a transformation of the corpse into a spiritual body. This underlies the depiction of Jesus' body in the Easter stories as one that could appear and disappear, but the assumption was not that this was a new body but that it was the old one transformed. That meant that no body would be left, for instance, in a tomb. If there was a resurrection, there had, therefore, to be an empty tomb.

Resurrection was expected to occur at the end of time. That meant that initially the claim that God had raised Jesus from the dead implied that the end of time had come or was about to come. This may explain Matthew's saying that some bodies were already emerging from their tombs (Matt 27:52-53). It was not as though Jesus' resurrection was seen as an isolated event with the end of time to occur some two thousand or so years later. They almost certainly understood Jesus' resurrection to be the beginning of the end times and hence they gathered in Jerusalem ready for the end. It did not happen, even though at least Mark, Matthew, and Luke held to the expectation that it would happen within a generation (Mark 9:1; 13:30; Matt 24:34; Luke 21:32).

Paul's mention of Jesus' appearance to Peter suggests that this might have been where it all began. This appears to find confirmation in our passage where Luke has the disciples affirm: "The Lord really has risen from the dead and has appeared to Simon [Peter]" (Luke 24:34), but also in Mark's account, which has an angel declare that Jesus would appear to Peter along with the disciples in Galilee (Mark 16:7). That would imply that his body would not be in the tomb, and it made sense to have the women go there to do the usual embalming and find nothing there.

Turning to the passage before us, Luke tells us that the crowds left the scene clearly impressed by what had happened and so, by implication, likely to be sympathetic. It reinforces Luke's message that Jesus' execution was seen to be a gross injustice. Jesus' acquaintances watched what was happening from a distance, doubtless because they would otherwise place themselves in danger, but then Luke mentions, as did Mark, that there were women there watching who had come down from Galilee, though unlike Mark, does not name them at this point. For Mark it is only the women. For Luke, it's men and women, probably including the disciples, because he omitted Mark's mention of their fleeing.

By depicting Joseph as righteous and as dissenting from the council's decision, Luke reinforces the message that what happened to Jesus was an injustice. In addition, by depicting Joseph as eagerly hoping for the inbreaking of the kingdom of God, Luke is reinforcing his central theme of hope for Israel's liberation. It echoes how his story began, namely with Zechariah and Mary and others also looking forward to liberation. Luke will reinforce this by having the two disciples on the road to Emmaus repeat this hope: "We were hoping that he would be the one coming to liberate Israel" (Luke

24:21). Similarly, in the beginning of Acts, Luke has the disciples ask Jesus: "Is this the time you will restore the kingdom to Israel?" (Acts 1:6), only to be told that the timing was not for them to know.

It was not unusual for female relatives or friends to surround the corpse with spices and ointments. Luke makes a point of underlining that the women faithfully observed the commandments about not working on the Sabbath, just as Mary had done in following the Law in bringing an offering for Jesus as the firstborn (Luke 2:22–24). Luke depicts followers of Jesus as upholding the Law. When the women finally arrived first thing on the Sunday morning, they found the tomb empty and met the two angels (not just one, as in Mark and Matthew), who assert Jesus' resurrection and remind them that he predicted it. Luke thus changes the story from what Mark told and omits the instruction that the women are to tell the disciples to head off to Galilee. It is at this point that Luke names the women, as Mary Magdalene and Joanna and Mary, James's mother, and other women (Luke 24:9). Mark names: "Mary Magdalene, and Mary, James's mother, and Salome" (Mark 16:1).

Unlike in Mark, the women do not remain silent, but instead inform the disciples, who doubt them, but then Peter runs to the tomb and also finds it empty. It looks like the author of John's Gospel adapted Luke at this point, adding that Peter was joined in the race to the tomb by the beloved disciple who got there first and believes first (John 20:1–9). To this point in Luke and John, Jesus has not yet appeared to anyone, unlike in Matthew.

Luke then inserts the story of two disciples on their way to Emmaus on that same day who are joined by Jesus incognito. Luke incorporates some of his key themes into the story and in doing so interprets the events that have occurred. That includes their hope for the liberation of Israel and Luke's explanation of Jesus' fate as foretold in the Scriptures. No specific Scriptures are cited, but in Acts, Philip cites Isa 53 as an example to the Ethiopian eunuch. So Luke helps his listeners come to terms with Jesus' death in two ways: it was the work of wicked men, an injustice, and it was meant to be, foreordained. What might sound like a kind of passive fatalism does not lead Luke to excuse the perpetrators.

Luke's interpretation of Jesus' death matches the way he has Peter and other disciples expound it in the speeches in Acts. He does not give emphasis to Jesus' death as a sacrifice or as vicarious, that is, as "for sins." This is somewhat surprising given his use of Isa 53 in the story of Philip's meeting with the Ethiopian eunuch, but even there he does not cite the verses that see the servant's death as for sins. Luke deleted that aspect from one of the two passages in Mark that speak of Jesus' death in this way (Mark 10:45 as used in Luke 22:27) and in the other, his traditional account of Jesus' last meal, Luke at most retains it as implied. He has used the dialogue in the Emmaus story to underline his key themes.

The two disciples realize that their dialogue partner is Jesus only after he is persuaded to join them and they come together for a meal. For then he breaks up some bread and gives it to them just as he had on the night of his arrest. At this point he vanishes, as a resurrection body could, and they make it back to Jerusalem, all still on the same day, and find the eleven disciples gathered there with the rest. It is at this point that Luke brings the traditional affirmation that the disciples have come to believe in Christ's resurrection because he appeared to Peter. Mark suggests this appearance occurred in Galilee. For Luke, this is clearly not the case, but in describing the events of this single day he does not tell us how or when this happened.

As Jesus suddenly vanished, so he suddenly reappeared among them with the greeting of "Peace." Luke has him confront their doubts and even eat a piece of dried fish, clearly as part of an attempt to say that it really was a resurrection, though leaving us with the puzzling question what became of the fish in a spiritual body when it disappeared again. Luke then has Jesus repeat his interpretation of Jesus' death, going on to point to the mission to all peoples, described as an offer of forgiveness of sins, for which the disciples would be empowered by the Spirit. So, again, Luke is having his key themes underlined, this time by Jesus. This is creative narrative, not atypical of biographers of the time.

The empowerment by the Spirit is something Luke had planned to bring much later, in his second volume, Acts. In the interim, before he begins this second volume, he simply portrays Jesus as blessing his disciples and then going up to heaven, apparently all on the same day of resurrection (Luke 24:50–51).

In his second volume, Acts, he begins again, and has Jesus ascend only after forty days and give the Spirit not on the day of resurrection (as in John's Gospel), but fifty days later on the Day of Pentecost, the Jewish harvest festival. "Pentecost" is the Greek word for fifty. Symbolic echoes of Israel's wandering in the wilderness for forty years and the promise of a new harvest inspire his historical artistry.

John's Gospel has Jesus ascend after meeting Mary Magdalene but before meeting the disciples (John 20:17). John appears to have known and adapted Luke's account of that meeting on the day of resurrection. He uses it as the occasion when Jesus commissions and empowers them for mission and church discipline, and in doing so has Jesus breathe the gift of the Spirit onto them (John 20:19-23). The gift of the Spirit is all part of the one complex event of Jesus' death, resurrection, ascent to the Father, and appearance to empower the disciples. John's account, however, splits the event as told in Luke and has Thomas absent and join the eleven only a week later and then have his doubts met by being able to touch Jesus' wounds (John 20:24-29).

Luke has Jesus tell the disciples to remain in Jerusalem, the hub of divine action. For Luke, it all began and will all end in Jerusalem, when Jesus returns. He feels free therefore to go his own way and delete references to the risen Jesus appearing to the disciples in Galilee, as Mark has Jesus promise (Mark 14:28) and as the angel instructs the disciples (Mark 16:7), and as followed also by Matthew, who then has Jesus send them on mission from a mountain in Galilee (Matt 28:16-20). And even John's Gospel, which adapts Luke's story of the resurrection evening, omits the demand they stay in the city, but instead has the disciples go fishing on Lake Galilee and Jesus encounter them there (John 21:1-14). Luke must have felt free to make such changes because he was aware that, beyond the basic affirmation of resurrection, detail was scant and authors were left to their own creative devices to imagine what might have happened and tell it in ways that brought out its significance.

Luke concludes where he began, namely with holy people praising God in the temple (Luke 24:53). This is in part Luke's way of underlining the continuity he wants to emphasize between the church and Israel. Having everything happen in Jerusalem is probably part of that agenda. Faithful, true Jews were there in the beginning: Zechariah, Elizabeth, Mary, Simeon, and Anna, and now again at the end, faithful, true Jews, the disciples, are praising God in the temple. They will feature also in the opening chapters of his second volume, Acts.

Many of these stories read more like creative reflections on how the authors saw the significance of Jesus' resurrection. This accounts for their diversity. Joining them all together, however, is the central claim. Hope was not extinguished by the death of Jesus. Where the interests of those in power said no, God said yes.

Reflection: What are Luke's special concerns as he seeks to fill out the story of Jesus' resurrection and its significance?

Where to From Here with Luke?

As we leave Luke's Gospel, we come away with a sense of persistent hope. We know that Luke will go on in a second volume to tell the story of the beginnings of the church, but beyond that, beyond the church, is this persistent hope. Luke looks forward to Jesus' return within a generation and his setting up God's kingdom in Jerusalem. All the people on the right side of Luke's story, the faithful ones, share this vision. It was there from the very first days when Zechariah and Elizabeth, Mary and Joseph, and then Anna and Simeon yearned for change and saw that age old yearning about to be fulfilled in Jesus.

While Luke had to imagine how these hopes would be fulfilled, he had reliable traditions about what it would mean, reaching back to Jesus himself. For he not only recorded that the kingdom was the central theme of Jesus' preaching, but also passed on what it would mean in substance. It would be good news for the poor and hungry. It would also mean more than that. It would mean the defeat of those powers that inflicted humanity with sickness and disability, the ultimate exorcism, foreshadowed in Jesus' saying about seeing Satan fall from heaven. Even more than that, it would mean community and belonging foreshadowed in Jesus' engaging in shared meals with the most unlikely and unloved and his invitation to all to embrace the hope of the great feast of belonging for which he had lived out his life and had given of his body and lifeblood.

Such was the hope that Luke has Jesus hold out to all, hinting already in his account of Jesus' ministry that this offer of life would extend beyond

Israel or at least find its fulfillment as the nations took their place, as the prophets foretold, at one with Israel, sharing in prayer and praise to God. The mission on which Luke has Jesus send his disciples to call Israel to faith would, as his parting words indicate, entail new strategies to sustain outreach, which went beyond what sufficed for itinerants going from village to village in Galilee.

From the beginning, Luke highlights the close connection between John the Baptist and Jesus, while making every effort to weight their significance differently. Both offered divine forgiveness, but Jesus moved from the place of waiting to the arena of God's inbreaking kingdom in the present, not least through exorcism and healing. Both see impending divine judgment and confront those rejecting God's call to change, but Jesus takes on a task in the interim to announce and enact good news in the present time.

Drawing on Mark, but also on the collection of teachings of Jesus found in the source he shared with Matthew, as well as his own independent sources, Luke brings much that would have been instructive for Christ-followers of his own day. That included teaching about prayer, trust, and commitment. His context appears to have been one where tension had arisen with fellow Jews who refused to embrace the belief that Jesus was their Messiah. Those troubles color the accounts of Jesus' rejection and project his demise as primarily brought about by the temple authorities.

The role of the real executioners, the Roman state, is minimized, and, if anything, attributed primarily to poor leadership on the part of Pilate, for having rightly recognized that Jesus was innocent of all charges, but then allowing himself to be swayed by a crowd. The Roman state through Pilate affirmed Jesus as innocent of all charges of subversion and so should do the same for the movement in Luke's time. Pilate's shameful failure in good leadership failed both Jesus and Rome itself.

While Luke's closing words look to the message of forgiveness of sins, John's and Jesus' message, being proclaimed to all the world, he does not link this to specific understandings of Jesus' death, but rather to what God offers to those willing to repent, to turn to God and embrace God's way. It is left then to his second volume to describe how this will eventuate. Israel's hope, centered on Jerusalem, widens its embrace as the truly faithful of Israel, as Luke portrays them, engage in mission and call all peoples to faith.

www.ingramcontent.com/pod-product-compliance
Lightning Source LLC
Chambersburg PA
CBHW031359230426
43670CB00006B/588